This book is rooted in hands-on, practical knowledge that TA leaders can put to use from day one to take their candidate experience to world-class levels. Grossman and Schoolderman have literally given you the cheat code for success!

Tim Sackett, President, HRU Technical Resources, Author of *The Talent Fix: A Leader's Guide to Recruiting Great Talent*

What Grossman and Schoolderman don't know about Candidate Experience isn't worth knowing! In *Candidate Experience: How to improve talent acquisition to drive business performance*, you will gain everything you need to deliver the best experience possible for the humans in the recruitment process. Why? Because people make businesses succeed and if you are giving the people you'd like to hire a poor experience, you are damaging the future of your company in more ways than you'd think. Based on 10+ years of research and full of case studies and easy to implement steps, this is the book you need to ensure your company delivers an exceptional candidate experience.

Katrina Collier, Author of *The Robot-Proof Recruiter*, Facilitator & Speaker

In today's talent-short labour market, providing superior candidate experience might be the advantage that makes the biggest difference to companies competing to hire. Few people know more about the topic than Grossman and Schoolderman. They prove it with this definitive guide that operates as a how-to on each aspect of candidate experience. It's a must-read, folks.

Hung Lee, Curator of the weekly newsletter *Recruiting Brainfood*

At last, the definitive book on the candidate experience! Built on the back of years of research and some compelling case studies, the book analyses the constituent parts of the candidate experience. It offers evidence-based, actionable insights to improve this vital element of effective talent acquisition. An absolute must-read for anyone looking to improve the way their company recruits.

Matt Alder, Producer and Host of *The Recruiting Future Podcast*

Grossman and Schoolderman have created a book that should become a foundational tool for all talent acquisition professional training. This book embarks on the candidate's journey relationship with a company. It delves into a decade of data and case studies to define who is a candidate and simply what is the best candidate experience they should have from world-class employers who seek to maximize their brand's long term success in retaining talent. I can't wait to share this book with C-suite executives to show how a 'customer' is treated after not being selected can be just as powerful as those you select to operate the company.

Cathy Henesey, SPHR, CHHR, SHRM-SCP, Vice President, Talent Acquisition, HR Shared Services, AdventHealth

Grossman and Schoolderman provide the reader with a methodical approach in understanding the candidate experience through a comprehensive question and answer framework. The authors focus on critical competencies of candidate experience, including employer branding and recruitment marketing which are essential to building a successful talent acquisition organization.

Jennifer O'Brien, Global Talent Acquisition Leader of Candidate Attraction & Experience, Booz | Allen | Hamilton

The authors are thorough professionals in the field of Candidate Experience. There is a judicious mix of storytelling with reference to theory, process and case studies. Organizations of any size that wish to acquire talent, irrespective of the scale and complexity, can leverage this book to enrich their candidate experience journey. This book sets the gold standard on how to use this framework as a platform for change in the new hyper-connected economy where the war for talent is intense. In short, this book can be called 'Candidate Experience Bible'.

E. Subramanian Subbu, Senior Vice President & Global Head of Talent Acquisition, Virtusa

In their first book together, titled *Candidate Experience: How to improve talent acquisition to drive business performance,* co-authors Grossman and Schoolderman, have created a treasure trove of valuable content and information centred around the candidate experience. Accessing over a decade of data from Talent Board, the research is validated throughout the book. This book is a leadership book for anyone in talent acquisition faced with improving their business and especially their focus on candidate experience.

Elaine Orler, Managing Director, Consulting, Cielo – Global RPO Partner

Anyone who questions how a poor candidate experience can negatively impact a business should read this book. The authors have spent years tackling this research and it pays off here. As you read, you will find very clear and practical ways to improve candidate attraction, screening, interviewing, and hiring for any company trying to figure out how to yield better results. Not only can this lead to a great hire, but an energized and motivated one too!

David Crawford, Vice President, Talent Acquisition, New York-Presbyterian Hospital

This book is a must-read for anyone wanting to positively impact candidate experience within your business or organization! The authors offer their subject matter expertise by sharing the inside scoop of why candidate and customer experience matters and what you can do about it. We've been working with Talent Board since early 2017 and have leveraged their expertise, counsel and research to advance our talent experience strategy at Comcast.

Lisa Bianchini, Director of Talent Strategy & Experience, Comcast

This book is a must-have resource as you develop and implement your ongoing talent strategy.

Steve Browne, SHRM-SCP, Chief People Officer, LaRosa's, Inc., and author of *HR on Purpose* and *HR Rising*

The content and direction provided in this book will help you develop a strategy for continual improvement.

Shuree Sockel, Talent Acquisition Systems Manager, Enterprise Holdings

This book combines research and real-life experiences to give you tangible actions to improve candidate experience in your organization today!

Wendy Dailey, Talent Acquisition Professional, Host of #HRSocialHour Podcast

This is a must-read for all TA and HR professionals, hiring managers and CEOs. Grossman and Schoolderman discuss this critical-to-business topic head-on and break the candidate experience down in a simplified way that helps business leaders understand why it's so important and best practices to improve, including details about the CandE Awards and benchmark research program. Because I never stop thinking about the candidate experience (and neither should you), this book is at my fingertips at all times.

Brandie Dawson, Director, Global Talent Acquisition & Candidate Experience, Valvoline, Inc.

Candidate Experience

*How to improve talent acquisition
to drive business performance*

Kevin W. Grossman
and Adela Schoolderman

KoganPage

First published in Great Britain and the United States in 2022 by Kogan Page Limited

2nd Floor, 45 Gee Street	8 W 38th Street, Suite 902	4737/23 Ansari Road
London	New York, NY 10018	Daryaganj
EC1V 3RS	USA	New Delhi 110002
United Kingdom		India

www.koganpage.com

Kogan Page books are printed on paper from sustainable forests.

ISBNs

Hardback   978 1 3986 0535 0
Paperback   978 1 3986 0533 6
Ebook   978 1 3986 0534 3

British Library Cataloguing-in-Publication Data

A CIP record for this book is available from the British Library.

Library of Congress Control Number
2022013464

Typeset by Integra Software Services, Pondicherry
Print production managed by Jellyfish
Printed and bound by CPI Group (UK) Ltd, Croydon CR0 4YY

This book is dedicated to Reinout, who creates the platform on which I can dream big.
Adela Schoolderman

For my daughters, Beatrice and Bryce. May their candidate experience always be positive and fair.
Kevin W. Grossman

CONTENTS

List of figures and tables xv
Foreword xvii
*Preface: About Talent Board and the Candidate Experience
Awards* xxi

01 What is candidate experience? 1

Candidate experience scenario No 1 2
Candidate experience scenario No 2 3
Candidate experience scenario No 3 4
Candidate experience makes an impact 5
The candidate experience is pervasive throughout 7
What impacts the business impacts candidate experience 15
Candidate experience competitive differentiators 16
Note 18

02 Why is the candidate experience journey so important? 19

The candidate journey 19
Attraction/research/brand 21
Application 23
Screen/interview 25
Non-selected (rejected candidates) 26
Offer and onboarding 27
Map the candidate journey 29
Then make the business case 35
Note 36

03 The business impact of candidate experience 37

What impacts the business impacts recruiting and hiring 37
The criticality of communication and feedback loops 39
Dr Reddy's Laboratories 43
Hoag Memorial Hospital Presbyterian 44

Syneos Health 44
Walgreens 44
Auburn–Washburn USD 437 45
BASF 45
Colorado Springs Utilities 45
Southwest Airlines 46
Stantec 46
The business impact of candidate experience 47
For all companies, referrals are critical 51
The impact is real 52
Notes 54

04 Improving the attraction phase: Employer branding,
     recruitment marketing and sourcing 55

What is the attraction stage of the candidate journey? 55
What are candidates looking for? 56
Where does attraction occur? 59
Who is involved? 60
Targeting ideal candidate profiles 62
Developing an employer brand 62
Utilizing recruitment marketing 62
Putting robust information at candidates' fingertips 64
Referral programmes and incentives 64
Employee ambassador programmes 65
Using video 66
Creating live virtual events 66
Encourage internal mobility 66
Create separate processes for internal candidates 67
Job postings 68
Passive sourcing basics and candidate experience 71
Contacting sourced candidates 73
'What's the pay range?' 74
Rejecting passively sourced candidates 74
Sharing passively sourced candidate profiles with hiring
     managers 75
Notes 76

05 Improving the application phase 78

What do candidates want? 80
Best practices for improving the application candidate
    experience 81
Internal applicants 85
Video interviews and assessments 87
Rejecting candidates who are not qualified 88
Notes 91

06 Improving screening and interviewing 92

Résumé/application screen 94
Pre-employment screening tools 95
What candidates want 97
Recruiter screen 99
Hiring manager interviews 102
Interviews 103
Decision 112
Notes 113

07 How to reject candidates with empathy 115

Why does it matter how we reject candidates? 116
Why is rejecting so hard? 118
What candidates want 120
Rejection prioritization 123
Silver medallists 128
Notes 130

**08 Get hiring manager support: Building strong relationships
from the beginning** 131

Why the recruiter–hiring manager relationship is important to
    the candidate experience 132
Why don't hiring managers care about candidate
    experience? 133
How can I build a better relationship with my hiring
    managers? 136
Note 144

09 Improving the hire phase: Offer and onboarding 145

What candidates want 147
Salary discussions 149
Offer prep and the pre-close 149
Extending the offer 152
Competitive and counteroffers 154
Negotiation 159
Prepare for a negotiation 161
When a candidate accepts the offer 163
When a candidate does not accept the offer 165
Best practices during offer and onboarding 166
Notes 167

10 Overcoming resistance to improving candidate
    experience 168

Resistance to candidate experience No 1: it's too expensive 168
Resistance to candidate experience No 2: compliance comes
    first 170
Resistance to candidate experience No 3: it's one more thing the
    recruiters must do now 172
Resistance to candidate experience No 4: it's too 'fluffy' 172
Resistance to candidate experience No 5: it's not how we do
    things 173
Note 175

11 Getting leadership buy-in to improve candidate experience:
    The nods have it – or do they? 176

Why measuring candidate experience is where you start 177
CandE case studies 179
Build your own business case 183
Gather your metrics 186
Presenting your case 189
Process improvements can ensure a quality candidate
    experience 190

12 **Diversity, equity and inclusion candidate experience considerations** 193

DEI under the microscope 194
DEI and the candidate experience 195
Implement strategies and tools for reducing bias 196
The business case for DEI 201
The latest CandE Benchmark Research underscores it all 202
The importance of perceived fairness 204
Other rays of hope and areas of opportunity 205
Notes 206

13 **Recruiting technology candidate experience considerations** 208

Technologies across the candidate journey 210
Recruiting automation 213
Technologies on the rise 214
The human touch still matters 222
Notes 223

14 **Working with recruiting agencies and improving candidate experience** 225

Considerations 225
Challenges with working with agencies 227

15 **The future of the candidate experience** 231

Where do we go from here? 231
Sustaining means more than maintaining 233
How to get the CandE-winning competitive edge 234
The future of candidate experience is now 237
Note 239

Index 240

LIST OF FIGURES AND TABLES

FIGURES

Figure 1.1   The Candidate Experience Journey and CandE
              Winner Best Practices 8

Figure 1.2   2020 North America employer/candidate perception
              gaps 11

Figure 1.3   2021 North America employer/candidate perception
              gaps 12

Figure 1.4   Business impacts that impact recruiting and hiring 14

Figure 2.1   The Candidate Experience journey and CandE
              Winner Best Practices 20

Figure 2.2   The Candidate Journey map 33

Figure 3.1   Great candidate experience over the years 41

Figure 3.2   Poor candidate experience over the years 42

Figure 6.1   This is an e-mail template that a recruiter can use to
              help prepare and align every interviewer prior to
              meeting with candidates. The intended use is for the
              recruiter to give a draft to the hiring manager.
              The hiring manager can then customize that draft
              before sending to the interview team 110

Figure 7.1   Rejection pyramid 127

Figure 13.1   Candidate Experience Journey technology
              considerations 211

TABLES

Table 1.1   Percentage of candidates sharing positive and negative
              experiences with their inner circle 6

Table 1.2   Candidates sharing positive and negative experiences
              publicly online 6

Table 2.1   Defining candidate personas 30

Table 2.2   Candidate Journey chart – Attraction/research/
             brand 32
Table 2.3   Candidate Experience success: areas for
             improvement 35
Table 2.4   Candidate Experience success: how to achieve
             improvement 35
Table 4.1   Critical online/interactive ways employers engage
             with candidates who have not yet applied (partial
             list) 59
Table 6.1   Because there is so much information to collect in a
             30-minute initial telephone screen with a candidate,
             we created a sample recruiter screen itinerary 99
Table 6.2   Different types of interviews have pros and cons and
             are best for unique company circumstances 106
Table 6.3   There are multiple ways to construct a candidate
             interview 107

FOREWORD

Before we dive into Kevin and Adela's ground-breaking book *Candidate Experience: How to Improve Talent Acquisition to Drive Business Performance*, let me take a moment of your time to pause and consider what we know about the first word in the phrase 'Candidate Experience'.

Humour me – quickly define the word 'candidate' in the context of your work as a recruiter.

What immediately comes to mind? What really makes a candidate a candidate?

How confident do you feel about what you just stated to yourself? Did you even say it out loud?

Dictionaries will offer little help, by the way, as they waffle over whether a candidate is a person seeking a job or just being considered for one. Nothing more. Nothing less. (All dictionaries downplay a candidate in a recruiting context as secondary to someone being considered for an honour or a wannabe politician.)

Wikipedia doesn't add anything and simply repeats a dictionary's conflicted point of view.

The test of whether your definition is acceptable is if a room full of your peers – say 100 recruiters – could come close to agreeing on a definition. Then, at least, we would all be on the same page about whose experience it is we should be concerned about.

Feel free to do that survey, although for nearly three decades I've enjoyed asking the question at the very beginning of my presentations and find the answers as relevant (and concerning) today as I did at the dawn of the digital revolution.

Picture that room full of recruiters tasked with answering, 'When is a prospect no longer a prospect but, instead, a candidate? What is it that makes her (or him) someone whose experience is now something for which you should be at least partially responsible?'

Typically, there is pregnant pause as each recruiter in the room considers whether this is a trick question.

It is.

After all, everyone in the room is dealing with them (candidates) every day. How could anyone who has ever recruited not know what a candidate is? Well, we all do know, it is just that we aren't bound to the same answer. There isn't a required standard recruiting language we were tested on when we first discovered hiring as our career path.

Responses to the question in a decent sized room arrive tentatively and then, boldly, to fill the void:

'Every prospect is a candidate.'

'All those who have the skills to do the job.'

'All applicants who meet our requirements.'

'Everyone who passes our screening.'

'The people we choose to interview.'

'The person I will offer the job to.'

The actual list is much longer, but you get the point.

Employers don't pay recruiters for candidates. They pay us for results – for hires. The only standard most employers are interested in is knowing we've sourced, selected and onboarded a new employee capable of doing the job at hand. Nuances about the workflow up to that point – identifying leads, keeping prospects warm, assessing candidates, etc. – are simply operational processes that need to be efficient and productive. Even the term 'applicant', with 20 years of regulation behind it, serves only to define how employers comply with demographic representation.

So, it is no wonder that differentiating leads from prospects from applicants and candidates has historically been just an internal functional approach to measuring the stops on the conveyor belt (or funnel if you prefer) of our hiring process.

Experience has long been nowhere to be found in a company stressed over cost, time and quality.

Until the twenty-first century, that is.

That we might want to consider improving the treatment of candidates (or any other word we use to describe the phases we attach to people on their way to becoming an employee) was and to a great degree still is ignored but changes are in the wind.

Because candidate experience really does make a difference in the success of our companies. A difference we can measure and connect to practices we can incorporate and technology that enables the practices to be efficiently executed.

Candidate Experience: How to Improve Talent Acquisition to Drive Business Performance is all about this difference, those measures and especially the practices and technology. Candidate Experience is still a work in progress but, after more than 10 years collecting and analysing data, we can be confident of the basics presented here as well as the cost and rewards of doing it well.

Fortunately, *Candidate Experience: How to Improve Talent Acquisition to Drive Business Performance* is built on a solid definition of a candidate that is drawn by substituting that room full of recruiters with a room full of job seekers.

Given a choice, 100 per cent of job seekers will always agree about the moment they become a candidate.

Every prospect is certain in their mind that they became a candidate the moment they formally expressed interest in an opening. Whether it is pressing 'send' at the end of a completed online application, posting a résumé in the mail or filling out a simple job interest form at a mall, they 'know' they are a candidate.

It is the job-seekers' definition that is the sole arbiter of when their experience starts to matter not the employers' definition.

Not you as recruiter but you as job seeker can now pivot to the only acceptable definition.

As candidate, you will form and increasingly share attitudes about your experience of every company where you have expressed interest. You will also increasingly behave in ways that actively and collectively impact that employer's brand as a place of work and the company's performance. (And, yes, even investors are now taking note and, while that is a much longer discussion, financial disclosures now require specific data about how we manage candidates and employees.)

Read this book thinking that a candidate is *anyone who has formally expressed an interest in working for you, qualified or not* and you will discover world-class solutions to fill the gaps in your hiring practices. Your employer will benefit by you stepping up to connect the candidate experience dots to their success. If they don't thank you, there are a growing number of employers who will. Shine a bright light on all of them.

Gerry Crispin, co-founder, CareerXroads and Talent Board
January, 2022

About Talent Board and the Candidate
Experience Awards

Kevin Grossman's candidate experience story: the upside down and candidate experience

Welcome to Talent Board's book about improving recruiting, hiring and the candidate experience. I'm one of the co-authors, Kevin Grossman, and I want to share a story with you about my own candidate experience. My co-author, Adela Schoolderman, and I are sure that many of you have your own visceral candidate experiences that you could share, and we'd love to hear from you after you read the book.

In early 2013, my professional life was upside down. I had left a great job in 2010 to pursue something new – to purchase and run a small leadership development firm – and failed quickly and miserably. I didn't even make it to the acquisition stage. Fear and uncertainty gripped me in the final steps, and I stumbled and gave up. The owner of the firm was definitely not happy with me, but it was a relief and a blessing in the end.

I decided to again double down on HR and recruiting technology marketing, which was the industry and primary role I had just left in that great job, and one I had been in since 1999. I consulted, briefly returned to the same great job (which really wasn't for me or them any more), became an industry analyst (very briefly), applied for another industry analyst position I didn't get and then worked for an HR technology startup that was wrong for me (and them) from day 1.

However, the other industry analyst position I didn't get was what became part of the trifecta of synchronicity for me. It was a well-known firm at the time, and at first everything was going well for me. I didn't have the HR and recruiting practitioner experience they were looking for, but they were interested in my technology marketing background and the fact that I was knowledgeable of the industry.

I had a phone screening and then another one, and then they scheduled an in-person interview for me to meet with the firm's founder, other principals and the team I'd be working for and with. I was so excited I couldn't stand it; this could be a breakout opportunity for me! The interview day was a little rocky because I was nervous and didn't think I did very well.

They notified me that same week that I was one of two top candidates for the position. Right on! They said they'd get back to me before the weekend.

And then they didn't.

The weekend came and went, and I sent an e-mail to them that very next Monday.

Nothing.

Another week went by.

Nothing.

More e-mails from me.

Nothing.

I finally called and got a pleasant run-around from one of the people I had interviewed with.

But nothing more.

And then I found out through industry backchannels that the other candidate got the job. It was nearly three weeks later when I finally got an apologetic e-mail from the founder apologizing for their team.

Too late, though. My candidate experience went from good to bad to upside down. Plus, I had to see these people at industry conferences and smile and wave and just deal with it, which I did.

I moved on, yes, but never forgot the experience. *Companies can definitely do better than this*, I thought. *They have to do better than this.*

Then the other two trifecta events occurred. I started working for another HR and recruiting technology company, commuting about one week per month to their headquarters in the Boston area. Around the same time, I got to know the co-founders of Talent Board, recruiting luminaries I had known for a few years: Elaine Orler, Gerry Crispin and Ed Newman.

Talent Board's origin story

Gerry Crispin co-founded CareerXroads over 25 years ago and has worked with many HR and talent acquisition leaders and their teams during that time. He couldn't help but notice that job candidates tended to be taken for granted in a variety of ways, but it was never really addressed as there was no incentive provided to recruiters. Unfortunately, he found that making these observations in the 1990s fell on a lot of deaf ears.

Ed Newman did a lot of work with companies on recruiting technology and automation from the early 1990s on. The very first return-on-investment that he ever received from a recruiting project was when his team changed the standard letter in an envelope that acknowledged the receipt of a candidate's résumé to a postcard. This reduced the postage by a third of the cost and was a huge cost benefit. The postcard said something to the effect, 'Dear Applicant, we regret this impersonal response. However, we receive too many résumés to give you something more personalized.'

At the time, this was an important step in ensuring that every job applicant still received a response, no matter how impersonal it may have been and, of course, saving recruiting budget as well. However, in 2009, when the pre-Talent Board conversation about candidate experience began, Ed realized that, after all those years since the 1990s working on automating and improving recruiting processes with technology, the industry had only progressed from postcard to e-mail – with the exact same message that goes to that candidate literally one second after they click submit. Not being able to scale a personalized response for every single applicant was (and still is) an absolute reality; the sheer volume of job applicants for most mid-sized to global enterprises just aren't qualified. But there still had to be a better personable way to respond to that volume of candidates.

Considering how much investment had been made in customer experience management, the recruiting and hiring experience was far behind. Candidate experience was woefully lacking and probably the most overlooked customer base on the planet.

In 2009, at the HR Technology Conference, Elaine Orler, who was the founder and CEO of a technology consulting firm called Talent Function (now part of Cielo), and Gerry agreed to a debate. The idea was to have a formal debate on stage in which they took time going back and forth, making the case for either that candidates should be treated with some degree of respect or they should not. Gerry agreed to take the role that they should not, that candidates were just pawns in this whole process and, by and large, interchangeable. Employers could do what we wanted with them, and they'd still line up to try to get hired. To this day, Gerry thinks he almost won. However, Elaine made the better case overall that they should be treated respectfully and fairly, but the audience reaction told them that the world wasn't necessarily ready to do something about it. There was enough interest, though, and the debate got many HR and talent acquisition leaders thinking about change.

Shortly after that, Elaine Orler had a conversation with Chris Forman (founder and CEO of Appcast, a programmatic job advertising platform that helps reach passive candidates) who had approached her at a conference and asked what they were going to do about candidate experience? She asked him to clarify, and he said, 'What are you going to do about candidate experience?'

She responded, 'Why me?' He told her why not and said he'd give her $5,000 to do something about it. She agreed and created a nonprofit and an awards programme. She recruited Gerry, also known as the Godfather of Candidate Experience, and Ed Newman to help her with this new educational nonprofit.

The idea was simple enough – create an educational research nonprofit and develop surveys for employers to answer on how they deliver recruiting and hiring and how they would rate their own candidate experience, and for job candidates to answer rating their experiences throughout the recruitment process.

The co-founders decided that putting a positive light on candidate experience was the primary mission; not to jeopardize or to challenge companies whose candidate experience was poor, but to shine a light on those that really cared and wanted to do something better.

A labour of love and data

Early on, Talent Board was a labour of love focused on elevating and promoting a quality candidate experience and continues to be to this day. The co-founders received valuable feedback from employer participants on what survey questions they'd like to see asked. I participated as one of many volunteers helping to develop, analyse and write up the research survey results.

During the first two years, the candidate experience ratings and benchmarks we measured (and still measure today) were finalized. Elaine, Gerry, Ed and a group of dedicated industry volunteers (I was one of those early volunteers), launched the Candidate Experience Awards programme and the survey research. We secured sponsors that were dedicated to recognizing a quality candidate experience offered by companies throughout the entire recruitment cycle (which we do every year). Our mission to forever change the way job candidates were treated began to flourish (and we publish this background information every year in our research reports that are free to download).[1] After about four years of the co-founders running this new educational non-profit with the help of the volunteers, I was fortunate enough to be recruited by Elaine Orler to grow and scale the programme and was only one of two full-time employees at the time. Besides the volunteers, we did have a part-time project manager and a full-time intern (who's now my global programme director managing all our marketing and the benchmark research process).

Each year our organization digs a little deeper into the candidate experience survey feedback we receive and shares what we find with the global HR and talent acquisition industry. Our benchmark research survey questions remain valid and reliable year after year. Our survey research is also anonymous and confidential for the hundreds of employers that participate each year and the hundreds of thousands of candidates that answer the feedback surveys.

Companies participating in our annual benchmark research each year send our candidate surveys to their candidates to ask for feedback on their experiences during the recruiting process, from pre-application to onboarding. The in-depth data analysis we do each year helps companies to see and understand their recruiting and hiring strengths and weaknesses compared to all the companies participating. Our candidate experience feedback and benchmark research helps companies big and small across industries raise the bar on their recruiting and hiring activities. Our measurements also set global standards for the candidate experience for HR and talent acquisition leaders and their teams.

The following has been previously published in Talent Board research reports but is important to share again here for readers to understand more intimately our overall methodology.

Talent Board works with employers from around the world (North America, Europe, Middle East and Africa (EMEA), Asia-Pacific (APA) and Latin America). The CandE Awards and our benchmark research are composed of two rounds of data capture: Round 1, the employer survey, and Round 2, the candidate surveys.

Round 1 is the employer survey designed to capture and evaluate the participating company's recruitment processes and practices that affect the candidate experience. We also ask participating companies to self-assess their own candidate experience – how they would rate themselves.

After that, companies participate in Round 2, which involves surveying a random sampling of their job candidates. These candidates are given several questions about their recruiting experience and were asked to rate their experience via 4- and 5-point Likert scales. Likert scales measure either positive or negative responses to a statement.

These scales are also easily converted to net promoter scores (NPSs). It's important to talk about NPSs here because more companies not only use NPSs to measure customer satisfaction, they're using it to measure their candidate and employee experiences. NPSs are based on an 11-point scale from 0 to 10. Respondents are then grouped as follows, based on their responses:

- **Promoters** (score 9–10) are loyal enthusiasts who will keep buying and refer others, fuelling growth.
- **Passives** (score 7–8) are satisfied but unenthusiastic customers who are vulnerable to competitive offerings.
- **Detractors** (score 0–6) are unhappy customers who can damage your brand and impede growth through negative word-of-mouth.

Subtracting the percentage of detractors from the percentage of promoters yields the NPS, which can range from a low of –100 (if every customer is a detractor) to a high of 100 (if every customer is a promoter).

When converting a 4-point scale to NPS, you subtract the 1 score (lowest) from the 4 score (highest). For example, when we ask candidates how likely they are to refer others, the scale looks like this:

- 4 – extremely likely;
- 3 – likely;
- 2 – unlikely;
- 1 – definitely not.

The resulting score is then an NPS. For a 5-point scale, you subtract the 1 and 2 scores from the 4 and 5 scores and that's NPS. We then simplify it even further for our CandE Benchmark Research and group results as follows:

- **Amazing** (scores above 50) are loyal candidates who will most likely keep referring others based on their experience.
- **Okay** (scores between 0 and 50) are candidates who are satisfied but may or may not be too enthusiastic about referring others based on their experience.
- **Not so good** (negative scores) are unhappy candidates who can damage your brand and impede growth through negative word-of-mouth.

Because most job candidates don't get hired, there's always negative sentiment in the foundation of recruiting and hiring, no matter how positive candidate experience is. Any NPS above 0, a positive score, is okay. Anything above 50 is amazing. Any negative NPS means there's work to be done. Our methodology and ratings will be referenced throughout this book to underscore why measuring candidate experience is so important. We measure candidate experience at every recruiting stage, from pre-application to onboarding, and the candidates' positive and negative ratings always align with their perception of fairness. Fairness is a critical yet subjective measure that impacts whether your job candidates, external or internal, will ever apply again, refer others, have continuing brand affinity or, for consumer-based organizations, whether candidates will make purchases or influence them.

Again, every year in our annual benchmark research reports we share our above and below methodology and those companies that win our CandE Awards. Whether we're looking at Likert scale averages or NPS averages, those companies that have the highest positive ratings in our benchmark research each year win our coveted CandE Awards and are the only companies we tout publicly. To qualify for a CandE Award, companies must commit to a specific, statistically significant candidate response and a set standard for the proportion of randomly selected respondents who were not hired. This means each company must first meet a minimum qualification for responses based on the size of the candidate population plus a minimum percentage of those not hired (80 per cent or more of the candidates didn't get hired and 20 per cent or less did get hired). These candidate responses include multiple touchpoints from the pre-application process to onboarding (if hired).

These responses and ratings are then scored and then normalized to a standard ratio of those 'Not Selected' versus those 'Hired' to eliminate any 'halo' effects and run through a statistical analysis and an algorithm that produces a final CandE score for each company. After that, we stack rank the scores and select the winners that have CandE scores above the lowest winning CandE score from the year before. This is in addition to the statistical analysis and algorithm applied above and the selection of the top CandE winners. For more information, download our latest research reports at TheTalentBoard.org.

Talent Board today

Since the very beginning, Talent Board's mission has focused on the elevation and promotion of a quality candidate experience with industry benchmarks that highlight accountability, fairness and business impact.

To date, Talent Board has worked with over 1,200 employers big and small across industries around the world. We've surveyed over 1.25 million candidates about their candidate experience from pre-application to onboarding. Every year we help employers understand their candidate experience impact by collecting their own candid candidate feedback and sentiment and then comparing them against all the other employers in our annual benchmark research program, anonymously and confidentially. This in turn helps reiterate to HR and recruiting teams that treating every person well who expresses an interest in working for them is not only the right thing to do but a compelling business necessity, which will become clearer as you read through this book.

Talent Board has also developed other education programs beyond the benchmark research to help companies improve their recruiting, hiring and candidate experience. Adela Schoolderman, the co-author of this book, has been in talent acquisition for over 15 years and began working with Talent Board a few years ago. She's been an invaluable advisor, consultant and even an employee for a time. With her help, we created our candidate experience audits, a multi-tiered deeper dive into a company's overall recruitment process, identifying strengths and weaknesses and making improvement recommendations.

We also developed a professional development course, in conjunction with HR.com, which is based on over 10 years of Talent Board candidate experience benchmark research and best practices. Our joint certificate program is designed to help companies gain a competitive edge in recruiting, secure top talent and improve their employer brand through improving candidate experience from pre-application to onboarding.

Talent Board also hosts public and private hands-on workshops, informative webinars and conferences each year sharing proven practices from innovative practitioners and companies big and small across industries.

Now that you've got to know Talent Board, its origins and its mission, in the next chapter we're going to further define what candidate experience is.

Adela Schoolderman's candidate experience story

We began the preface with one of my candidate experience stories and how Talent Board came to be, and now we want to end this section with one story from Adela. Again, every single one of us has both positive and negative candidate experience stories, enough to fill volumes of books on the subject.

I found my future career during my junior year at Arizona State University. I took an Industrial Organizational Psychology class, and this was my first exposure to applied psychology. However, I returned home at the end of the school year and transferred to University of Washington, and there were no I/O programs at the time outside California. Instead, I got a master's in human resource management.

I thought HR was fine. I was still mostly interested in the strategic aspects of it. I really didn't like recruiting because it felt like a conveyor belt process to me. The same thing over and over and over. Of course, the only positions available as I entered the workforce were in recruiting. Over the years, I tried to go back to the HR side but was never successful. I was quite frustrated by it and didn't know what I was lacking. It wasn't until I worked for a mid-sized community bank that I realized my value: managers didn't want me to leave the recruiting role because I was good at it. One staffing partner told me, 'You've almost single-handedly built the IT department of a bank. That's not sexy work, but you did it. Feel proud of that!'

I was successful because I cared about people, and I did exactly what I told them I would do. During the great recession, I struggled financially but I knew the one thing I could give people that was of value was my word, so I made it a point to always keep it. It really was that simple.

In 2014, I discovered Talent Board through an article about egregious LinkedIn Inmails sent from recruiters to developers. The article quoted one of the benchmark research reports, and I read the entire thing. I read about the CandEs and finally discovered my edge: candidate experience. Treating people how they want to be treated. In the business world, this is a concept so removed from modern practices that we needed to train people how to do it! The following year, I entered my company in the CandEs and we won. I was hooked. My career developed around candidate experience when I learned we can succeed in getting candidates to say yes to our offers over others, not because we paid the most but because we cared the most. I learned to coach talent acquisition practitioners and hiring managers on how to elevate recruiting through the concepts we share in this book,

I don't understand why someone would want to be in talent acquisition if you don't have an interest in leaving candidates in a little better place than where you found them. A few pieces of feedback can literally change the trajectory of someone's career. You might open an opportunity for them that changes their life. There is someone I hired 12 years ago who still messages me on her work anniversary and thanks me, reminding me that she wouldn't be where she is if I didn't give her the chance.

How lucky am I?

Note

1 Talent Board. 2021 Global candidate experience research reports, December 2021, thetalentboard.org/benchmark-research/cande-research-reports/ (archived at https://perma.cc/8UX9-XDXN)

01

What is candidate experience?

Now we've talked about the background, we'll move on to looking at exactly what candidate experience is. How is it defined, and what does it encompass? Recruiting and hiring has evolved dramatically over the years, especially with the technologies implemented, but candidate experience continues to be a struggle for many organizations. Defining it is one thing. Measuring it and improving it are at a whole different level, which we'll get to in this book.

Let's talk about what it is first. According to Miles and McCamey:[1]

The candidate experience emanates from an exchange between job seekers/candidates and the organization to which employment is being considered. The job candidate is seeking employment and the organization is seeking (recruiting) talent. The candidates' focus is on securing desirable employment for themselves. Subsequently, they engage in activities that present themselves in a manner that is desirable to their targeted organizations. Candidates invest an enormous amount of time preparing for and assembling materials to assist in moving from decision point to decision point during their job-search process, purposefully encountering organizations – sometimes even before the candidate has the requisite knowledge to qualify for a position. Subsequent decision points made by the candidate include whether to apply, to go through assessments if invited, to continue the process, or to disengage from the search with a particular organization. The job candidate evaluates information and experiences to form perceptions regarding the processes, practices, and people representing the organization.

Job candidates, both external and internal, evaluate their experiences that form perceptions about a specific business and brand they're interested in gaining employment at. While the above definition is good, it's predicated on active job-seeking. It doesn't include all the interactions a prospective candidate has with a business and a brand before they actively apply for a job and how those interactions impact their brand perception throughout the active stages. We'll talk a lot about this throughout the book.

Based on our research over the past 10+ years, we've distilled even further the Talent Board definition of candidate experience:

> Candidate experience is essentially every interaction in recruiting and hiring, such as social, digital, in person, and/or experiential, between an individual (the candidate) and an organization over time (recruiters, hiring managers, the business and the brand), from before the candidate applies to as far as they get in the process, which ultimately impacts the candidate's perception of fairness and the measurable attitudes and behaviours of those experiences. The resulting candidate sentiment and perception of fairness determines whether or not the job seeker will apply again, refer others, have any brand affinity and/or make purchases and/or influence purchases if the business is consumer-based.

We're going to talk a lot in the chapters to come about these various interactions throughout the recruiting and hiring process and the ultimate business impact. In the meantime, to further add context to the above definition of candidate experience, let's give you three different scenarios below based on accounts we've heard over the years that highlight just how impactful these candidate interactions can be.

Candidate experience scenario No 1

Anup is an engineer at an aerospace company. He's moderately happy with his job but has been there for three years and was promised that by now he'd be managing a team, which hasn't happened. Plus, he's just not excited about his work anymore. One day while at work he's doing some industry research online when he comes across a competitor developing fascinating lunar landing technology for a future moon mission – an area he's particularly interested in. He clicks through to the aerospace competitor and reads on. He discovers they're hiring as well! So, he checks his network to see if he's connected with anyone there and digs deeper into learning more about the company. He finds mixed reviews online about what it's like to work there and hears even more mixed reviews from a few people in his network.

He decides to apply online anyway and awaits the automated response, which he receives, but then later that same afternoon he gets an e-mail from one of the competitor recruiters. The recruiter actually reviewed his résumé and wants to schedule a phone call. Anup's excitement builds after the phone screening as the recruiter tells him he really thinks he's qualified and wants to schedule an interview with the hiring manager next.

And then nothing. A week later Anup contacts the recruiter to see when the interview is going to happen. Nothing. Another two weeks go by. Nothing from the recruiter. Then, a full month later, Anup receives an automated rejection e-mail saying they filled the position. A week later Anup sees that the job he applied for is still open on the website.

While his anger and frustration won't translate into affecting his purchasing decisions – he's not going to be buying lunar landing technology anytime soon – when asked by other engineering friends about whether they should apply or not, Anup's answer was definitive and clear: no.

Candidate experience scenario No 2

Jenny thought she found the job of her dreams. She's a recruiting operations professional looking for her next career opportunity. She felt she had the skills and experience the company was looking for. So, after researching the company and checking with her network, she applies.

However, the application process is long and arduous. It asks for the same information multiple times during the process and still asks her to upload her résumé and post her LinkedIn profile. She must save where she is in the application a few times (fortunately, the company she was applying to allowed for that functionality) and go find information she didn't have at the ready. She plods through the obscure and obtuse application, which is followed by a personality assessment, something she never found any value in as a recruiter.

All totalled, it takes Jenny about 2.5 hours to complete the application process. She hesitates for a moment prior to hitting submit, crosses her fingers, then pushes enter. Having dealt with clunky applications before as a recruiter, she half-expects to get an error message.

Instead, 30 seconds later, she receives an automated rejection e-mail. This in turn makes her livid – 2.5 hours of her life gone for an automated e-mail half a minute later. She tries to get an answer from the company as to why she was rejected so quickly, that it was obviously the auto-screening settings in the application tracking system (ATS), but she never hears back.

From that point on Jenny knew she would never apply again to that company, and she would also actively encourage others not to.

Candidate experience scenario No 3

Beth was struggling. The COVID-19 pandemic forced the hotel she worked at to close indefinitely, and she lost her job as a shift supervisor at the hotel restaurant. Her unemployment benefits helped but not enough for her to take care of her young children long term. She was fortunate she had childcare help from her family, but it was still hard being a single parent. The local food packaging plant for a well-known brand was hiring again, after being closed the first few months of COVID-19 and, while she wasn't sure if she qualified for a job, she looked at what was open.

On the company's career website there was a statement that stated, 'Due to COVID-19, we continue to follow the Centers for Disease Control and Prevention (CDC) guidelines to ensure the safest work environment possible. We hope you consider applying to one of our currently open positions.'

Beth found a position she was interested in and applied. She knew she wasn't as qualified for the supervisor role as others with industry experience might be, but she really needed a job. She had already been applying for other open jobs in her area and just wasn't hearing back from anyone.

She applied, received the automated 'thank you for applying' message and then actually got a nice personal response from a recruiter a week later. The recruiter thanked her for her time, but then said she's not qualified for the role she applied for.

But instead of that being the end, the recruiter encouraged her to apply for another job that was linked in the e-mail message. Not only that, the recruiter gave her some coupons that she could use to buy the very food products the company sells. Coupons she could really use right then.

Beth thanked the recruiter and decided that she'll definitely apply for the suggested position.

Candidate experience makes an impact

The above candidate experience scenarios are played out millions of times each year around the world, each with the potential outcome being negative, positive or neutral. The fact is, the sheer volume of candidates who apply for jobs anywhere will not be hired. That's why Talent Board states repeatedly that recruiting and hiring teams are in the business of 'no'. They are saying no much more often to external candidates as well as current employees looking for internal mobility opportunities.

The cumulative candidate experience impacts the job candidates' perception of fairness about a business and its brand. Candidates are clear about whether they'll share their positive and negative experiences with their inner circles (close family and friends, significant others and close peers and colleagues they share their life experiences with). Table 1.1 shows just how much candidates share both in North America through 2021.

Each year the Talent Board candidate experience benchmark research is made up of different companies (although 60 per cent of the same companies participate year after year) and different populations of hourly, professional and management candidates. So, it's always fascinating to us how consistent the responses are year after year. Sharing negative candidate experiences decreased in 2020, and then increased again in 2021, as indicated in Table 1.1. It did the same in EMEA but not in APAC and Latin America where candidates are less likely to share their negative candidate experiences year after year.

Candidates are also asked if they'll share their positive and negative experiences publicly – meaning posting reviews on Glassdoor, Indeed, Fairygodboss, Kununu, Seek and many others. This also means they might share their experiences via social media sites, in blog posts they write, in videos they film, among other opportunities to share. Table 1.2 shows just how much candidates again share both in North America. Sharing positive candidate experiences publicly online increased in 2020, and then decreased again in 2021, as indicated in Table 1.2.

Again, the consistency of responses year after year is fascinating. However, when asked about sharing publicly, the willingness to share publicly decreases for both positive and negative experiences. And while not as high as their willingness to share with their inner circles,

TABLE 1.1 Percentage of candidates sharing positive and negative experiences with their inner circle

	2021	2020	2019	2018	2017
Positive experience	75%	77%	76%	78%	77%
Negative experience	57%	52%	72%	66%	66%

TABLE 1.2 Candidates sharing positive and negative experiences publicly online

	2021	2020	2019	2018	2017
Positive experience	50%	57%	50%	50%	51%
Negative experience	32%	31%	35%	35%	35%

it's still a significant percentage of individuals. Sharing the negative experience publicly is lower as there's another 35 per cent+ of candidates every year who tell us this information is private, and they don't share it publicly. This is understandable, because most of us don't shout from the rooftops that we didn't get hired, no matter how bad the experience was.

The candidate experience is pervasive throughout

All these candidate interactions we're talking about are all touchpoints along a common set of six stages in which candidates move in the recruiting process. We refer to this collectively as the Candidate Experience Journey (see Figure 1.1).

Talent Board didn't create these stages; they've been a part of the recruiting and hiring process for decades. But what we've found over the years is that every interaction a candidate has from pre-application (the attraction stage), through being rejected (most candidates), through being made offers and being hired (less than 10 per cent of all interested job candidates) again impacts their perception of fairness.

There are also perception gaps we help companies identify each year – how they feel they're delivering recruiting and hiring to their candidates versus how candidates actually perceive the experience and how they rate those experiences. (We'll talk more about the best practices in the following journey graphic throughout the book.)

Pre COVID-19, perception gaps year after year looked like our 2019 CandE Benchmark Research throughout North America, EMEA, APAC and Latin America – revealing more employers rating themselves higher than their candidates from attraction, to interview, to being rejected. We'll talk more about the best practices in Figure 1.1 throughout the book.

FIGURE 1.1 The Candidate Experience Journey and CandE Winner Best Practices

Talent Board | CANDIDATE EXPERIENCE AWARDS

CANDIDATE EXPERIENCE JOURNEY
CANDE WINNER BEST PRACTICES

ATTRACTION / RESEARCH / BRAND	APPLICATION	SCREEN / INTERVIEW	NOT SELECTED	OFFER	NEW HIRE / ONBOARDING
— MAJORITY OF CANDIDATES —	— MAJORITY OF CANDIDATES —	— FEWER CANDIDATES —	— MAJORITY OF CANDIDATES —	— 10% OF CANDE CANDIDATES —	
Align employer and corporate brands	Apply for your own jobs!	Leverage AI and automation screening and tests	Timely automated and recruiter and/or hiring manager rejections	Timely offers after final interviews	Be accountable for the entire hiring process
Market culture, testimonials, diversity, inclusion, values	Different process for internal mobility	Prep candidates for video interviews	Thank candidates for their time	Negotiate wisely if necessary	Engage new hires before day 1
Automation to answer questions (chatbots)	Mobile apply	Ensure candidates can present skills and experience	Ask for candidate feedback	Expectation setting and next steps	Ask for new hire feedback
Referrals and brand ambassadors	Personalize the experience by job type	Stick to schedules	Offer feedback	Ask for candidate feedback	Offer feedback
Customer-centric approach	Ensure personable acknowledgement and closure	Expectation setting and next steps	Nurture silver medalists	Offer feedback	Expectation setting and next steps post-hire
Ask for candidate feedback	Expectation setting and next steps	Ask for candidate feedback		Nurture declined offers	Keep re-recruiting to retain
	Ask for candidate feedback	Offer feedback			Shift to employee experience
		Nurture silver medalists			

DECLINED

NOT SELECTED

For example, whether candidates spend five minutes or five hours researching a company, even if they did end up applying for a job, what they were looking for didn't quite align with the employer's perception of what they were delivering – i.e. the job and marketing content shared on their career sites, via social media, via search engine searches or found on employer review sites.

After researching, many interested candidates still may apply for jobs they're interested in. This is usually done via an online application but could be done via kiosk or mobile device in a store, office, etc., as well as completing a paper application. As mentioned, this is as far as most job candidates get in the recruiting and hiring process, and where most are either rejected or never hear back from the employer. This is a huge perception gap we find every year in our benchmark research. Candidates not hearing back from employers always skews negatively for employers.

For the smaller percentage deemed qualified, the job candidates are then screened (test, assessment, phone call, video interview, etc.) and an even smaller percentage may be interviewed live in person or live virtually, as many more companies had to do due to COVID-19. Another perception gap exists here year after year as well. Although the candidate ratings are usually higher at the point of being screened and interviewed due to more human engagement and communication at this stage, there can still be perception gaps. For example, employers not following up after the interview, especially when the candidates were told otherwise.

For some of the finalists, offers are made and negotiated, which not all candidates accept in the end. This is where the perception gap either disappears altogether, or it flips to where the job candidates rate the employers higher. Most employers are all in at this point in the hiring process, doubling down on communication and feedback to ensure the close, and there's also a halo effect for the candidates getting offers and being hired.

And then there are the very few finalists who do accept the jobs. These are the new hires, and everything that happens leading up to being hired, and beyond, sets the tone for their ongoing employee experience, however long that will be.

The biggest perception gaps we see each year are the candidates who are rejected and how they perceive that experience versus the employer's perception. This is always a negative skew, from being rejected at the point of application to being a finalist during the interview stage, no matter what employers do, including definitive acknowledgement and closure, the job candidates will always rate the rejection experience lower than employers.

It's important to reference the experiential differences we found in our benchmark research in 2020 and 2021. Once COVID-19 officially became a pandemic, employers were put into a forced level of transparency like no other. They had to ask themselves things like:

- What do we tell potential candidates (and current employees) now that the business has been hit with this pandemic, and we have to freeze hiring indefinitely?

- What do we tell our candidates who were supposed to be interviewed in person and now we have to virtualize them all?

- What do we tell our new hires who were supposed to start but now we have to push out their start dates or rescind the offers altogether to do the business contracting?

- What do we tell our current employees we're doing to prevent furloughs and layoffs?

Those companies that did their best to keep candidates and employees updated as the pandemic wore on communicated with much more empathy than we've seen in our benchmark research to date. Combine that with all the social upheaval of 2020 – social and racial injustice and inequality – upheaval that continued in 2021, and it

FIGURE 1.2 2020 North America employer/candidate perception gaps

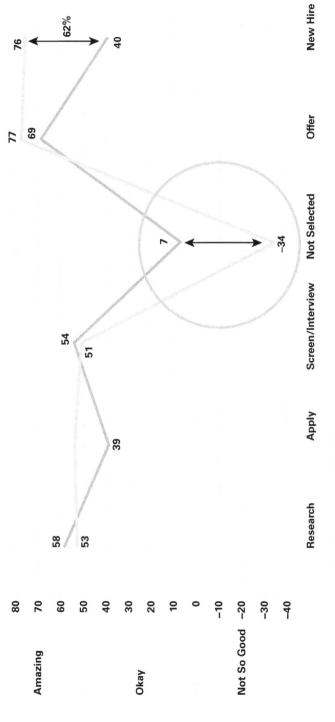

FIGURE 1.3 2021 North America employer/candidate perception gaps

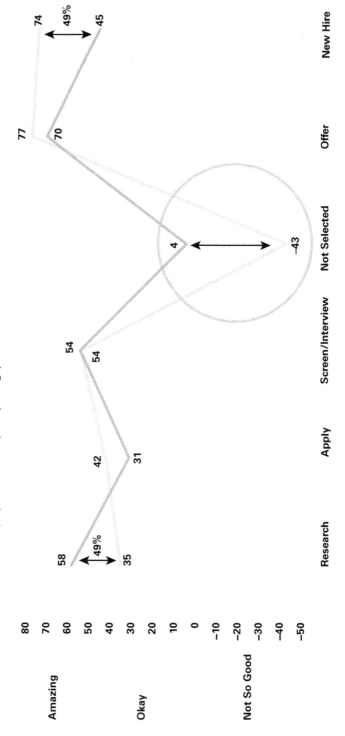

became even more critical for organizations to continuously communicate. And with millions of people out of work, candidates definitely had to be more patient and forgiving of what was happening in the world.

Which is why we saw a greater alignment of perception in 2020. Negative perception gaps actually collapsed in 2020 (except for when candidates were rejected), with more trending positive instead, as you can see in Figure 1.2 for North America (you can view the similar global perspective in our research briefs from EMEA, APAC and Latin America).

As you can see, many of the negative perception gaps we saw pre-COVID virtually disappeared, with only those not selected having the big red circle of negativity, which isn't unusual. No matter what the world looks like, each year we see a negative skew with those candidates not selected, which is always most individuals interested in any given job.

We saw these dramatic changes all over the world and through much of the ratings data we captured in the benchmark research. And although not every region we measure candidate experience in collapsed all the negative gaps, we saw more changes in experience and perception than the previous nine years. No matter what the world looks like, not even the highest rated companies in our research can do everything right all the time when you consider the changes impacting businesses year after year.

What's interesting is how similar the alignment of awareness is for 2021 (see Figure 1.3), even though candidate resentment has increased in North America to pre-COVID levels. Again, we see the same pattern in the Offer and New Hire (onboarding) ratings, where the gaps level out and flip positive. We also continue to notice over the past few years that employers feel they have work to do at the onboarding stage and with the continuing virtualization of onboarding and the focus on retention, which will mostly likely extend well into 2022.

FIGURE 1.4 Business impacts that impact recruiting and hiring

RECRUITING
TEAM CHANGES

MERGERS &
ACQUISITIONS
ACTIVITY

SO MUCH
MORE

LEADERSHIP CHANGES

THE BUSINESS

ECONOMIC
FLUCTUATIONS

NEW
PRODUCT/SERVICE
LAUNCHES

COVID-19

CHANGING
PRIORITIES

What impacts
the business
impacts recruiting

Talent Board

CANDIDATE
EXPERIENCE
AWARDS™

What impacts the business impacts candidate experience

Who plans for a global health crisis? Besides the World Health Organization, the Centers for Disease Control and Prevention, US National Institute of Allergy and Infectious Diseases, and other healthcare and infectious disease organizations, most employers do not. As we've already seen, positive communication during downturns and stressful times goes a long way with candidates.

As noted in the preface, Talent Board was founded a couple of years after coming out of the Great Recession. Since 2011, we were in nothing but a growth market, with month after month job growth and, until February/March 2020, the lowest unemployment rates in decades. And while we did see a modest improvement in a positive candidate experience over the years, communication and feedback loops – the primary differentiators we see every year in our research – weren't as consistent and, in turn, impacted candidate perception negatively. We'll look at more of our CandE Benchmark Research throughout this book, but the point here is that there are many other events that impact a business, recruiting and hiring, and ultimately the candidate experience (see Figure 1.4). Consider these other examples:

- leadership changes in the C-suite and other levels;
- recruiting team changes;
- merger and acquisition activity;
- economic fluctuations;
- new product and/or service launches;
- expansion;
- downsizing;
- changing business priorities;
- the list goes on and on…

Many HR and recruiting leaders and their teams are the first to be impacted when these kinds of events strike. One day you're emergency surge hiring during a pandemic (depending on your industry), the next day you're furloughing thousands of employees. And candidates, external and internal, are not shielded from the rollercoaster of positive and negative experiences.

Candidate experience competitive differentiators

Let's revisit again our definition of candidate experience in the beginning of this chapter, break it down and highlight the key items from it outlined in this chapter:

> **Candidate experience is essentially every interaction in recruiting and hiring...**
>
> ... such as social, digital, in person and/or experiential...
>
> **... between an individual (the candidate) and an organization over time (recruiters, hiring managers, the business and the brand)...**
>
> ... from before the candidate applies to as far as they get in the process...
>
> **... which ultimately impacts the candidate's perception of fairness and the measurable attitudes and behaviors of those experiences...**
>
> ... The resulting candidate sentiment and perception of fairness determines...
>
> **... whether or not the job seeker will apply again, refer others, have any brand affinity and/or make purchases and/or influence purchases**
>
> ... if the business is consumer-based.

After over 10 years of conducting candidate experience benchmark research, we know the following are clear competitive differentiators in recruiting and hiring and all the interactions your organization has with job candidates. You'll be reading a lot more about these throughout the book, so we wanted to introduce them to you here:

1 **Consistent communication from pre-application to onboarding.** This includes automated messaging for most job candidates and

human interaction for the smaller numbers of people who are screened, assessed, interviewed, made offers to and hired. When the communication is professional yet personable, timely and definitive, candidates are more likely to rate their experience as positive, have a higher perception of fairness overall and are more likely to engage the employer again in the future.

2 **Expectation setting.** Another exchange that goes hand in hand with consistent communication is setting proper expectations. What happens after the application process? What happens after the screening, assessing and interviewing process? What happens after the offer and my start date? When the next steps are defined and consistently followed through on?

3 **Feedback loops.** This includes asking for candidate feedback in continuous feedback surveys and/or our annual benchmark research programme. The act of asking for feedback implies the employer cares and wants to improve its recruiting and hiring practices. Providing feedback is also important, especially for finalists. Most employers won't give feedback for the great percentage of candidates who apply and don't go any further, but for those who were screened, assessed and/or interviewed, feedback goes a long way with candidates. Most of the highest-rated employers in our research each year provide feedback to finalists and, again, these candidates are more likely to rate their experience as positive, have a higher perception of fairness overall and are more likely to engage the employer again in the future.

4 **Being more accountable and transparent.** Just as we saw with how many employers responded to candidates during COVID-19, being more accountable to job candidates and transparent about the hiring process usually translates in higher positive ratings, a greater perception of fairness and candidates more likely to engage the employer again in the future.

5 **Perception of fairness.** While it's inspirational to hear companies state that 'happy candidates make for happy customers', especially consumer-based companies, it's not very realistic in the end. Job candidates are only going to be happy if they get hired, and most

do not for any given job. In fact, you could provide the best candidate experience in the world, and at the point of telling a candidate you're no longer going to pursue them, their experience can turn negative. This is why the point of rejection always results in the lowest ratings in our research. However, all the differentiators above and all the examples we share in this book can lead to positive outcomes for the business and the brand.

What's clear is that candidate experience is pervasive throughout the recruiting and hiring process, even before candidates apply for one of your jobs. We'll take a more in-depth look at why the candidate journey is so important in Chapter 2.

Note

1   Miles, Sandra and McCamey, Randy (2018) The candidate experience: Is it damaging your employer brand? *Business Horizons*, 61 (5), 755–64.

02

Why is the candidate experience journey so important?

The candidate journey

Similar to how we defined what candidate experience is in Chapter 1 – *essentially every interaction in recruiting and hiring from pre-application to onboarding* – the candidate journey is a perpetual cycle that loops back on itself again and again for most job seekers. Why? Because most job seekers don't get hired for the jobs they're interested in. While historically the candidate journey is viewed in a linear fashion, meaning candidate researches, candidate applies, candidate gets screening, candidate gets interviewed, candidate may get rejected or candidate gets an offer, candidate gets hired – most candidates only make it to the application process and are either rejected or they don't hear back. In fact, on average in our benchmark research, 50 to 60 per cent of candidates who apply never make it to the screening and/or interview stages.

In fact, what really happens can be quite nonlinear. For example, let's use Anup as an example from Candidate experience scenario No 1 in Chapter 1. Anup is an engineer at an aerospace company. He's moderately happy with his job but has been there for three years and was promised that he'd be managing a team by now, which hasn't happened. Plus, he's just not excited about his work anymore. One day while at work he's doing some industry research online when he comes across a competitor developing fascinating lunar landing technology for a future moon mission – an area he's particularly interested in.

FIGURE 2.1 The Candidate Experience journey and CandE Winner Best Practices

Talent Board | CANDIDATE EXPERIENCE JOURNEY
CANDE WINNER BEST PRACTICES

ATTRACTION / RESEARCH / BRAND — MAJORITY OF CANDIDATES

- Align employer and corporate brands
- Market culture, testimonials, diversity, inclusion, values
- Automation to answer questions (chatbots)
- Referrals and brand ambassadors
- Customer-centric approach
- Ask for candidate feedback

APPLICATION — MAJORITY OF CANDIDATES

- Apply for your own jobs!
- Different process for internal mobility
- Mobile apply
- Personalize the experience by job type
- Ensure personable acknowledgement and closure
- Expectation setting and next steps
- Ask for candidate feedback

SCREEN / INTERVIEW — FEWER CANDIDATES

- Leverage AI and automation screening and tests
- Prep candidates for video interviews
- Ensure candidates can present skills and experience
- Stick to schedules
- Expectation setting and next steps
- Ask for candidate feedback
- Offer feedback
- Nurture silver medalists

NOT SELECTED — MAJORITY OF CANDIDATES

- Timely automated and recruiter and/or hiring manager rejections
- Thank candidates for their time
- Ask for candidate feedback
- Offer feedback
- Nurture silver medalists

OFFER — 10% OF CANDE CANDIDATES

- Timely offers after final interviews
- Negotiate wisely if necessary
- Expectation setting and next steps
- Ask for candidate feedback
- Offer feedback
- Nurture declined offers

NEW HIRE / ONBOARDING

- Be accountable for the entire hiring process
- Engage new hires before day 1
- Ask for new hire feedback
- Offer feedback
- Expectation setting and next steps post-hire
- Keep re-recruiting to retain
- Shift to employee experience

DECLINED

NOT SELECTED

Let's change the scenario, though. Anup applies to the job, gets a phone screen, then is asked to take an assessment and an engineering test, gets an interview, gets a second interview, but then is told the company has hired someone else with more experience that they're looking for. One week later, another recruiter in the company that rejected him is sourcing for another engineering role in another department and finds him in their applicant database. This time Anup gets the offer, and he takes it, as he's still very interested in this new company. Imagine all the different job types companies big and small across industries hire for and all the different permutations of candidate experience from pre-application to onboarding. It can go here, there and everywhere, and as we mentioned above, loop back on itself again and again. In a sense, a portion of semi-qualified candidates are recycled, which isn't really the best term, but is true. They may have applied for other jobs at the same and/or different companies, and smart recruiting technologies today allow them to be more accurately matched to other jobs recruiters are sourcing to fill.

When you look at Figure 2.1, our candidate experience journey best practices, you'll see a set of activities at each recruiting stage that companies with the highest candidate experience ratings in our research each year put into practice regularly. We'll review each stage briefly below and then in more detail in future chapters.

Attraction/research/brand

The candidate journey begins before anyone ever applies. Whether candidates spend five minutes or five hours researching the jobs they're interested in, they're also checking out the business and the brand that they're interested in prior to applying. As mentioned earlier, Talent Board believes that the candidate experience is a 24/7 interactive experience, whether it's for passive candidates or those actively looking for a job.

Overall candidate experience, diversity and inclusion, and employer branding are the top recruiting initiatives or activities employers have been focused on the past few years. And attracting candidates is one area of talent acquisition (TA) that has been given more and more attention and investment due to such a strong job market in the past few years, at least until the impact of COVID-19, with many more employers big and small across industries understanding just how competitive attracting and sourcing quality candidates truly is. In fact, diversity, equity and inclusion, along with redeploying people to retain them, have become some of the most important initiatives of recruiting throughout the pandemic.

Employer branding is a critical component of talent attraction (which we'll go into in more detail in Chapter 4). The employer brand is a big part of the reason why someone wants to work for an organization. It encompasses the culture and the employee value proposition. A strong, descriptive and transparent brand will help companies attract talent and alleviate some of the challenges that recruiting the right candidates can create. A weak brand, on the other hand, can deter talent or misrepresent the employee experience, which can lead to new hire turnover and low performance once onboard.

Organizations must think like traditional marketers more than ever. Just as consumers have evolved, candidates have become savvier in their job search and per our research are more likely to have previous relationships with employers and conduct their own research. Candidates are also diving deeper into career sites, social media and employer review, and job sites like Glassdoor, Indeed and Fairygodboss to get a clear picture of an organization before making a connection and applying.

Candidates today are doing their research. They want to be prepared and take ownership of their journey, and organizations need to be prepared as well, regardless of what the world looks like. Whether millions are out of work or millions are choosing to work elsewhere, companies need to provide clear and consistent information so candidates can self-select based on their interests and needs.

Quick-hit best practices

- Align employer and corporate brands.
- Market culture, testimonials, diversity, inclusion and values.
- Implement automation to answer (chatbots).
- Leverage referrals and brand ambassadors.
- Take a customer-centric approach.
- Ask for candidate feedback.

Application

The application process is driven primarily by whatever applicant tracking system is being utilized and thankfully has improved significantly (which we'll go into in more detail in Chapter 5). Recruiters are able to handle an increased volume of applications and better manage the administrative side of the application process. Plus, automated communications can be triggered at various disposition stages, screening and assessment tools can be integrated throughout the application process, and applicants can be notified of their status and connected with nurturing recruitment marketing systems.

It's still not without its limitations and shortcomings, however. There are still too many candidates who don't hear back from employers months after they applied. And when most candidates only make it this far in the recruitment process, that's a very limited interaction and mostly automated candidate experience. Each year when we ask candidates in our benchmark research what's the last step they remember completing in the recruiting process, over 60 per cent of them said they had applied, and less than 10 per cent said they had been informed they did not get the job. This means that a good portion of candidates simply don't remember receiving the automated message telling them they weren't going any further or, worse, they didn't actually hear back after they first applied.

Even with the sheer number of unqualified candidates who apply for jobs every year, if some level of communication isn't provided, it can impact a candidate's perception of that employer. And no matter the level of automation, if it includes definitive closure by letting candidates know they won't be pursued any further, it can help to keep the perception of fairness at least neutral, if not positive.

Of course, not all employers want everyone to apply again – some companies have and will face heavy candidate volume and some serial applicants are nowhere near qualified. But most employers do want those candidates who could be deemed as future fit to apply again for other jobs. Thankfully, more employers have collapsed the time it takes to initially apply, with the majority of all candidates in our research saying it took less than 15 minutes. However, that allows for a greater volume of mostly unqualified applications on average, which is the conundrum.

On average, the reality for most companies is that a third to half of the candidates who apply for all position types are just not qualified. It's no surprise that high-volume hiring companies can become cynical about the vast number of unqualified candidates, but that doesn't mean that not acknowledging applicant interest and ensuring definitive closure leads to the best outcomes for the employer. Plus, many companies have 'banned for life' codes, or something similar, to block those unqualified serial appliers.

Quick-hit best practices

- Apply for your own jobs.
- Development a different process for internal mobility.
- Implement mobile apply options.
- Personalize the candidate experience by job type.
- Ensure personable acknowledgement and closure.
- Ensure expectation setting and next steps.
- Ask for candidate feedback.

Screen/interview

A strong connection exists between how candidates are treated during the screening and interviewing stage and whether they'll continue to associate with the business and the brand (which we'll go into in more detail in Chapter 6). By the time potential candidates make it through general screening, and perhaps an assessment or two, to get to the interview stage, positive ratings tend to increase, even if it's not the best experience. This is because when there is more communication and opportunities for engagement because candidates are 'in the running', they tend to rate their experience higher.

That's not to say they won't rate employers lower if their experience is bad, because they will. It's just that this is where companies can win or lose with candidates they definitely want to apply again and refer others.

Through strategic recruiting, organizations can make sound investments in applicable tools, assessments and tactics, expand their local and global reach, improve the candidate experience and strengthen their overall quality of hires. We're finding most organizations in our research say they use pre-employment assessment and selection tests during the interview stage.

Screening and interviewing are often the deciding factors in hiring a candidate. After screening all the applications and early assessments and conducting early phone screenings and/or video interviews, this is where the final list of candidates is evaluated by the recruiters, hiring managers, potential colleagues and other leaders and individuals in the organization. When recruiters and managers have the right tools and use best practices, interviewing can be a powerful process that determines the best fit for the organization.

However, few organizations have a standard approach for how interviewing is conducted. A broken, disconnected interview process has a negative impact on both the quality of hires and the candidate experience, especially when recruiters and hiring managers don't prepare ahead of time.

Obviously, during the pandemic, most employers had to completely transition to virtual environments for interviewing and hiring, and continue to use virtual systems. Some employers fared better than others in doing this. Plus, the number one negative reason candidates withdraw themselves from the recruiting process is because their time was disrespected during interviews and appointments.

This is why, whether it's in person or virtual, when companies help candidates prepare, ask relevant questions and communicate with candidates throughout the interview process – while adhering to schedules overall – the candidate experience skews positive.

Quick-hit best practices

- Leverage AI and automation screening and tests.
- Prep candidates for video interviews.
- Ensure candidates can present skills and experience.
- Stick to interview schedules.
- Ensure expectation setting and next steps.
- Ask for candidate feedback.
- Offer candidate feedback.
- Nurture silver medallists (those candidates who are finalists but didn't get the job).

Non-selected (rejected candidates)

This is a pivotal point of the recruiting and hiring process because it's here, no matter how far a job candidate makes it in the process, where negative sentiment abounds. No one wants to be rejected from a job opportunity they feel they might be qualified for. Yet, the reality is that over 90 per cent of candidates in our research do not get the job, which reflects the real world as well. Your organization could deliver the best candidate experience from pre-application to whatever the final stage is, and yet, when the candidate isn't selected, it skews negative.

But let's not call it rejection. Let's call it non-selected. Because applying for any given job is conditional based on the experience and skills for that particular job; the very same candidate could be qualified for another similar job in the near future (which we'll go into in more detail in Chapter 7). There are job candidates who are not selected who then get fast-tracked into screening and interviewing, and even silver medallists who end up getting offers because the new hire withdrew or didn't work out. This is why it's important for organizations to consider all candidates, external and internal, to be perpetual candidates. In fact, we're all perpetual candidates, whether we're actively looking for work or not.

At every stage of the recruiting and hiring process, there are many who become the non-selected. As we wrote in Chapter 1, your candidates' collective experiences, positive and negative, can and will impact your business and your brand. Asking for candidate feedback and providing feedback as to why you won't be pursuing them will go a long way to protecting your brand. That's why empathetic communication to those you aren't selecting at any stage is so critical over time.

Quick-hit best practices

- Timely automated and recruiter and/or hiring manager rejections.
- Thank candidate for their time.
- Ask for candidate feedback.
- Offer candidate feedback.
- Nurture silver medallists.

Offer and onboarding

Once an organization decides to hire a given candidate, it first sends an offer letter and proceeds to negotiate, either in print or electronically (which we'll go into in more detail in Chapter 9). However, this intricate and emotionally charged final step in the process can bring frustration since the organization may not succeed in closing the deal – especially when the process takes too long overall. Time continues to be a big frustration factor with final-stage candidates.

This is why organizations must continue to provide a positive candidate experience and communicate with candidates throughout this process and beyond the new hire experience via onboarding. Onboarding is the final stage in talent acquisition, and when new hires have a positive onboarding experience, they are more productive in their first few weeks and may be more likely to stay with their new employer. The good news at this stage is that most employers are 'all in' with those they want to hire, and we see little to no difference in overall ratings during offer and onboarding compared to CandE winners in any year.

For some companies, however, after making a heavy investment in earlier stages of talent acquisition, human resources and hiring managers ignore candidates (now employees – but candidate experience is perpetual) once they've been hired.

When onboarding goes well, the benefits directly impact organizational success. When onboarding goes badly, employee morale and retention is at risk.

Quick-hit best practices (for offer)

- Timely offers after final interviews.
- Negotiate wisely if necessary.
- Ensure expectation settings and next steps.
- Ask for candidate feedback.
- Offer candidate feedback.
- Nurture declined offers.

Quick-hit best practices (for new hires)

- Be accountable for the entire hiring process.
- Engage new hires before day one.

- Ask for new hire feedback.
- Offer new hire feedback.
- Ensure expectation setting and next steps post-hire.
- Keep re-recruiting to retain.
- Shift to employee experience (which is also internal candidate experience!).

Map the candidate journey

Journey mapping the customer experience was first introduced by Oxford Corporate Consultants in 1998,[1] to help Eurostar establish and implement their corporate mission and brand proposition. Customer journey maps help companies understand how their customers behave and ultimately how they want them to behave by considering all the various processes, people and technologies that impact the customer experience, business and the brand.

The same can be done with your candidate experience journey outlined above. Visualizing your company's recruiting and hiring processes that your candidates go through can be extremely valuable to make critical improvements over time. Combined with continuous candidate experience feedback, these analyses can give your organization an intimate understanding of not only how the experience impacts your business and brand, but where positive and negative impacts occur.

By leveraging the Figure 2.1 The Candidate Experience Journey and CandE Winner Best Practices guide, you could create your own journey maps by candidate persona types. We recommend developing personas first, since there are many different job types you're hiring for. Defining what the ideal candidate could be for each job type can help you further develop a journey map that in turn can help you better design your recruiting and hiring processes.

For example, developing a candidate persona could include defining the following for each candidate and job type you hire for.

TABLE 2.1 Defining candidate personas

Store associates persona	
Personal attributes (values and motivations)	Looking for part-time flexible work Make extra money while going to school Make extra money while raising a family Looking for training/growth opportunities
Professional attributes (skills and experience)	Previous retail experience Previous customer service experience Excellent communication skills Is empathetic and compassionate
Job search behaviour (preferences and challenges)	Looking for nearby work Able to take mass transit to work Looking for COVID-19 safety protocols Looking for a living wage

Let's say you're hiring store associates for your retail operations. Create a matrix for these personas that include the following (see Table 2.1):

• personal attributes (values and motivations);

• professional attributes (skills and experience);

• job search behaviour (preferences and challenges).

Once you have key personas developed, then you can start mapping the journey for each one. Whether you're a one-person shop, or a team of 150, developing personas and journey maps takes time, but in the end it will be time well spent. There are many different iterations of candidate experience journey maps on the market today, and your organization may have already used one of these.

We're going to share our own unique approach by combining the competitive differentiators in Chapter 1, which we've found to be constant year after year in our benchmark research and the candidate journey guide from Figure 2.1 in this chapter. As a reminder, here are those competitive differentiators again:

1 **Consistent communication from pre-application to onboarding.** This includes automated messaging for most job candidates and human interaction for the smaller numbers of people who are

screened, assessed, interviewed, made offers to and hired. When the communication is professional yet personable, timely and definitive, candidates are more likely to rate their experience as positive, have a higher perception of fairness overall and are more likely to engage the employer again in the future.

2 **Expectation setting.** Another exchange that goes hand in hand with consistent communication is setting proper expectations. What happens after the application process? What happens after the screening, assessing and interviewing process? What happens after the offer and my start date? When next steps are defined – and consistently followed through on – candidates are more likely to rate their experience as positive, have a higher perception of fairness overall and are more likely to engage the employer again in the future.

3 **Feedback loops.** This includes asking for candidate feedback in continuous feedback surveys and/or our annual benchmark research programme. The act of asking for feedback implies the employer cares and wants to improve its recruiting and hiring practices. Providing feedback is also important, especially for finalists. Most employers won't give feedback for the great percentage of candidates who apply and don't go any further, but for those who were screened, assessed and/or interviewed, feedback goes a long way with candidates. Most of the highest-rated employers in our research each year provide feedback to finalists, and, again, these candidates are more likely to rate their experience as positive, have a higher perception of fairness overall and are more likely to engage the employer again in the future.

4 **Being more accountable and transparent.** Just as we saw with how many employers responded to candidates during the pandemic, being more accountable to job candidates and transparent about the hiring process usually translates in higher positive ratings, a greater perception of fairness and candidates more likely to engage the employer again in the future.

5 **Perception of fairness.** While it's inspirational to hear companies state that 'happy candidates make for happy customers', especially

consumer-based companies, it's not very realistic in the end. Job candidates are only going to be happy if they get hired, and most do not for any given job. In fact, you could provide the best candidate experience in the world, and at the point of telling a candidate you're no longer going to pursue them, their experience can turn negative. This is why the point of rejection always results in the lowest ratings in our research. However, all the differentiators above and all the examples we share in this book can lead to positive outcomes for the business and the brand.

Now let's set up an example journey chart to complete. We'll just share segments below for brevity and will make an entire CandE journey chart available in the downloadable resources from this book. Again, let's use the store associates example (see Table 2.2). This example focuses on the Attraction stage.

TABLE 2.2 Candidate Journey chart – Attraction/research/brand

Store associates Attraction/ research/brand					
Consistent communication	How the candidate thinks/feels (survey feedback, anecdotal feedback, opinion)	How you want the candidate to think/feel	People (who's responsible and what do they do)	Strengths: Challenges:	Outcomes: Opportunities:
			Processes (what are they and how do you measure their effectiveness)	Strengths: Challenges:	Outcomes: Opportunities:
			Technologies (what are they and how do you measure their effectiveness)	Strengths: Challenges:	Outcomes: Opportunities:

FIGURE 2.2 The Candidate Journey map

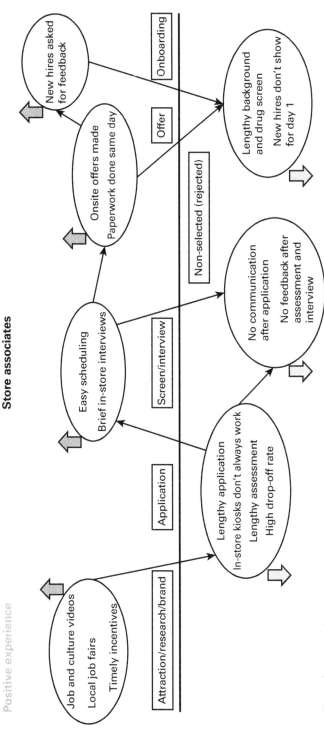

Positive experience

Store associates

Job and culture videos
Local job fairs
Timely incentives

Attraction/research/brand

Easy scheduling
Brief in-store interviews

Application

Onsite offers made
Paperwork done same day

Screen/interview

New hires asked
for feedback

Offer

Onboarding

Non-selected (rejected)

Lengthy application
In-store kiosks don't always work
Lengthy assessment
High drop-off rate

No communication
after application

No feedback after
assessment and
interview

Lengthy background
and drug screen

New hires don't show
for day 1

Negative experience

This is a powerful exercise to do for all five of the key differentiators listed above. Of course, there will be overlaps for each differentiator – similar processes, team members and technologies involved. The goal is to get to the strengths, challenges, outcomes and opportunities for each one and distil commonalities that you can focus on improving.

You can then map these key highlights and commonalities across the continuum from attraction to onboarding. Figure 2.2 illustrates this based on our store associates example. This exercise will help you visualize and better understand perception gaps in your recruiting and hiring processes, which we discussed in Chapter 1.

If creating personas and mapping the candidate journey seems too complex and cumbersome to pull off with your team today, especially if you've never done an exercise like this before, or if you're a one-person shop or on a small team, then you may want to start with an easier activity.

Based on where you're at today with your recruiting and hiring processes and your candidate experience (or as much as you understand), brainstorm three areas that you want to improve in candidate experience. Then describe why you want to improve these areas. For example, improving communication with rejected candidates, prepping candidates for the interview process, etc. (see Table 2.3). We recommend that you get feedback from anyone else in your department, including your hiring managers and your business leadership if possible. You may want to create an ad-hoc committee to complete this experience.

Then move onto another exercise of defining how you'll go about accomplishing one of these. Based on the three areas that you want to improve in candidate experience, pick one and outline three steps on how you'll achieve it. Focus on how you will achieve it (specific, tangible, action oriented – see Table 2.4).

Each year we help companies understand that many candidate experience improvements are incremental and usually don't require huge change management initiatives. Understanding some if not all of what candidates experience in your recruiting and hiring processes is the first step to identify even one area you want to improve and that you can improve within your current resources, staffing and technologies.

TABLE 2.3 Candidate Experience success: areas for improvement

Area for improvement	Why do you want to improve this
1.	
2.	
3.	

TABLE 2.4 Candidate Experience success: how to achieve improvement

The area you want to improve is:
How you will achieve it (specific, tangible, action oriented)
1.
2.
3.

Then make the business case

In the next chapter we'll talk about the business impact of candidate experience, and then, after deeper dives into recruiting, hiring and the candidate experience in Chapters 4 to 9, we're going to talk about making the business case and getting leadership buy-in in Chapters 10 and 11. But making the business case is going to be highly dependent on one thing: data. Data that show what your recruiting and hiring process strengths and weaknesses are. Whether or not you participate in the CandE Benchmark Research or do your own continuous candidate feedback surveys, you're going to need to understand what the candidates experience every step along the way. After the next chapter we're going to give you even more details and insights on how to improve your candidate experience journey from pre-application to onboarding.

Invest the resources and the time to ask for candidate feedback, develop your candidate personas, map the candidate journey, identify your perception gaps, identify one improvement you can make today, work on overcoming internal resistance – and then make the business case!

Note

1 Yoo, J and Pan, Y (2014) Expanded customer journey map: Interaction mapping framework based on scenario, in *HCI International 2014 – Posters' Extended Abstracts. HCI 2014. Communications in Computer and Information Science*, **435**, ed C Stephanidis, Cham: Springer.

03

The business impact
of candidate experience

What impacts the business impacts recruiting and hiring

Think about this for a minute: pre COVID-19 we were in nothing but a growth market globally with the lowest unemployment rate in decades. In fact, as mentioned earlier in the preface, Talent Board has been measuring candidate experience since 2011, and at that point we were already well on our way out of the Great Recession of 2007/2008. Businesses across industries were thriving, growing and hiring.

It was a candidate market as well; qualified, sought-after job candidates were able to leverage better jobs and pay. Unfortunately, the phenomenon known as ghosting, usually applied to dating when one person never again contacts the person they had been seeing, had been increasing in recruiting and hiring. And not just from employers ghosting candidates either; candidates were ghosting employers. According to job search engine Indeed in 2019,[1] four in five employers (83 per cent) had experienced being 'ghosted' by a job candidate who either didn't show up for an interview or stopped replying to hiring managers entirely. Nearly 70 per cent of employers had stated that being ghosted had only started in the previous two years. This behaviour included not showing up for interviews, stopping replying to recruiters and/or hiring managers, accepting the job offer then not showing up and accepting a verbal offer but never signing the paperwork.

This accelerated in 2021 while millions voluntarily left their jobs for other jobs or to start their own businesses, creating a tight labour market that recruiting and hiring professionals had never before seen.

What's even more interesting is that pre-COVID, in the growth market we experienced over the past decade, candidate resentment was actually increasing globally. We define candidate resentment as an unwillingness to apply for another job at a specific company, to never again refer anyone to work at that company, to never again have any future brand affinity and/or to never make or influence purchasing decisions at that company (if a consumer-based company) based on the candidate's experience applying for a job. According to our annual Talent Board CandE Benchmark Research, candidate resentment increased dramatically in North America and EMEA from 2016 to 2019, and again from 2020 to 2021. We define candidate resentment as the percentage of candidates not willing to ever apply again, refer others, or have any brand affinity with a specific employer due to a poor candidate experience. Candidate experience ratings have been more positive in APAC and Latin America over the years, primarily because candidates in many of the countries in these regions are less likely to share negative feedback.

Companies around the world invest billions of dollars or pounds each year on improving their customer service and customer experiences. According to International Data Corporation (IDC),[2] worldwide spending on customer experience (CX) technologies totalled $508 billion in 2019 and was expected to increase to $641 billion in 2022. Yet, according to research from Aptitude Research and Talent Board[3] (sponsored by Symphony Talent), only 10 per cent of companies have a dedicated budget for candidate experience.

So, when we think back to January 2020, employers big and small across industries were poised for a banner year. Until the global pandemic happened. Businesses were locked down. Candidates prepping to be interviewed were put on hold. New hires ready to start were put on hold. Companies had to quickly triage and flip to a virtual world – if they could – and figure out how to keep the business moving forward. Industries like travel and leisure, consumer goods, restaurants, food and beverage, some services sectors and others were hit hard very fast.

Plus, coronavirus wasn't the only disrupter in 2020 and 2021. Social and racial injustice and inequity, political divisions and just overall upheaval everywhere continue into 2022. Here's the bigger point: who plans for a pandemic and social upheaval? There are so many things that impact your business and in turn impact your recruiting and hiring efforts. All the above-mentioned events impacted businesses dramatically, plus consider the following that can occur at any time that also will impact your business, which we first mentioned in Chapter 2:

- leadership changes;
- recruiting team changes;
- mergers and acquisitions;
- new product and service launches;
- changing business priorities;
- economic fluctuations.

Any of these kinds of events can happen at any time. One minute your company might be surge hiring (what we're seeing today at the time of writing, with COVID-decimated industries ramping exponentially again), and the next you're freezing hiring, furloughing and laying people off. And, through it all, every single interaction with your candidates, external and internal, impacts their perception of fairness and their perception of your business and your brand. This is why communication and feedback are such important competitive differentiators in recruiting and hiring.

The criticality of communication and feedback loops

As mentioned above, candidate resentment was growing pre-COVID, so we were expecting to see much of the same in 2020. What we weren't expecting, was to see such a surge in a positive candidate experience globally. But that's exactly what our data showed in 2020. Then, in 2021, the great experience decreased dramatically in North America and EMEA, and increased dramatically in APAC and Latin America.

One of the key rating questions we ask candidates each year is what we call 'the relationship question' (what kind of relationship will you have with the employer going forward based on your experience?). Those who answered said they had a great experience and were willing to increase their relationship, meaning to apply again, refer others and, for consumer-based companies, make purchases (see Figure 3.1).

Conversely, those North American candidates who said they had a poor experience in 2020 and were no longer willing to associate with an employer actually decreased dramatically and then increased dramatically again in 2021 (see Figure 3.2). What we know now is that 2020 brought out a greater level of empathetic communication between employers, candidates and employees like never before. Candidates also became more forgiving since it was no longer a candidate market in many hard-hit industries. Because hiring ramped up again everywhere in 2021, combined with the continuing pandemic and social upheaval, the above swing was due to the fact that candidates and employees felt like employers' transparency decreased from 2020. Candidates and employees also demanded positive and supportive experiences and wanted to work more on their own terms going forward. We'll have to see what happens in 2022 and beyond to this upside-down recruiting and hiring world.

As mentioned in Chapter 2, consistent communication from pre-application to onboarding is critical for a positive candidate experience. This includes automated messaging for most job candidates and human interaction for the smaller numbers of people who are screened, assessed, interviewed, made offers to and hired. When the communication is professional yet personable, timely and definitive, candidates are more likely to rate their experience positive, have a higher perception of fairness overall and are more likely to engage the employer again in the future.

FIGURE 3.1 Great candidate experience over the years

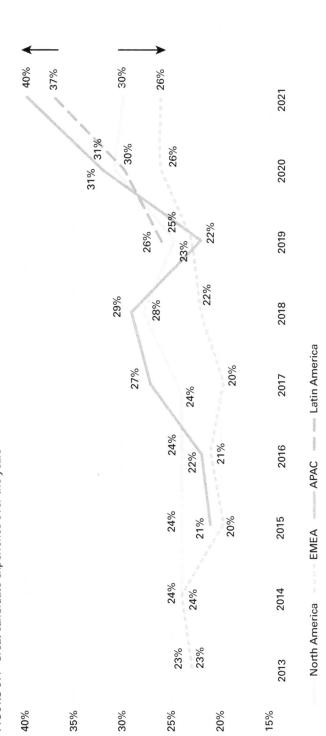

FIGURE 3.2 Poor candidate experience over the years

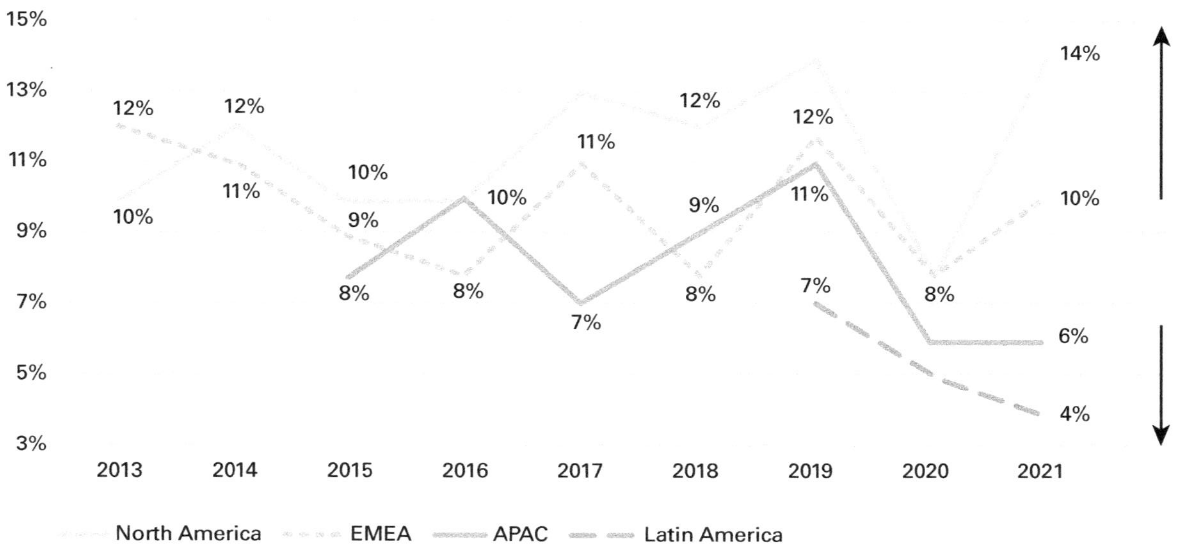

Legend: North America, EMEA, APAC, Latin America

Y-axis: 15%, 13%, 11%, 9%, 7%, 5%, 3%

X-axis: 2013, 2014, 2015, 2016, 2017, 2018, 2019, 2020, 2021

Data labels: 14%, 10%, 12%, 12%, 11%, 12%, 10%, 11%, 8%, 9%, 10%, 11%, 12%, 10%, 9%, 8%, 7%, 8%, 11%, 8%, 6%, 7%, 4%, 8%, 7%

Also, feedback loops are just as critical. This includes asking for candidate feedback in continuous feedback surveys and/or our annual benchmark research programme. The act of asking for feedback implies the employer cares and wants to improve its recruiting and hiring practices. Providing feedback is also important, especially for finalists. Most employers won't give feedback for the great percentage of candidates who apply and don't go any further, but for those who were screened, assessed and/or interviewed, feedback goes a long way with candidates. Most of the highest-rated employers in our research each year provide feedback to finalists and, again, these candidates are more likely to rate their experience as positive, have a higher perception of fairness overall and are more likely to engage the employer again in the future.

Here are just a few examples of improving communication and feedback loops from past CandE winners (companies that have the highest positive candidate ratings in our benchmark research each year). Although many companies do some of the following, the key is sustaining communication and feedback consistently over time, something that many companies struggle with. We'll share case study excerpts from our research throughout this book.

Dr Reddy's Laboratories

Dr Reddy's ensures transparency on their careers site regarding their application process, and this includes clear automated communications and notifications from their ATS to each candidate that applies. They make their rejection notifications more friendly and personal to explain the various reasons why a candidate may not be selected. Their recruitment team makes commitments to follow-up with considered candidates in a reasonable timeframe, even if the job has not been filled. Their recruiters speak directly with candidates not selected at the interview phase – by phone whenever possible.

Hoag Memorial Hospital Presbyterian

One of Hoag's biggest impacts was their 'Talent Huddle' biweekly newsletter. Their engagement/click-through rate (CTR) skyrocketed, and they received an overwhelmingly positive response from their talent community regarding the newsletter. Their team was building and curating content for job seekers that gave them the tools and resources to improve their career search and job interviewing skills and inform them of overall market trends related to professional advancement.

Syneos Health

Syneos Health developed and launched effective microsites within their career pages in order to engage, provide details and guide prospective candidates toward a positive experience, and in return drive more quality applicants to apply. These microsites included, but are not limited to, early career, interview tips and preparation and learning and development pages. They understand their candidates want to know why they would want to work for Syneos Health, and they may prefer communication that is personalized. These micro- sites allow their prospective candidates the opportunity to receive more relevant information and an overall candidate experience that is unique to them. They can see that candidates are reading and digesting the information versus just clicking in and out of the sites.

Walgreens

For Walgreens, follow-up throughout the process is critical, so they established strict parameters that their recruiters and hiring leaders operate within. They require all hiring leaders to provide candidate feedback, whether at the point of submission or after an interview, within 48 hours. Additionally, their recruiters update candidates within 48 hours of receiving hiring leader feedback. To ensure the candidate experience remains best in class, they survey candidates monthly. The survey data are then shared with their recruiters to help them recognize areas of opportunities to improve that candidate experience.

Auburn–Washburn USD 437

With the move to more virtual recruiting during the pandemic, Auburn–Washburn USD 437 updated and increased their candidate communication by creating templates within their applicant tracking system to better ensure that their candidates were receiving consistent communication in a timely manner. They knew their changes made a difference, not only through anecdotal candidate comments but also in their CandE survey results.

BASF

BASF identified a need to educate and connect with their candidates in a more intimate way. They started creating fun explanatory videos, which detailed their company, post-application expectations, interview overview, and offer/close the deal. After COVID-19 hit, they made further changes in the correspondence to their candidates to create full transparency on new interview processes, positions that were put on hold, changes in travel, interviews needing to be cancelled/postponed or interview health screens, so they had all the necessary information.

Colorado Springs Utilities

Colorado Springs Utilities re-evaluated their candidate communication templates and automated notifications based on both requisition status changes as well as candidate status changes within a requisition to ensure not only timely delivery of these messages but also to create consistency between recruiters. They did the same with communications sent to hiring managers throughout the recruitment and selection process. Their results across all key indicators from the CandE survey research showed improvement, and recruiters are spending less time keeping applicants and hiring managers informed during the hiring process.

Southwest Airlines

Southwest Airlines identified, mapped out and rewrote the communication their candidates receive along every step of their hiring journey from start to finish. They also changed and added processes to ensure that candidates receive timely, consistent communication from their recruiters immediately after applying. They want to ensure that no candidate falls through the cracks in terms of follow-up, and this has been and will continue to be a priority.

Stantec

Stantec created COVID-19 e-mail templates and added them to their ATS system to allow their TA team to provide real-time updates to candidates on how their application might be affected by COVID-19. They also increased communication with their candidates to ensure transparency with regard to the requisition status, application status, any delays and what changes to expect. They used virtual hiring tools to minimize the impact on candidate engagement, and they used Microsoft Teams to enable digital interviewing and rolled-out virtual interview training to make the process as close to in-person interviews as possible. A centralized location was also created to help their various stakeholders answer and ask questions that pertained to hiring in these challenging times. This included guidance on how to respond to incoming inquiries as it related to hiring during COVID-19.

The business impact of candidate experience

The above examples were from our benchmark research reports from the past few years. There are many more case studies you can read in our latest research reports. So, what will the future bring? No matter what the world looks like today and tomorrow, we at Talent Board continue to focus our research on the business impact of candidate experience from pre-application to onboarding. Every time we share the potential impact we find, each year, we get more and more nods of acknowledgement – this is quite real.

Also, as mentioned above, candidates who believe they have had a 'negative' overall experience tell us every year they will take their alliance, product purchases and business relationship somewhere else. This means a potential loss of revenue for consumer-based businesses, hurts referral networks for all companies, and determines whether future-fit and silver medallist candidates will apply again.

However, the good news is that those who had a 'great' overall experience say they'll definitely increase their employer relationships – they'll apply again, refer others and make purchases and/or influence purchases when applicable. These aren't just the job finalists either or those hired. The majority are individuals who research and apply for jobs but who aren't hired.

What's important to keep in mind is that the sheer number of candidates employers reject during the recruiting process can quickly impact the business and the brand (whatever the world looks like), in both positive and negative ways. That's not to say that those hired aren't important to the business. Of course they are – they're the individuals who help grow and sustain the business. While all candidates, hired or not, can impact how the business is perceived by other potential candidates, it's simply those candidates who are not hired that need more attention paid to their perceived overall experience.

But don't just take our word for it. Josh Bersin, principal and founder of Bersin, now part of Deloitte LLP, and the Josh Bersin Academy, explained that in today's world social media is like a nuclear weapon: 'A single employee could impact the health of a company's brand – and ultimately its success. One only needs to look at recent videos gone viral of employees making dramatic exits and being touted as heroes.'[4]

According to Society for Human Resources Management (SHRM), as many as 76 per cent of job seekers research a company online before submitting an application and 83 per cent rely on publicly available company reviews to decide whether to apply there.[5] This aligns with our research on how candidates research companies and how it impacts their perception of the business and the brand based on what they find.

For consumer-based businesses, where candidates are customers and vice versa, the potential revenue impact looms large. A commonly referenced case study (and one of the few public, case studies touting actual negative fiscal impact) conducted by Virgin Media and Ph. Creative a few years ago showed that Virgin Media was losing more than $6 million annually in sales revenues due to poor candidate experiences – which they were then able to turn into a $7 million revenue stream.[6]

Most companies, particularly publicly traded companies, aren't willing to share this kind of quantitative data publicly, and for good reason. But many today are internally quantifying the cost of a poor candidate experience, which can be in the millions of dollars or pounds per year, and incremental improvements to recruiting processes and candidate experience can go a long way to increasing revenue and referral networks.

Another case study from our Talent Board research a few years ago features Kimberly-Clark and how it turned candidate experience into a profit centre. Kimberly-Clark is a consumer product company with big brands like Huggies, Kleenex, Cottonelle, Kotex and Scott. Nearly one in four people globally use its products every day. So, it's essential that it has a candidate-centric experience, as its candidates are consumers of its products.

It built support and commitment from the top down with business leaders. Two of their leadership sponsors were presidents of their largest business unit, who were accountable for about $6 billion in revenue. It then tied the candidate experience back to its business results. It estimated that it had interaction with over 200,000 candidates a year, and all of them are potential customers of its products. What it realized was that:

- If it provided a good experience it could increase revenue.
- If it provided a bad experience it could lose revenue.
- It also pointed out the other implications of providing a poor experience – including the percentage of people that would tell a friend, talk negatively about the company on social media and stop buying its products.

Another key element of its change management plan was to gain support from the team executing and driving its processes: the recruiters, hiring managers and administrators who helped with scheduling interviews. It made a lot of friends within its administrative community because it made its processes better, which made their lives better.

One of the most important things it embraced as a recruiting and hiring team was recognizing that the job candidate was its No 1 customer. At the time, it calculated that the lifetime value of a paying customer was $30,000. So, if it could convert 5 per cent of the annual rejected candidates to be paying customers, it could generate another 10,000 customers for a total of $300 million in revenue.

And that's exactly what it did. It improved its overall candidate experience and offered rejected candidates coupons for the company's products.

To help companies better understand the potential negative impact, Talent Board created an online candidate resentment calculator for HR and talent acquisition professionals that generates potential lost annual revenue by plugging in some simple recruiting and hiring numbers. According to the latest Talent Board benchmark research, the overall candidate resentment rate – those candidates willing to sever the relationship with a prospective employer based on their experience – is at about 9 per cent globally (North America, EMEA, APAC and Latin America).

While the resentment calculator only produces a rough estimate based on the hiring numbers used, it helps to make the business case that improving the recruiting process benefits companies' bottom lines. Even business-to-business (B2B) companies can use it as a conversation starter because, ultimately, if they don't have the candidate referrals needed to grow and sustain their businesses, it will potentially impact their revenue.

To give you an example of how it works, let's walk you through some numbers:

In 2021, according to our benchmark research, the average global resentment rate was 9 per cent. That means 9 per cent of all our candidate responses, mostly rejected candidates, were extremely negative. However, we know not everyone will put their money where their complaint is.

So, according to Microsoft research, 47 per cent of consumers have made the choice to switch to a different brand due to bad customer service within the last year.

Assumptions:

- You make 10,000 annual hires.
- Your applicants-per-hire ratio = 100:1.
- Your average annual value of a paying customer = $500.

That means for every 100 candidates... according to our projections:

- 10,000 annual hires means 99 rejected applicants per hire.
- Total annual rejected applicants = 990,000.
- Potential lost customers at 9 per cent resentment rate: 89,100.
- 47 per cent of 'detractors' who really leave the brand: 41,877.
- Average annual customer value = $500.
- Potential annual loss = $20,938,500.

That's nearly $21 million dollars in lost revenue. No company wants to lose that kind of revenue by treating their customers poorly. But, as you can see above in the Kimberly-Clark and Virgin Media examples, improving recruiting, hiring and the candidate experience can also lead to increasing revenue for your business. Even if you're a B2B company, this resentment calculator can help start internal discussions about the potential fiscal impact of candidate experience (think referrals).

For all companies, referrals are critical

Candidate referrals are a cornerstone of smart recruiting for a good reason. For lots of magnetic reasons.

As *Harvard Business Review* put it, 'referred candidates are of higher quality than applicants from the general public and are more likely both to receive and accept an offer, stay at the job longer, and perform better. This all adds up to spending less time on the hiring process, reducing turnover, and increasing overall productivity.'[7]

Employers across the globe received some additional good news about referrals from Talent Board research: the majority of candidates said they were likely to extremely likely to refer other candidates based on their experiences over the years.

What's astonishing here are the facts that:

- On average, nearly 90 per cent of the candidates in all global regions did not get hired for the jobs they applied to.
- And 50 to 60 per cent of the candidates in all global regions did not get any further than applying for a job.

In other words, candidates didn't hold it against employers for not giving them the job. They were still willing to make referrals when their candidate experience was efficient, timely and respectful, which isn't easy to do at the point of application. According to our research, one of the main reasons employers don't get referrals is because they've delivered a poor candidate experience at one or more stages of their recruiting process. Just like they may lose revenue if they're a consumer-based business.

Based on the above percentages, you might be thinking that employers are doing a good job at providing positive candidate experiences.

While it's true that the overall quality of the candidate experience is on the rise, it can and does still fluctuate year after year; who plans for a pandemic?

Plus, there's still plenty of room for employers to improve when it comes to getting referrals, especially when you consider there will be many more candidates entering talent pipelines as the post-pandemic recovery continues. As the number of job openings rise and more candidates apply, employers can maximize potential referrals and sustain those killer percentages noted above by delivering a positive experience every step of the way.

Not all referrals are equal. Employee referrals and referrals from people who have worked together or know each other well are typically more likely than referrals from people who are connected only through social media. Also, those candidates who get screened, assessed and interviewed have a higher level of human engagement than just applying for a job, which in turn increases the likelihood of a stronger referral. We don't know too many organizations who think of rejected candidates as a potential referral source, but they should. Especially when their experience is positive, and their perception of fairness is high enough.

The impact is real

As we've already shared, people will still talk to one another about their good and bad candidate experiences, especially when we consider their inner circles (i.e. significant others, close friends, colleagues, peers, etc.). The percentages drop when we look at how many candidates share their positive and negative experiences publicly online (i.e. social media posts, Glassdoor reviews, Indeed reviews, etc.), but there are still significant populations willing to share their experiences publicly.

We should also mention losing candidates in the later stages of the recruiting process due to a poor experience. When it comes to candidates withdrawing themselves from the recruiting process, there are many reasons as to why. But when we look at Talent Board data, for those candidates who have an overall poor experience, the most negative reasons candidates withdraw year after year are:

- Their time was disrespected during interviews and appointments (trends the highest in North America).
- The recruiting process just took too long.
- The salary didn't meet expectations.
- There was poor communication and rapport with recruiters and/or hiring managers.

Although it's not the same pool of candidates year to year, what's interesting is how consistent year after year these reasons are globally, even considering the impact of COVID-19.

Even with all the potential business impact highlighted above, whether candidates will apply again and/or refer others based on their overall candidate experience is a vitally important outcome of the candidate experience. And while most companies would argue that they don't want all the candidates applying again, they do want those deemed future fit to apply again. They most certainly want their final interview silver medallists to apply again and to refer others who may also be the right candidates for future roles.

At the time of this writing, the world continues to try to manage and move beyond COVID-19, and hiring has again ramped exponentially. But the candidate resentment rate we measure increased again unfortunately, as we mentioned earlier. Companies are struggling to recruit people competitively as well as retain the people they have, professional and hourly, and all sorts of incentives are being offered like:

- flexible work schedules (remote/hybrid);
- higher salaries and hourly pay rates;
- stronger COVID safety protocols;
- bonuses and other monetary incentives;
- medical benefits or enhancements to current package;

- professional development and tuition reimbursement;
- childcare benefits;
- non-monetary incentives (phones, computers, etc.);
- unlimited vacation.

Ultimately, making and sustaining improvement investments in recruiting and candidate experience today can ensure a greater return on employment brand and quality of candidate tomorrow, no matter what the world looks like, or what the future brings.

Notes

1 Lewis, L. The ghosting guide: An inside look at why job seekers disappear, Indeed, August 2019, indeed.com/lead/ghosting-guide (archived at https://perma.cc/R3PR-QX5B)

2 International Data Corporation (IDC). Worldwide semiannual customer experience spending guide, IDC, August 2019, businesswire.com/news/home/20190806005070/en/Spending-on-Customer-Experience-Technologies-Will-Reach-641-Billion-in-2022-According-to-New-IDC-Spending-Guide (archived at https://perma.cc/D4Q3-QEF4)

3 Allioto, G, Laurano, M and Grossman, K. Exceptional experiences research report, Symphony Talent, May 2021, resources.symphonytalent.com/exceptional-experiences-research-report (archived at https://perma.cc/L9TW-V7UH)

4 Bersin Insights Team. Insights from IMPACT, Josh Bersin Academy, April 2018, www2.deloitte.com/content/dam/Deloitte/ca/Documents/audit/ca-audit-abm-scotia-insights-from-impact-2018.pdf (archived at https://perma.cc/NFT8-Y2SV)

5 Wilkie, D. Was your company trashed online? What to do with workers' negative reviews, SHRM, June 2019, shrm.org/resourcesandtools/hr-topics/employee-relations/pages/negative-workplace-reviews-.aspx (archived at https://perma.cc/K36N-CAXK)

6 Adams, B. How Richard Branson plans to make over $7 million a year from… recruiting, Inc, June 2016, inc.com/bryan-adams/how-virgin-media-plans-to-make-over-7-million-a-year-from-recruiting.html

7 Gautier, K and Munasinghe, L. Build a stronger employee referral program, *Harvard Business Review*, May 2020, hbr.org/2020/05/build-a-stronger-employee-referral-program (archived at https://perma.cc/Y85B-A2AE)

04

Improving the attraction phase

Employer branding, recruitment marketing and sourcing

For a company to successfully grow, a company must be able to attract talent. Attraction is defined as the pre-application stage of identifying and engaging with candidates before they apply for a position, and it includes employer branding, recruitment marketing, social media, job posting and passive candidate sourcing. In other words, it is the ability of an organization to draw people in. A *recruiting* function fills job vacancies. A *talent acquisition* function works alongside leadership, and together a strategy is devised by which you can identify key roles and personas and proactively attract them to your company now and for future job openings. In this chapter, we will discuss helping your organization hone an authentic employer brand that compels candidates to learn more about your company and consider working for you.

What is the attraction stage of the candidate journey?

Attraction is now arguably the most important aspect of recruiting since it prepares organizations to fill current growth goals and shortages as well as prepare for future talent needs. It also gives most candidates that first impression of an employer and what it's like to work for the company.

Research shows that job search behaviour is ongoing, whether a worker is in fact actively seeking a job change or not. Search intensity will no doubt vary, from those who are merely curiously perusing career sites to those who want out of their current company now, but it is estimated that up to 71 per cent of the global labour force is looking at available company information at any given time.[1] Humans are curious by nature.

The desired outcome is that your prospects and potential candidates can begin to picture themselves working for your company, desire employment in your environment and decide to take action and apply.

What are candidates looking for?

People are looking at much more than just the job spec and matching their experience to desired skills when searching career options. Today's talent market is seeking companies that match their lifestyle and values. In the following sections, we'll look at how you can make the best impression on candidates by offering them the information they're searching for.

Clear communication and transparent information. Candidates want communication, transparency and authenticity in their interactions with you. Companies are using multiple mediums of communication to reach a larger audience and allow candidates to consume content where they want to find it. The authenticity they're seeking includes hearing directly from your employees, in their voice. They want to hear from workers other than the recruiters and it can be in the form of 'passing the mic' to targeted workers to engage them in crafting content and videos and writing reviews that help engage candidates.

Company insight. They also want realistic job previews, information on potential career paths, tips on successfully interviewing with your company, and, in some cases, for you to provide links to online learning to close any skill gaps between their experience and the profile your company is seeking. Internal mobility, the movement of employees to other roles within an organization, is becoming more critical to organizations as we seek to retain and develop our existing talent and keep them engaged; and internal applicants are more engaged when companies provide these tools via a separate, internal career portal. External candidates are looking for details on benefits and total rewards, and information on the company's outlook, growth and what is in it for them regarding career mobility and total rewards. For workers who are in extremely high demand and short supply, it could also be about who pays the highest salary.

An acknowledgement of current events. Candidates expect organizations to at least acknowledge current political, social and economic events or environmental causes. Many organizations are taking this a step further with detailed messages about their stance on issues, and public action plans with goals around key topics like diversity and community impact pages, along with regular updates on progress. In the 2020 Talent Board CandE Benchmark Research Survey, we found that global positive candidate experience rose and negative candidate experience decreased, in correlation with companies posting COVID-19 related public marketing communications plans around ways that their businesses and operations were shifting to keep patrons, employees and candidates safe.[2] Companies who stay quiet on current events may miss out on top talent. This is not a trend that is going away either, and we strongly recommend that companies do not 'turn off' social impact messaging. This is now our baseline, our new normal.

Connection to the company. Candidates are also looking for a clear understanding of company culture, a compelling place to work and a sense of connection with the overall brand. Company culture continues to be the most important marketing content for 35 per cent of candidates who responded to the 2021 CandE Benchmark Research survey. They want insights into the company experience, a 'day in the life' of current employees, including the company's mission statement, vision and values. According to McKinsey and Company experts, 'as long as the pay is competitive, an inspiring mission and value proposition is what motivates the best talent'.[3] There is also a trend in companies' career content shifting towards workplace attributes such as balance and well-being, financial compensation, the structure, mission and purpose of the workplace, and being transparent about change and stability, to which candidates are responding favourably.[4]

Diversity, equity and inclusion. Candidates want information on diversity, equity and inclusion (DEI) initiatives at your company for a few key reasons. Workers want to be part of organizations where they feel a sense of belonging, that they are represented and that they have an equal pass to success. They want to be part of a company whose people reflect the community in which it operates and leadership that upholds social responsibility. They also want to work for a company that understands how diverse companies consistently financially outperform less diverse companies by up to 36 per cent.[5]

There are a few places where this information may exist. One place that is out of our control is on publicly available review sites like Glassdoor. For better or worse, the fruits of our efforts may end up in a public review, so it is crucial for an organization to be earnest about the DEI strategy and to be transparent about its successes, failures and current state.

We can control the information shared on the company career sites and social media pages, and we should see this as an asset. Companies should highlight all diverse employees who represent their community demographics, including underrepresented and Black and Indigenous people of colour (BIPOC) minorities, military veterans, workers from non-traditional backgrounds, and the generational and gender differences that abound. Some organizations even post social impact statements, such as corporate pledges, to create inclusive environments, including accompanying action plans detailing how the company is supporting DEI and goals. Other companies have also publicly tracked progress towards their goals and listed their achievements, diversity statistics and equitable practices. Of course, global companies must familiarize themselves with DEI issues in all markets to ensure their strategy and approach is localized to each of their regions. We'll cover DEI more in Chapter 12.

Where does attraction occur?

The recruiting and attraction activities of an organization take place both inside and outside its domain. This involves the direct and intentional ways that your company communicates with the talent market, including the career site(s) and job postings, external job boards, LinkedIn outreach and ads, social media, SEM/SEO, mobile texting campaigns, marketing efforts such as Best Places to Work awards and passive candidate sourcing. It involves employer branding efforts, such as targeting, thought leadership and storytelling.

CandE global research shows that the number one investment that companies are making to engage with candidates, pre-application, is their own external career site (see Table 4.1). Other top recruitment marketing investments are LinkedIn, job boards and other micro-career sites, videos, Facebook pages, building talent communities and mobile texting platforms.

TABLE 4.1 Critical online/interactive ways employers engage with candidates who have not yet applied (partial list)

	2021	2020	2019	2018	2017
Career site (primary)	70%	76%	68%	77%	72%
LinkedIn outreach	60%	63%	58%	62%	62%
Job board/other site company pages (job/career specific)	54%	52%	53%	52%	47%
Videos (across websites and social channels)	37%	31%	26%	21%	20%
Facebook pages	36%	26%	23%	29%	29%
Mobile career/job apps	33%	29%	26%	30%	27%
Career site (micro-sites)	30%	32%	29%	33%	33%
Talent community	30%	30%	31%	26%	25%

(continued)

TABLE 4.1 (continued)

	2021	2020	2019	2018	2017
SEO/SEM paid advertising (social and search)	25%	32%	27%	31%	N/A
Mobile text messaging campaigns	24%	17%	12%	5%	N/A

It also includes the organic ways that people become aware of your jobs, such as browsing your career site after seeing media coverage, publicly available employee rating sites, or advertisements for your products or services. They might learn about your company's corporate reputation because they are former employees or customers, or they met one of your employees through networking, get a referral or simply word of mouth. Remember, research shows that candidates share both their positive and negative candidate experiences with their inner circle.[6] Best-in-class employers are '...creating a [talent] community of individuals who are already aware of your organization and are inclined to think well of it'.[7]

Who is involved?

Every employee has an important role in attracting candidates, but the workers most directly involved with attraction are the marketing/ recruitment marketing teams, talent acquisition/HR teams, and diversity and talent inclusion specialists.

While the candidate's first impression of an organization might come from a job posting, social media or even consumer content, the interaction with the recruiting team will leave the biggest impression, whether it is positive or negative. As Miles and McCamey explained in their scholarly article, 'The candidate experience: Is it damaging your employer brand?': 'The candidate experience stems from both the recruiter and recruitment process, which forms the candidates' perception of the employer brand and influences the candidates' decision to continue a relationship with the organization.'[8] Recruiter behaviour can have an impact on whether or not that candidate continues to be interested in working for the organization, continues being a customer, refers others and whether they leave positive or negative reviews on publicly available sites like Indeed and Glassdoor. Each recruiter/candidate interaction (and hiring manager/recruiter interaction) is an opportunity for one-to-one marketing for your organization. It is not just a conversation about whether the candidate is a fit for the role.

As candidates interact with companies through the recruiting process, that process and those people can build a deep, lasting relationship for current or future benefit – which in turn strengthens the employer brand. It can potentially be damaging if the candidate has a negative experience. Every practice and process used by the organization throughout the candidate journey and recruiting process influences the candidates' perception of, and future behaviour towards, the organization.

Indirectly, every interaction an employee has with someone outside the organization has the potential to be an attraction activity. As we stated earlier, up to 71 per cent of the current labour force is looking at available company information and that includes observing the way workers represent the organization in both professional and social settings. If a worker shows up at a neighbourhood park clean-up event with a big smile, a branded sweatshirt and a strong work ethic, others may be more interested in exploring career opportunities at that company versus being interested in the company of someone who says at a networking event, 'Yeah, I work there', and gives a half-hearted shrug. Across the organization, all employees are potential marketers, from sharing company content, creating content of their own, participating in company-sponsored community and culture events, to embodying the culture when talking to candidates. Companies who use third party recruiter/search agencies should ensure those firms are good representatives of your employer brand and are sharing the right message in their initial outreach, since they are potentially responsible for the first impression that candidates have of your organization.

Here are some best practices:

Targeting ideal candidate profiles

In marketing, persona creation is frequently used in targeted marketing strategy. Personas are fictional characters created to represent market segments and their usual behaviours, and to help create and drive targeted messages to those segments. Talent acquisition teas can similarly create candidate personas to help identify the traits and characteristics of ideal candidates. Personas can be used for either passive candidate sourcing by segmenting talent, or for reviewing applicants. In his article, '6 Simple Steps to Revitalizing Your Candidate Experience', Adams explains how to use personas effectively and why it works: 'Research, understand, and love every persona of your audience so you can design an authentic experience to suit them and build real brand loyalty because you care.'[9] We must be able to explain why a company is great, why an opportunity is exciting and why a candidate should consider it; and it has to all sound authentic if we want it to resonate with our target audience.

Developing an employer brand

Why do employees want to work for particular organizations? The employer brand is a large part of your 'why' statement and encompasses the company culture, mission, vision, values and the employee value proposition (EVP). A strong, descriptive and transparent brand will help companies attract talent and hire the right people faster, and authenticity is key. One way to ensure you have an authentic brand is to spend as much effort on candidate experience as you do on branding, so candidates can experience it for themselves as well as hear or read about it from you.

Utilizing recruitment marketing

There are a few places in talent acquisition where our processes can be elevated by emulating our business partners, and the attraction phase in the candidate journey is one of them. Larger organizations may have recruitment marketers who own this function, but talent acquisition leaders in small- to medium-sized organizations may need to drive this initiative with marketing, or even own it completely. Either way, adopting marketing best practices will elevate the way our brand is perceived by candidates and result in a greater reach. Here are some to try:

1 Create a content library to store articles, ideas, quotes, employee profiles and inspirational content from other sources that you can either share or emulate in your own future posts. This is also where posts that are not tied to a specific time can be written and saved for future use.

2 Create a recruitment marketing calendar. Start by identifying key dates (holidays, planned volunteer and community service activities, both experienced and campus recruiting events, etc.) and then plan a regular schedule for other content, for example perhaps employee highlights are posted in the first week of each month, and a health tip is scheduled for the third week of each month.

3 When possible, use a marketing automation tool. If not, sticking to this schedule will allow you to manage it manually.

4 Step into the shoes of your users or get feedback. Is your content resonating? If they are not engaging, perhaps there is an opportunity to weave in more calls to action. This goes beyond sharing a link to a job posting and writing, 'Apply now!' It's about engaging them in ways that they care about, and this could be around community events like park clean-ups and dog walking, celebrating diversity or even injecting humour from time to time.

5 Regularly review your posts and messages for content and errors (just like with job postings) and devise a strategy for responding to follower comments in a meaningful way.

Putting robust information at candidates' fingertips

Attracting candidates involves sharing as much information as possible, through the sites and on the platforms where they want to find it. Candidates are looking for details on many aspects of an organization: the financial health of the organization, growth opportunities, the facility, how flexible the environment is, total rewards and benefits including the little perks, how the company gives back to the community and diversity initiatives.

When it comes to company culture, the message is perceived as most authentic when delivered directly by the employees themselves. Any chance to highlight the voice of employees through video testimonials or even through live in-person or virtual events will resonate.

Candidates also want to receive answers on demand. This could mean that a company dedicates an employee to reviewing social media posts and responding to candidates as part of their responsibilities to drive candidates to the career site. On the career sites themselves, more companies are investing in chatbot technology and implementing them to answer frequently asked questions (FAQs). Chatbots can respond in real time as well as free up time that recruiters would otherwise spend responding to e-mails. Year after year in the Talent Board CandE Benchmark Research, implementing chatbots on career sites has been increasing steadily.

Referral programmes and incentives

It is important to find a way to create a culture of referrals within the organization while placing emphasis on encouraging the right referrals. Companies need a quick and easy referral process that is simple to use, yet has enough framework so that enough key data are captured.[10] When the TA team posts new jobs, they should share it with the hiring manager and encourage them and their teams to post and share to their own social networks. If a referral comes through e-mail instead of through the ATS, the recruiting team should send out an encouraging but educating note such as, 'Thank you, we love referrals! Make sure that you submit this person via [our ATS] so that

I can take action. You'll also get credit for the referral that way! Let me know when they're in the system, and after that I'll copy you on communication to them.'

If you work for an organization that commonly hands out business cards, consider creating generic business cards for wide distribution among your employees that say, 'We're hiring', and have a QR code that links to your career site. That way, your employees can give the cards to people they want to refer and recruit, and those prospects can access your career information via their mobile devices.

Research shows that the stronger the referrer's connections to the company and the candidate, the better a matchmaker the referrer should be. Year after year in the CandE Benchmark Research, candidates cite employee referrals as a valuable channel, and referred candidates are much more likely to increase their relationship with a potential employer (apply again, refer others, and make purchases if and when applicable) if referred by an employee.

Find a reward amount that is meaningful but also sustainable. You want employees to be incentivized to make referrals because it grows the business, not because they'll get rich. It's a good rule to pay referral bonuses after the referred new hire's 90-day mark and find a referral bonus amount that is relevant to the position. For example, you may pay $1,000 for a college hire or entry level referral, but the amount might change to $5,000 for an experienced technical referral hire.

Employee ambassador programmes

Employee ambassadors have more impact on a candidate's future relationship with a company than conducting their own search or receiving unsolicited outreach from a recruiter.

Southwest Airlines uses 'Culture Committees' to foster the Southwest culture internally and promote their company values. There is a Culture Committee in each Southwest location, with a 'national committee' made up of representatives from each local committee These groups 'teach employees the Southwest way of life'. They also use public relations efforts and external advertising to deliver a consistent brand through both formal and informal channels.[11]

Using video

Companies are using more video content, including authentic and unscripted testimonials from employees, to deliver that content as well as shine spotlights on career paths and success stories within the organization. Video 'shows' as well as 'tells' and depicts the diversity of the firm through real pictures and stories of actual employees. You can nominate recruiting champions or use your employee ambassadors and ask for their participation in creating content to share through videos on the company careers site, YouTube and through posts on other social media channels.

Creating live virtual events

Live virtual events are used for question and answer (Q&A) sessions with recruiters on upcoming hiring events, in place of traditional in-person career fairs and as networking tools with hiring managers to share information about different teams as well as the company culture. Live virtual events are becoming a popular platform to engage passive job seekers and share information about your company, roles and employer brand, without requiring an immediate commitment from them other than attendance. Attendees appreciate networking with hiring managers and actual employees, and not just the recruiting team.

Encourage internal mobility

Creating opportunities for upward internal mobility and a culture where employees can learn about other departments and explore transfers, gives employees a reason to stay with a company longer, work harder and also have higher rates of engagement and morale because they are invested in the organization (and the organization is invested in them). Encouraging career growth and upward mobility 're-recruits' current employees and leads to higher morale and employee engagement.

Benefits to the company include:

- Lower costs to hire, less time and budget spent recruiting hard-to-fill roles when you can fill internally.
- Deeper relationships formed within, such as between employees and hiring managers of other groups.
- Higher reviews on career sites.
- More participation in company initiatives, community events, recruiting efforts, etc.
- More visibility into what you're getting and higher rates of predicted success. You have access to information such as annual reviews, performance records and internal referrals.
- A strong internal mobility programme attracts external candidates, especially when you can use actual employees' stories to highlight in your attraction social media posts and on your career site.
- Employees are already engaged, have company knowledge and existing relationships, which means they get up to speed faster.

Traditional organizations historically had one path for employee mobility – up – but today's organizations are thinking about how skillsets span responsibilities and can be valuable to different departments. Rather than thinking of their organizations as hierarchical, more companies are matrixed and have multiple paths employees can take without hitting a ceiling in their development, and lateral moves are not frowned upon.

Create separate processes for internal candidates

Having a separate internal candidate career portal and application process allows you to post more information about ranges, give the candidates more visibility into and access to the team, and creates a platform for deeper engagement.

Internal employee-specific job descriptions allow you to share more detail about the role, which can inspire more to apply and more effectively allow others to self-select out of consideration if a particular job is not the right fit for them.

The internal mobility portal becomes a tool through which you can develop employees and further groom them for future openings when they are not currently qualified. While we encourage custom rejections for as many of your candidates as possible (we will discuss rejection messages in Chapter 7), internal candidates need to be rejected with special care. Each time an employee applies for an internal position and is rejected, it could negatively impact their employee engagement. Internal candidate rejection will be discussed more in Chapter 7.

Some CandE winning companies have created special programmes for internal candidates, such as hiring an internal mobility specialist who serves as an 'internal career concierge', holding résumé-writing sessions at different times of the day so that employees can find a session to attend that doesn't conflict with their work shift, and internal job fairs that teach employees about different parts of the business.

Job postings

Job postings can be responsible for a prospective applicant's first impression of your organization and have an important place in the attraction stage of the candidate journey.

A good job posting should help candidates that we want to attract understand what their company does better than they did before, explain why the particular job we are advertising is key to organizational success, help them picture themselves in the role and start to get them excited about the prospect of joining the company. A good job posting should also help unqualified candidates self-select out of applying for that job and instead look for one that is more suitable to their skills and experience. (While we want candidates to apply again when they're not selected for a position, ideally it is to roles for which they are qualified. We can do less rejecting when we are able to guide them towards the right openings and away from those they are not qualified to do.)

Differences between job postings and job descriptions. Job descriptions are *internal* documents created with the purpose to describe the responsibilities, type of work performed and qualifications of a particular job within an organization in detail. They are used to organize job families, do workforce planning, research compensation ranges and more. Job descriptions are also used to create job postings (job ads), which are *external* documents purposely written to attract candidates to apply for an opening.

Sometimes recruiters post the existing job description itself. That is fine, but it is not a best practice because the job description may be overly concise and is not designed to be an advertisement. There could be key aspects missing that may attract more candidates. Creating a well-written job posting starts with the following considerations:

- **Ideal length.** Job descriptions can be quite lengthy. We cannot expect every candidate to read our postings word for word, and we know that many will review them on mobile devices with a finite tolerance for scrolling. It is a best practice to keep the length somewhere between 300 and 600 words.

- **Job title.** The title of a job posting should be spelled out (it can be abbreviated throughout the rest of the post) and descriptive. A company might be hiring what is known internally as a BSA II; however, when posting the job opening, it should be titled: IT Business System Analyst (BSA). Now that it has been identified, later throughout the document it can be called a BSA. The 'II' is not relevant to the posting unless it can be replaced by a descriptor like 'senior' or 'lead'.

- **An introduction to the company.** What is your company, what do you do, why is it important and why is it great to work there?

- **An introduction to the job and why it is important.** This is the chance to tie the open job to the company mission.

- **A concise list of responsibilities.** Strive to keep the list of responsibilities and requirements to a maximum of 10 each. If this is a challenge, you can always share the complete job description with candidates who are moving on to interviews.

- **A separate list of 'must-haves' from 'nice-to-haves'.** One of the most vital ways any company can improve their job postings is to ensure that their section for 'basic' or 'minimum' qualifications only contains must-have experience. Any candidate who moves forward to the next round must meet those requirements, otherwise they are not qualified. All non-vital qualifications are nice-to-have and need to be moved to the 'preferred' qualifications section.

  This is important for two reasons: (1) To promote an unbiased workplace, each candidate's knowledge, skills and experience should be measured against the needs of the company's role rather than comparing candidates to each other. (2) If a candidate were to argue about why they were not selected for a position, you can point to a clear and consistent selection practice and explain how they were not qualified.

- **Removal of the phrase '...or related'.** Many job postings list qualifications such as, 'Bachelor's degree in marketing or related', but there are no standards for us to determine what degree is actually related to marketing, nor for us to communicate that list to candidates. A business degree makes sense, but an English composition degree also might, especially if the company is seeking a strong writer. Be as specific as possible while ensuring that you will not rule out a candidate you might want to consider: 'Bachelor's degree in business, marketing, journalism or English, along with writing samples of internal communications material you have created.'

- **Gender-neutral language.** Avoid using pronouns and adjectives that do not directly describe the position in order to keep your job posting free of bias and encourage all qualified candidates to apply.

- **Abbreviations and acronyms.** Define these the first time you use them in a document, just like with the job title.

- **Formatting and errors.** Always review what you've posted. Look for formatting errors, ensure consistency with bullets, fonts, line spacing and punctuation.

Pay transparency in job postings. More states in the United States are passing legislation related to equal pay among workers and requiring companies to post compensation information publicly in the job postings. At the time of writing, Colorado had recently passed the Equal Pay Transparency (EPT) Act. While the intent of this legislation is to combat gender and racial disparities in pay, it creates a hardship for employers who fear that more candidates will self-select out if they are not offered a salary at the top of that range. When this legislation first passed, some organizations either attempted to get around the law or buy themselves some time to work through it by excluding Colorado employees from consideration for roles, even remote positions, so they did not have to post the salary range. The downside of using this tactic to avoid the law or postpone complying with it is that it can seem inauthentic for a company to exclude certain states' workers from consideration while at the same time promoting a policy of inclusion. It's important to note that in the 2021 CandE Benchmark Research, 80 per cent of North American employers asked about salary expectations, and 6 per cent of employers avoided asking altogether. Candidates told us that they were asked about expectations 33 per cent of the time, while 8 per cent were asked what their most recent salary was, and 17 per cent were told what the salary was without requesting it. For those candidates who were told, their positive interview perception of fairness increased 30 per cent. Transparency continues to pay candidate experience dividends.

Passive sourcing basics and candidate experience

A company can have an excellent employer brand, a good social media presence and expertly written job descriptions, and still have job openings that are not attracting enough candidate interest. Or, you may have a decent applicant flow but no one is applying who is actually qualified. If so, it is time to source for candidates. Passive candidate sourcing is when a recruiter or sourcer proactively looks for qualified prospective candidates, whether they are currently employed and/or looking for work, and contacts them in an attempt to solicit interest and attract them to apply to a job opening.

According to Bersin research, 'Low-performing TA functions tend to fill jobs one at a time using a "post and pray" approach, while high-performing TA teams seek candidates who "fit" with the organization's culture and are viewed as having long term potential with the company.'[12] When these efforts are successful, it can significantly lower the time to fill, save potentially thousands of dollars or pounds from the recruiting budget and also help to create a more engaged employee since there was a pre-established relationship with the candidate.

Sourcing is an important skill in today's market, when we cannot afford to wait for the right candidates to apply. It also continues to build trust between you and your hiring manager because you are demonstrating your effectiveness, adaptability to market conditions and understanding of the job requirements. Building the talent pool by sourcing passive candidates tells the hiring manager, 'I know what you are looking for and I can find them.'

It is important to note: When used strategically, staffing agencies are valuable partners who help companies fill key roles quickly. However, sometimes when companies are behind their hiring plans, they fall into a pattern of using agencies for many roles. When multiple agencies are working on your positions, recruiters can find themselves spending more time managing agency relations and less time with candidates, which causes them to enjoy their job less. If you learn the necessary skills and can deliver results and instil confidence in your hiring managers, the demand to use agencies will decrease.

Cold sourcing can be daunting and unpleasant, but warm lead generation is not. Two of the most accessible places to source are your company's ATS and LinkedIn. Even when sourcing from your ATS, it is a good practice to cross-reference LinkedIn to see if they've made a recent job change or if they are still potentially looking. Also, if the ATS doesn't contain detail about their last interviews, try to contact the last recruiter to find them out, especially if the candidate ended up not being a good fit. There are numerous free sites that have tips on sourcing the internet for résumés and lists of people with certain professional certifications and conference attendees.

In the following section, we will discuss some additional candidate experience considerations for passive candidates. Because we are soliciting them before they express interest in our opportunities or perhaps before they even know they exist, the way that we engage with them is important to set ourselves apart from all the other 'recruiter noise' and represent our organizations well.

Contacting sourced candidates

When calling a sourced candidate and they answer the phone, ask if they have a few minutes before launching into a pitch. When e-mailing, keep it brief to minimize the need for scrolling if they are reading on their mobile device. Keep your demeanour natural and approach it as a networking conversation rather than a screen until they agree that they want to be considered.

Identify yourself, how you found them and why you are reaching out. Include a link to a job so they can review for themselves. Historically, sourcing has been done to help build a candidate pool for a current, active job. However, many companies and recruiting firms are adopting an ongoing 'evergreen' search approach in response to the tight supply and competition for talent. The intent of searching for candidates without a specific role in mind is to build a pipeline by growing and nurturing a network of pre-warmed and pre-qualified engaged candidates until there is a suitable role opening, whether it is weeks or months before the right opportunity is presented. The challenge is candidates who are in the market for a job now do not always perceive fairness in this process. This method can erode trust if the candidate perceives they have been misled into thinking that a role already exists when it does not. Furthermore, prospective candidates who have in-demand skill sets will be contacted and courted by many recruiters – this includes corporate recruiters who 'own' a position, external recruiters who have been retained to help with a search and/or a slew of agencies who may be competing for the same talent to fill contingent roles. Candidates may experience recruiter fatigue, which triggers them to respond less to talent acquisition professionals.

You can combat recruiter fatigue by referencing LinkedIn to see if you have shared connections. LinkedIn Recruiter insights tell you whether a candidate is engaged with your talent brand and following your company already. Another method is to partner with the hiring manager for a 'sourcing party' – if you can get your hiring manager to reach out to key prospective candidates, there is a higher likelihood they'll respond to someone who could be their manager or peer and not just 'another recruiter'.

Your goal in the initial conversation is to generate interest and to close them on taking a next step, whether it be applying for the position directly, agreeing to speak to the hiring manager to learn more; or even letting them peruse more company information and following up with you with questions before committing.

'What's the pay range?'

This question gets asked quite often when candidates hear from many recruiters with a role that isn't real, or when they hear from multiple recruiters who are advertising opportunities that pay too low of a rate. The best answer to this question is to be as transparent as possible, share a dollar or sterling amount and not a range (naturally, if you give a range, they will want to be offered a rate at the top of it), leave a small amount for negotiation and tell them there is some opportunity in there depending on skills and experience.

We will discuss salary negotiation more in Chapter 9.

Rejecting passively sourced candidates

The most important candidate experience consideration for passive candidates is rejection. (We recommend that everyone who has a formal interview with a company and is not selected gets a phone call rejection, and we will give tips on this in Chapter 7.) When you or your hiring manager screens a passively sourced candidate and decides not to move them forward, they should always get at least a rejection e-mail. The best practice is to create a separate rejection e-mail template for passively sourced candidates that is different from your company's standard rejection e-mail template. Since you got them interested and solicited them, it is a very nice touch to send a personalized e-mail.

Sample passively sourced rejection e-mail template

Dear [Candidate First Name],

Thank you so much for taking the time out of your busy schedule to speak with us and learn about [Company Name].

I called you with the [position title] role in mind, but after our conversation I got a much clearer understanding of what you are seeking. While this role is not a good match, the door is certainly open here. I hope we can connect on LinkedIn and stay in touch, especially when a suitable role emerges here.

Please check us out on [social media platform links] where we often post about upcoming roles and community events.

Until we chat again, if there is assistance I can provide or an introduction I can facilitate, please don't hesitate to ask.

Thank you again.

Sincerely,

[Recruiter Name]

[Company Name] Talent Acquisition Team

Sharing passively sourced candidate profiles with hiring managers

When you contact and screen passively sourced candidates, you might not have their résumé when you want to present them to the hiring manager. It is fine to share their LinkedIn profile while waiting for a copy of their résumé. If you do, explain to the hiring manager that they are viewing a general LinkedIn profile that hasn't been updated and a résumé is on its way. That distinction is important because hiring managers who are not familiar with the concept of sourcing may start criticizing the content and formatting of the profile. Explain that once a candidate has expressed interest, you expect the résumé to be updated and tailored to the role, but not everyone maintains their LinkedIn profile, especially if they are not actively looking for a new role.

A company that invests in attraction and building an employer brand will be most successful when they also focus on the rest of the candidate journey in conjunction with building attraction. Investing in attraction and ignoring a candidate journey, so that it feels more like a transactional process, could leave the impression that your brand is not as authentic. A holistic approach to aligning all the stages of the candidate journey is the best strategy. Now that we have learned about attracting prospective candidates to our companies and job opportunities, in our next section we will learn how to successfully engage them in the application stage of the candidate journey.

Notes

1 Miles, SJ and McCamey, R (2018) The candidate experience: Is it damaging your employer brand? *Business Horizons*, **61** (5), 755–764.
2 Grossman, K, Fox, J and Schoolderman, A. How recruiters can help when companies aren't hiring, Talent Board, 21 May 2020, thetalentboard.org/article/ how-recruiters-can-help-when-companies-arent-hiring/ (archived at https:// perma.cc/32XN-HSCS)
3 Bhens, S, Lau, L and Sarrazin, H. The new tech talent you need to succeed in digital. McKinsey, 30 September 2016, mckinsey.com/business-functions/ mckinsey-digital/our-insights/the-new-tech-talent-you-need-to-succeed-in-digital (archived at https://perma.cc/G76B-9RZ3)
4 Sundberg, J. Covid-19's impact on employer brand, Link Humans, 2020, linkhumans.com/covid-impact-employer-brand/ (archived at https://perma.cc/P6BD-9B9Z)

5 Dixon-Fyle, S, Dolan, K, Hunt, V and Prince, S. Diversity wins: How inclusion matters, McKinsey, 19 May 2020, mckinsey.com/featured-insights/diversity-and-inclusion/diversity-wins-how-inclusion-matters (archived at https://perma.cc/S4WK-HH6Q)

6 Grossman, K. It's time to improve our post-application responsiveness, Talent Board, 20 April 2021, thetalentboard.org/article/its-time-to-improve-our-post-application-responsiveness/ (archived at https://perma.cc/9CDK-FFJZ)

7 Aberdeen Group. Talent acquisition 2014: Reverse the regressive curse, A⁺ Edge, 6 August 2014, abriedeswardt.com/talent-acquisition-2014-reverse-the-regressive-curse/ (archived at https://perma.cc/LZW7-X5DC)

8 Miles, SJ and McCamey, R (2018) The candidate experience: Is it damaging your employer brand?. *Business Horizons*, **61** (5), 755–64.

9 Adams, B. 6 simple steps to revitalizing your candidate experience. ERE Recruiting Intelligence, 9 September 2016, ere.net/5-simple-steps-to-revitalizing-your-candidate-experience/ (archived at https://perma.cc/5LHB-C8M9)

10 Gautier, K and Munasinghe, L. Build a stronger employee referral program. *Harvard Business Review*, 26 May 2020, hbr.org/2020/05/build-a-stronger-employee-referral-program (archived at https://perma.cc/XJ2C-EQ8K)

11 Miles, SJ and Mangold, WG (2005) Positioning Southwest Airlines through employee branding. *Business Horizons*, **48** (6), 535–45.

12 Erickson, R and Moulton, D Six key insights to put talent acquisition at the center of business strategy and execution, HR Daily Advisor, 16 January 2018, hrdailyadvisor.blr.com/infographic/infographic-insights-highly-mature-talent-acquisition-team/ (archived at https://perma.cc/SN3Z-Y2L7)

05

Improving the application phase

The job application is when candidates formally decide to take action and notify the company of their interest in a position or when they make it official after having a couple of networking calls or being solicited by a recruiter. It involves the application itself, the instructions and communication that an organization sends them afterwards and any assessments or tests that immediately follow the application. The pool of applicants is reviewed by a company's recruiting team and divided into three categories: unqualified, qualified/not pursuing and qualified/pursuing.

The application is an important but often overlooked part of the candidate journey. Why?

Before the internet, applicants would answer a job posting in the newspaper or other publication by mailing or faxing their résumés to companies for consideration. Their résumé would be reviewed by a recruiter (more likely, a personnel officer), and if they were qualified they'd be contacted to fill out a lengthy application asking for detailed information on demographics, work experience (history, supervisor name and title, last position held, wage, responsibilities, reason for leaving), education experience, professional licensure, at least three professional references and a short essay-form response about why they want to work for the company. At this point in time, the application was lengthy because companies needed to get all the information in one shot.

After the internet became commercially available and widely adopted, companies turned away from print advertising and to online job boards. Suddenly, it was much easier to advertise jobs and the number of candidates increased exponentially because of greater visibility and the ability to apply with a few clicks. It was a nice problem to have, but we saw that more candidates didn't necessarily mean better candidates. Next, with the advent of applicant tracking systems, companies became able to put their job applications online. The long applications didn't go away, either. Employers were starting to be required to collect some information by law, and they loaded it all on the front end – the application – to get all the information in one shot, whether they needed to collect it from all applicants or not. During this time, employers were thinking more about their process than the candidates' experience, and collecting more information was better.

As recruiters got bombarded with more and more applications, the length of an application was sometimes used to weed out people who weren't serious about the opportunity. What we found was that people we'd want to hire were withdrawing at this stage. According to a CareerBuilder report in 2016,[1] at least 60 per cent of job seekers quit in the middle of filling out an application due to its length or complexity. At time of publishing this book we did not find an updated statistic for that metric, but a 60 per cent dropout rate in 2016 is still significant. There are still applications out there asking for information that is not necessary to determine whether a candidate is qualified for a position, for example, we do not need to know their last salary (in some states, we are forbidden by law to ask that question now) nor collect professional references at application.

Organizations are investing large sums of money into creating interactive and splashy career landing pages where applicants can watch video employee testimonials and interact with chatbots to ask some basic questions, yet sometimes when those candidates click 'apply' and the backend workflow takes them into the ATS vendor to apply for a job, the change in the user interface from the modern career site to the older ATS technology is jarring. There are still many issues with ATS applications and parsing from résumés, displaying résumés properly depending on their format and more. There are still applications that are not optimized to be mobile-friendly. There are still text fields that do not register an applicant's choice and return an error message rather than saving the text. For as much as we talk about candidate experience, the application seems much more like a transaction.

Think for a moment about visiting an ecommerce site to buy a pair of shoes. We can filter on shoes for work or fitness, quickly find the right size and if it's in stock and order them with a couple of clicks and a swipe. Why is it so challenging to apply for the right role? The technology exists. It is our responsibility, as a talent acquisition industry, to overhaul this experience that can seem clunky and painful – and is certainly outdated – and create an application experience that helps them to determine whether they are qualified for a position, allows them to submit their information with ease and gets us the pertinent information that tells us whether a candidate is qualified. It is the right thing to do, and it will help us to hire quickly and more successfully, too.

What do candidates want?

Speed and ease of application, including options to apply, such as from a mobile phone or with a LinkedIn profile. Whenever possible, we should collect information about candidates when we are sure they are moving on to interviews, rather than asking for everything in one shot at the beginning. Remember, we only hire about 1 per cent of our total applicants. Why are we collecting unnecessary data on the 99 per cent that we will not hire?

Their information to be reviewed and to perceive fairness. Candidates spend hours preparing their résumés (in response to recruiters asking them to tailor their experience to their target roles), then more time applying for the job. After investing hours, they want their information to at least be reviewed.

Communication, including acknowledgement of application, as well as clear next steps and a timely decision on their candidacy. The more personal, the better. Even if rejected, candidates are continually asking for a clear and definitive response. Most negative reviews come from candidates who simply never heard back after application. 'If you are a fit, we will contact you,' is not an acceptable response. After all, they are applying because they think they are a fit.

Their time to be respected. Many applicants are taking time away from their current jobs to pursue your opportunity – if they make it beyond the application stage. In return, candidates expect a simple and straightforward process with some level of acknowledgment of next steps after they apply. They deserve closure, and this is also a missed opportunity to connect them back to us via the career site, talent network, social media or live virtual events where they can stay engaged with us and our brand.

Best practices for improving the application candidate experience

Companies that view talent acquisition as relationship building rather than gatekeeping, including those that have won Candidate Experience Awards, use this approach to influence all their actions and processes. Just like companies take customer-centric approaches for customers, they do the same for candidates, and approach every step of the candidate journey with greater transparency. Here are some of their best practices:

More communication about next steps. Candidates want to know where they are in the evaluation, and do not want to be left hanging. Talent acquisition leaders should strive to exceed candidate expectations at every touchpoint and set better expectations with candidates. Automated e-mail responses are a helpful way to share basic information quickly with them. Auto responses might include the acknowledgement after a candidate's résumé or application is received. It is even better when they include a range of days in which candidates can expect an answer, such as five to seven business days after the application is submitted. Auto responses can also include invitations to take initial steps in the screening and evaluation process, like scheduling time for a phone screen or taking an assessment.

Whenever possible, it is best practice to utilize technology to ease the candidates' experience by limiting the number of clicks and logins they'll need to accomplish something you're asking of them and doing so will also help to minimize abandonment rates.

Crafting messages to build relationships with each candidate. Writing the auto responses, and all e-mail templates for that matter, in the voice or tone of the company is an excellent way to transform communication that feels transactional, like a form letter, into something that becomes a good candidate experience. Take time to craft meaningful responses that can be consistently used. Examples of meaningful auto responses use links to social media, words of encouragement and tips for interview success. Sometimes organizations want to remain hyper professional, but it can be perceived by candidates as being impersonal. When there is an opportunity to be both professional and colloquial in written conversation, it is received well.

It is a candidate experience best practice to follow up with all candidates and officially provide closure when they are not qualified. Sometimes companies send a message that tells candidates, 'We will be in touch if your résumé is a fit,' but we must understand that the candidate applied because they thought they were a fit in the first place. Sending a firm but encouraging rejection message is informative and gives them closure. In Chapter 11, we will discuss how to craft rejection messages.

Creating different evaluations for different levels. Job applications and assessments are more likely to be competed when talent acquisition can tailor their applications for different job or experience levels and omitting questions that are not relevant for certain groups. For example, some workers, especially hourly, might not have a résumé and can fill out their job history in an online application. However, it is highly unlikely that senior manager or executive level candidates would need to fill out their job history when these candidates most likely have a detailed résumé and the ATS should be able to parse their information into the system.

When it comes to assessments, or pre-employment tests that are often administered online, ensuring that they are job-specific and relevant increases the likelihood that candidates will complete the evaluations instead of abandoning them (recall that at least 60 per cent of applicants withdraw during the application). When choosing an assessment platform, McKinsey suggests: 'Vendors should have technical documentation describing the reliability, validity and prescribed uses of their assessments. Also pay attention to any information on test bias, administration requirements and potentially available databases for scoring and test interpretation.'[2] A company's assessment needs to be a tool that uncovers the best candidates for a given job through a standardized means of collecting information about them. Talent acquisition professionals must use assessments for the purpose of selection rather than a means to simply 'weed out' some of the candidate volume. The risk of 'weeding out' the highest qualified is too high. If reducing candidate volume is a goal, we need to rethink our strategy and go back to the beginning – the job posting – to ensure that we are explicit about the requirements to help people decide whether they should apply. And remember that it is vitally important to close the loop and notify candidates who have not passed an assessment to let them know they are no longer being considered.

For today's job applications, best practices include:

- **Welcome your candidates.** Post an intro message that says, 'Thank you for your interest in applying! We are pleased you have decided to apply.' This is an excellent place to introduce warmer, more colloquial written language.

- **Giving an estimated completion time.** Let candidates know how much time they need to set aside to successfully submit the application. When the workflow directs candidates from the application directly into an assessment, be sure to include the time it takes to complete both parts. Talent Board has 'mystery shopped' various company job applications that estimate a 15-minute completion time, which is accurate for the application; but then sadly candidates must go straight into an assessment that can take an additional 30+ minutes. Abandonment rates are more likely in this situation because candidates would have to start the assessment over again if they did not keep going.

- Speaking of length, **keep job applications brief.** Use the application to gather only what is necessary to determine if candidates are qualified for the job. Traditionally, job applications have asked for professional references, but what is the point of collecting them at this stage when we know that as many as 99 per cent of applicants will be rejected? If an organization checks references on their finalist candidates, references should be collected on or after the interview. This small adjustment to the recruiting process could translate into an improvement in the candidate experience. In a SHRM article, Dave Zielinski explained that shortening the application can significantly increase the completion rate. He wrote, 'The idea is to balance what's convenient for recruiters with what's user-friendly for applicants.'[3] Talent Board recommends that applications should be able to be completed in 15 minutes or less.

- **Give candidates the option to apply on a mobile device.** Giving candidates multiple options when it comes to how they can complete an application improves their perception of the company's employer brand. In turn, candidates want to increase their relationship with those organizations. In the annual CandE Benchmark Survey, we always see an increase in positive sentiment and fairness based on multiple methods of applying.

- **Tell candidates where they stand in the application process and how much is left to complete.** As we mentioned in the last section, setting accurate expectations of application completion time can significantly improve the candidate experience. Jacobs, an international professional services firm, is a multi-year CandE winner that made significant changes to the candidate journey in the application stage and shared the results in a case study:

  ○ We've added a page that tells candidates how long the application process should take, what pieces of information they'll need, and how they'll best complete the application. While we can see through

Google Analytics that there is some drop off at these pages, we assume that some people may not want to go through the hassle of the full application process. Others may not be on the right device at the time (e.g., tablets or mobile devices), and others may need to gather the required information. This serves as a bit of a self-selection point, in which some candidates may opt-out entirely based on knowing more about our full process, while others may return later to complete their application.[4]

- **Technology can add value**: chatbots can answer job-seeker FAQs and free up recruiters' time to focus on more meaningful touchpoints with top candidates.

- **Acknowledge the completion of the application** with an auto-response from your ATS that thanks them, tells them it has been received, states next steps and timeframe. An example would be: 'Thank you again for applying with our company. A recruiter will review your application in seven business days if you are selected to move to our next step, a screening interview. Either way, we will be in touch to let you know the outcome.'

- **Send well-crafted auto-response rejection messages** for candidates who are not a fit. In the next chapter, we discuss rejection messages in more detail.

Internal applicants

Internal mobility, the ability a company gives its employees to move across roles – not just 'up' – or to a different role altogether, is gaining more momentum. Historically, companies were hierarchically organized, and employees were not able to get promoted unless someone above them, usually their manager, left or retired. In modern organizations, we are starting to see a matrixed organizational structure, where employees are aligned more like a grid and may have multiple managers or points of reporting. This structure has created more opportunity for employees to move, and lateral moves are not seen as undesirable. In fact, some large organizations are starting to build rotational programs so that employees, and especially recent hires, can get exposure to various parts of the business. Internal mobility benefits companies that have many employees and complex business structures with a high degree of collaboration involved.

In Chapter 4, we discussed the many benefits that companies are realizing by focusing effort on internal mobility programs. To get started, talent acquisition and HR teams can develop organizational and succession plans for business units, including identifying key skills that need to be retained, and skills gaps that must be hired externally. According to Erickson et al (2018), many organizations recognize how valuable their internal talent pools are, but often face structural barriers or discouraging cultures to making use of that value. Therefore, it's important to ensure internal mobility is recognized and promoted at all levels of the business.[5]

Best practices for internal mobility include:

Build a culture of internal mobility within the organization and promote the benefits to gain buy-in from hiring managers who might favour hiring externally rather than training a current employee on skills they lack.

Create a separate process or portal for internal job seekers to apply. This way, you can give the internals more of a white glove treatment. You can collect less information than an external job application. You can share more information about pay ranges and more access to the team so they can decide whether the move they are considering is a good fit for their goals. Internal employee-specific job descriptions allow you to share more detail about the role, which can inspire more to apply and also more effectively allow others to self-select out of consideration if it is not the right fit.

Educate workers on career options and how to get there. You can create development programs, internal job fairs, résumé workshops and other employee-specific programs to help workers build their careers without leaving the company. These activities can keep their employee engagement level and morale within the organization high especially when someone else is selected for the opening. If an internal employee applies for multiple positions and gets rejected over and over, they will get discouraged and it will affect their engagement and desire to stay.

Create feedback loops. Ask internal candidates for feedback, whether they have been selected to fill an open position. Be sure to always give them feedback on their interview and the decision. A best practice from multiple CandE winners is to have the hiring managers deliver the decision and feedback to the internal candidate, always within a specific timeframe.

Compassion International, a multi-year CandE winner, tells us: 'For our internal candidates, we've started a class that we now offer four times a year. It covers interviewing tips, resumes, cover letters – all the things our internal candidates sometimes wanted more support with. We're trying to be more proactive and doing more corporate communications to show our internal candidates they have our full support.'[6]

Video interviews and assessments

Job assessments are used at various stages, from the application through the interviews, to measure the most critical work functions and competencies, and predicted success. They are used to evaluate candidates in a consistent method on anything from 'hard' skills like math and driving, to 'soft' skills like presentation style and emotional intelligence. Assessments are usually hosted by a third-party vendor that integrates with the ATS and the workflow leads candidates from the end of the application to the start of the assessment.

Assessments are another place where applicants might abandon completing their application due to length, complexity or simply not understanding what is being measured. One best practice is to include the 'why' – why they need to fill out certain questions, conduct video interviews (we'll discuss video interviews in greater detail in Chapter 10) or do certain assessments. CandE-winning employers said they explain why they're using a specific assessment during the application process 61 pe cent of the time versus 46 per cent for all employers combined.[7]

Year over year, candidates tell Talent Board that the biggest factors in ensuring they had a good experience included ensuring their time was respected, their perceived fairness in the assessment tool and its relevance to the job, and they received helpful information and feedback following the assessment. As we mentioned earlier in this chapter, it is imperative to give candidates some estimate of how long the entire application should take, especially when the workflow makes a candidate start the assessment immediately following the application without the option to save their work and complete it later.

Rejecting candidates who are not qualified

Rejection messages are crucial communications that we'll discuss more in Chapter 7. For now, we will focus on auto-rejection messages that recruiters send after a candidate applies and they are not selected to be screened or interviewed.

Not every company is notifying candidates when they are not qualified for open positions. Some companies do not acknowledge the application submission at all. Others send a message that says, 'Thank you for applying. If you are a fit, someone will contact you.' This type of communication is not ideal to send to a candidate for three reasons: 1) Human beings need closure, so why wouldn't we give it to them if it can be done with a couple of mouse clicks? 2) It's a missed opportunity to engage with an individual who could potentially have great deal of influence over others applying to our company or purchasing goods or services from us, or it could be someone we might want to consider reviewing in the future or for a different opening. 3) It gives the company all the power in the situation and does not give the individual the opportunity to engage and connect with us via social media or talent communities to learn more.

Another common mistake, but much less egregious, is to send a rejection message that seems 'canned' or insincere. It could be written like, 'Thank you again for applying for [opening]. We reviewed your résumé and you are no longer being considered for the position. Sincerely, [Company] recruiting team.'

A rejection e-mail, even a template sent to candidates who will not be selected for a screen, can be another place to continue building a relationship with candidates (who could be your customers) and continue marketing our company and employer brand. Here are some best practices:

- **Use a tone aligned to your company culture.** A rejection letter should be consistently branded with other communications and have a similar voice.

- **Use an auto-delay for rejection messages when dispositioning candidates.** When a candidate applies to an opening and the recruiter reviews and dispositions the candidate the same day, the auto-rejection message should be delayed for a minimum of 24 hours. As we discussed earlier in the chapter, candidates often spend hours tailoring their resume to the open job, or at least making updates to it. After working on the application for hours, it is very discouraging to receive a rejection within minutes.

- **Have a separate template for internal candidates.** A standard auto-rejection message should not be sent to internal candidates. It is a best practice to forward all internal candidates to the hiring manager, even if they appear to not be qualified, so the manager can decide whether to speak to the internal candidate. If they are not a fit, they should receive individualized feedback.

- **Have a separate template for passively sourced candidates.** When a sourcer or recruiter passively sources a candidate via LinkedIn or other means and can convince that person to apply for a role, it is not perceived well when those candidates receive the same auto-rejection that direct applicants receive. There is a bit of courting involved with the candidate when we directly solicit them. If they decided to spend time talking to us when they weren't looking or interested in the first place, we owe them a more personalized and softer message of closure.

- **Disposition candidates regularly** rather than waiting for a role to be filled. Think back to the time when you received a rejection message from a company that you applied to six months to a year ago, or maybe you don't remember applying to them. Again, candidates expect and deserve closure, and it is always more palatable when it can be done swiftly.

- **If a recruiter has taken too long to disposition a candidate, they might have already moved on to other opportunities.** If they feel like they withdrew from consideration and then you send a standard rejection e-mail that they aren't qualified, it could cause negative sentiment. Also, after time goes by, it is easy to forget which candidates were screened and recruiters may send the wrong templates to candidates.

The best rejection e-mails express gratitude that they applied, regret that they will not be considered, encouragement to continue searching for a role that matches their skills and experiences, and an invitation to connect via social media and a talent network.

As we learned in this chapter, the job application is a critical part of hiring that is historically overlooked from a candidate experience perspective. The standard job application has not changed drastically over the years except getting longer in some cases when it is used as a single repository where employers collect information from candidates or more complex in cases where assessment tools are added. When we start to break down the purpose of each of the application components, we start to see that there is a lot that can be improved over what has traditionally been done here. We can discuss whether certain questions are even necessary. When we stop to place ourselves in the shoes of a candidate, we understand how little tweaks can make such a big impact for a candidate, for example, shortening an application and then communicating the length of time it will take to finish it. For the modern talent acquisition professional, the job application is a place where strategic changes can lead to a large change more qualified candidates and an increase in positive candidate sentiment. In Chapter 6, we move to the next stage of the candidate journey: screening and interviewing.

Notes

1 Dave Zielinski. Study: Most job seekers abandon online job applications. SHRM, 8 March 2016, shrm.org/resourcesandtools/hr-topics/technology/pages/study-most-job-seekers-abandon-online-job-applications.aspx (archived at https://perma.cc/A3YS-N9SS)

2 Imose, R, Potter, J and Schrah, G. The 4 biggest assessment myths undermining your hiring process, McKinsey, 3 May 2019, mckinsey.com/business-functions/organization/our-insights/the-organization-blog/the-4-biggest-assessment-myths-undermining-your-hiring-process (archived at https://perma.cc/UZX8-MC52)

3 Dave Zielinski. Study: Most job seekers abandon online job applications. SHRM, 8 March 2016, shrm.org/resourcesandtools/hr-topics/technology/pages/study-most-job-seekers-abandon-online-job-applications.aspx (archived at https://perma.cc/2AZ8-Q548)

4 Talent Board (2018, February). 2017 APAC candidate experience research report, February 2018, thetalentboard.org/benchmark-research/cande-research-reports/ (archived at https://perma.cc/F32X-V6ZK)

5 Erickson, R, Moulton, D and Cleary, B. Are you overlooking your greatest source of talent?, *Deloitte Review*, (23), 30 July 2018, https://www2.deloitte.com/us/en/insights/deloitte-review/issue-23/unlocking-hidden-talent-internal-mobility.html (archived at https://perma.cc/28L3-DZK6)

6 Talent Board (2017, February). 2017 North American candidate experience research report, February 2018, thetalentboard.org/benchmark-research/cande-research-reports (archived at https://perma.cc/F32X-V6ZK)

7 Talent Board (2019, December). North American candidate experience research report, December 2019, thetalentboard.org/benchmark-research/cande-research-reports/ (archived at https://perma.cc/F32X-V6ZK)

06

Improving screening and interviewing

When candidates have met the minimum requirements for our job openings, it is likely that they will be screened by a recruiter and then the hiring manager, followed by interviews. During the screen and interview stage, candidates go through a series of evaluations that help recruiters and hiring managers determine the best candidates to hire for an opening. For each candidate, there is one of two outcomes: The candidate is offered the position or rejected. (We will discuss both outcomes in future chapters: rejections in Chapter 7, and offers and onboarding in Chapter 9.) In this chapter, we are going to examine the recruiter interview, some of the more common subsequent initial screening steps, as well as formal interviews, both conducted by the hiring managers and the interview teams. Companies that practise good candidate experience tactics use the screening and interviews to build relationships with candidates in addition to assessing them for qualifications.

If a candidate is considered qualified and invited by the company to move on to screening and assessments, the candidate is conducting more specific research as they look for information to help determine if the company and role are a good fit. This includes evaluating their experience at every touchpoint, with every company representative. Basically, candidates are interviewing us as we are interviewing them, looking for a company with an employer brand and an employee value proposition (EVP) – 'what's in it for me?' – that aligns with their personal values, as well as career potential, a team they like and work that is interesting to them, among other things.

This stage is arguably the most important in the candidate journey, but interviews can be a 'danger zone' for candidate experience because, at some point, recruiters must 'hand off' candidates to hiring managers and interview teams for periods of time. There are a few variables, and it does not always go the way we envision or plan. Even though most companies have some sort of interview training that usually cover the basics, like what questions you are legally allowed to ask a candidate, many do not cover candidate experience.

We will discuss candidate experience in interviews, such as:

- How to prepare both candidates and interviewers for the interview.
- Tips to avoid bias in interviews.
- Remembering that candidates will be interviewing us as we are interviewing them.
- Setting expectations with your interview team about delivering feedback after the interview.

By the end of this chapter, you will be able to successfully form and manage interview teams to screen candidates for your open roles. At the same time, you will set your candidates up for success and, whether they are selected for the role or not, they will retain a more positive view of your company and their interview experience even if they are rejected.

Screening and interviewing generally includes the following process flow:

- résumé/application screen, along with disposition and communication:
  - (optional) assessments and/or on-demand, recorded video interviews;
- recruiter interview (phone, on-demand, or live video);
- hiring manager interview (phone or live video);
- interview team interviews (panel or loop in-person or virtual):
  - final interview (optional);
- decision.

Specific screen and interview steps differ from company to company, so our goal is to introduce universal concepts for you to customize for your specific processes. If candidates pass each step, they move to the next; if they fail, they are rejected. (We have given rejection its own chapter because it's something that can happen at any step and is arguably the single most important piece of communication that influences candidate sentiment.)

Screen and interview steps can look different within a single organization, perhaps between different business lines or regions. If an organization has a centralized recruiting model, there is a higher likelihood that recruiting and evaluation steps are similar across all open positions. Sometimes organizations have a decentralized recruitment model, where recruiting is 'localized' to different parts of an organization and can be managed at a regional or functional level. For example, a large, regional retailer may manage corporate recruiting at its company's headquarters, but each store/district, manufacturing site and distribution centre may manage its own recruiting in a very different way.

We will look at each of these steps in greater detail below.

Résumé/application screen

We discussed the application stage at length in Chapter 5, but the biggest impact you can make in this stage is to review and disposition applicants in a timely manner. Candidates should be receiving an auto-response message from your ATS that acknowledges the application is received. In addition, setting internal service level agreements (SLA) for your team to review applicant résumés and reject the unqualified ones. For example, two weeks of application submission signals to your candidates that you are invested in hiring for the position and in reviewing their qualifications.

Sometimes recruiters want to wait until they have several qualified candidates so they can interview the group in quick succession and move all through the evaluations at the same time. While this certainly makes for a more orderly process that is easier to manage, we must ask ourselves what impression does that give candidates who are actively looking for a job now? Any delay in evaluations may send a signal to candidates that you are questioning their fit or experience, or that they are not your top choice. Or, they might already be interviewing with other companies by the time they apply with you and waiting two weeks could mean you do not get to interview them because they have already accepted another offer. Even if they just applied to your open position, you don't know when they started looking, and they might have started their search weeks ago, either just coming across our posting or just deciding to apply. In the case that you want to wait a few days to interview candidates more closely together, we suggest adding an extra point of communication: Send an e-mail explaining that you have reviewed their résumé and will be in touch to schedule a phone screen in the next two weeks. Remember that candidates ask for more communication and feedback, so a simple gesture like this will go a long way.

Whenever possible, we strongly recommend that you screen candidates as they apply and communicate in that conversation that next steps will be a couple weeks out. While you still may lose candidates to other opportunities, you have already engaged with them and started building a relationship.

Pre-employment screening tools

When implemented correctly, prescreening tools can be an effective way to quickly review a high number of candidates in a short period of time and also increase candidate experience. CandE-winning organizations use pre-employment assessment tools designed to help hiring managers make better hiring decisions and increase fairness in the hiring process. Humana, a multi-year CandE winner, told us: 'We are increasing the use of prescreen questions. We are refining and scaling them across more of our jobs so that people can see what is important to us. Applicants can answer when it is convenient for them. For example, a single parent working full time may find that late in the evening works best to respond to our questions.'[1]

Assessments

Assessments can happen immediately following an application, or at any point during the interviews. As we mentioned in Chapter 5, companies should strive to communicate as much information about the assessment as possible upfront, especially the estimated completion time. Sometimes companies use a modern ATS that tracks where a candidate is in the application process, but then the application flows into an assessment that has an older interface and does not have the same quality user experience. If that is the case, upfront communication can help by setting the expectation early with candidates and preparing them for what they will see.

Any feedback you can give candidates following their evaluations is encouraged, especially when candidates do not pass. There should be an auto-delay built into any rejections that are automatically sent when a candidate does not pass an assessment – the last experience you want is for a candidate to spend an hour taking an assessment only to receive a rejection message 15 minutes later.

Video interviews

Video interviews are an extremely helpful tool but are often met with mixed reviews from candidates. There are several reasons, including:

- **Candidates feel like it is impersonal.** Prevent this by finding a way to tell candidates why you are using video interviewing and how it helps both the company and the candidates (for example, it allows them to take the interview any time or place it is convenient for them) and consider using company branding to bring as much of your company's 'look and feel' as possible to the video interviewing platform. Rather than writing questions that candidates must record themselves answering, have someone on your team record themselves asking the questions, also giving an intro to themselves and the team. Perhaps choose to use video interviews only for certain positions, such as high-volume roles.

- **Candidates feel they might get discriminated against.** Prevent this by incorporating everything written above and also linking frequently back to your corporate DEI message and goals. Highlight real employees' stories, videos and pictures on the careers site and in social media. (Look back to Chapter 4 for more on social media and career site best practices.) Consider giving the option to contact your team if they feel so uncomfortable with video that they prefer a phone interview first.

- **They do not have the chance to interview the company.** Prevent this by incorporating everything above, plus consider the addition of a chatbot or even a microsite that can answer FAQs, talk about how to be successful in the interviews, what the teams look for and more. Using AI and automation may seem counterintuitive, but turning a talent acquisition team into augmented recruiters by using technology to help with general functions and mass communication means they can white glove the most crucial and strategic candidates.

What candidates want

Candidates who withdraw do so for three reasons, according to Talent Board CandE Benchmark Research: 1) their time was disrespected during interviews and appointments; 2) the recruiting process just took too long; and 3) salary didn't meet expectations. In this stage of the candidate journey, candidates ask for the same considerations that we discussed in the application stage:

- **Respect for their time.** Reviewing résumés and dispositioning candidates in a timely manner. Setting expectations with hiring managers and interview teams that they must show up on time for interviews and that no-shows and last-minute cancellations cannot be tolerated if we are to successfully hire. This is not an easy conversation to have with an interview team, especially since recruiters are unlikely to have authority over interviewers. This is where a recruiter must build a strong relationship with the hiring manager to get their partnership and set these expectations with the team, as we will discuss in Chapter 8.

- **Speed and ease.** Candidates can be working professionals, actively interviewing or have personal events and cannot always work within our timeline or wait for our decisions. Strive to help your team understand that flexibility may be needed and whenever possible, have backup interviewers. Make swift decisions and let candidates go if they are not qualified rather than delay the inevitable bad news.

- **Transparency and clear expectations on next steps.** Candidates look for and expect respectful communication and feedback at each step (We will get into specific rejection communication and feedback in Chapter 7.) Whenever possible, communicate to the candidate at the beginning of the candidate journey what the series of steps will look like, rather than introducing one step at a time.

- **Sometimes candidates feel as if they are being asked to jump through hoops.** This happens because hiring managers/teams are indecisive and want more input from colleagues with whom they collaborate. Sometimes this happens when an organization has a lot of employees who expect input into certain hiring decisions even when it is not on their team. Sometimes it is even used to bridge a gap between two conflicting teams – if this is the case, the candidate will probably sense the tension. Whatever the situation, tacking on one step after another almost automatically makes the candidate feel like there is a flaw with their experience or fit, rather than assume that there is internal misalignment.

- **Perceived fairness.** Candidates want to feel confident about the interview process and their fit, through communication and interview preparation, and are more satisfied about being able to present their skills and experience. According to CandE Benchmark Research data, in 2021, 32 per cent of North American candidates reported receiving little to no preparation before the interview (it's closer to 20 per cent for EMEA, APAC and Latin America).[2] Interview questions, tests and evaluations must be fair and relevant to the job duties. Candidates want to be evaluated fairly against job qualifications and receive feedback on what was not in line with the requirements. Provide communication consistently before and after the screening and interview stage.

- Aerohive, a CandE winner, told us: 'We believe in prompt, consistent and transparent communication with each job applicant who makes it to an initial screening and beyond. It's that simple. We understand what it's like to be a job applicant and so we "put ourselves in the applicant's shoes" and deliver the same respect and care to them we would want for ourselves.'[3]

Recruiter screen

The purpose of the recruiter screen is to choose which of the candidates who have met the job's minimum requirements will be selected to have a deeper evaluation by the hiring managers. Recruiters ask qualifying questions about candidates' skills, experiences and interests, to ensure that they align with the position and that the candidates are a good potential addition to the company itself. There is a lot to fit into 30 minutes, so we have created a suggested itinerary in Table 6.1.

TABLE 6.1 Because there is so much information to collect in a 30-minute initial telephone screen with a candidate, we created a sample recruiter screen itinerary

Time spent	Topic
2 min	Grace period: Allow the candidate a couple of minutes to recover from back-to-back meetings/calls if they are currently working or to find a private room to conduct the call
3 min	Break the ice, reiterate why you reached out or why their information is interesting
5 min	Interviewer provides the company/role description
10 min	Interviewer asks questions
5 min	Allow the candidate time to ask questions
5 min	Wrap up the call and explain next steps

Following a format like this allows a recruiter to stay on track and gather pertinent information while maintaining a conversational style that can help build a relationship. It also allows the candidates to learn more about the role and helps start to get the candidate excited about the possibility of working with your company. The recruiter is practising one-to-one marketing and selling the opportunity to the candidate, and, at the same time, assessing the candidate for alignment to company values, the company and the opportunity, and soft skills that are important to the team and the organization. You will also learn about their motivations.

Ask a few questions that confirm candidates are at least minimally qualified for the position based on skills and experience, and maybe a 'knockout' question or two. A knockout question is one that a recruiter can ask to help determine immediately whether a candidate should move to the next step. An example of a knockout question for an hourly role is, 'Are you willing to work overtime?'

Salary/wage discussions

Money questions can be challenging to ask. There are a few states in the USA that do not allow recruiters to ask for salary history. Instead, recruiters can ask for a candidate's target salary range instead.

At the same time, the recruiter should be prepared to give some information at this point to the candidate about the target salary that the company expects to pay. In fact, pay transparency continues to be a competitive differentiator, with job candidates calling for it and many states and cities across the US enacting their own salary transparency laws for employers. There are employers that, in turn, have chosen not to promote jobs in those states, deliberately avoiding having to share salary information.

Many states also limited the kinds of salary questions employers can ask candidates (salary history, for example). In the 2021 CandE Benchmark Research, 80 per cent of North American employers asked about salary expectations instead from candidates, and 6 per cent of employers avoided asking altogether. Candidates told us that they were asked about expectations 33 per cent of the time, while

8 per cent were asked what their most recent salary was, and 17 per cent were told what the salary was without requesting it. For those candidates who were told, their positive interview perception of fairness increased 30 per cent. Transparency continues to pay candidate experience dividends.

While it is not a good idea to lock anyone into a rate at this point, before they've learned more about the role, recruiters need to do their best to ensure that both parties are on the same page regarding salary. Be prepared for salary to be a dealbreaker. For example: A small startup may want to hire technical talent out of a large enterprise organization, such as Microsoft, but may not be able to match the candidates' current salary or benefits package. While some candidates may be drawn to the opportunity and say that money is not a primary factor, there are many candidates who would not be able to lower their cost of living to make this transition. It is always better to find out early rather than after investing time in the interviews.

If a recruiter has passively sourced a candidate, the initial conversation may not be the right time to talk about salary. There might need to be an informational interview before a passively sourced candidate decides whether to act and apply to the open position. That is when a candidate may ask more questions to receive information about the company and position rather than be thoroughly screened for the role.

If your application form asks candidates to input their ideal salary range, understand that candidates expect a negotiation and may be starting high. They might be listing base plus salary. Rather than disqualify a candidate with a great résumé for listing a desired salary above the target, talk to them to see if they have flexibility. Rule them out after a conversation if they cannot flex.

Other 'dealbreakers'

Besides salary or rate, there might be other aspects of the open position that are dealbreakers for candidates. For example, if a candidate has been working remotely for the past year, they may be less willing to travel to an office five days a week. Start talking about dealbreakers early, including collecting some idea of rate range, travel expectations and time spent in office.

The company itself may have dealbreakers that make certain candidates not a fit for the organization. There are a few healthcare organizations, for example, with a strict no tobacco policy. It is a candidate experience best practice to be transparent upfront and make sure candidates understand the policy rather than waiting until the final stages when they might receive an offer contingent upon a drug screen. When this happens, neither the company's nor the candidate's time has been respected. The screen state is the optimal time to allow candidates to self-select out if they are not able to meet a company requirement.

For the greatest perceived fairness, a company can always use its career site to explain the 'why' behind policies that may rule certain candidates out.

Hiring manager interviews

From the kick-off meeting, we are working to establish strong and trusted relationships with our hiring managers. Continue to meet with them on a weekly basis while the search is ongoing, meet their expectations, deliver insights and intel that can inform their decisions and counsel them on the state of the talent market. From time to time, recruiters will have to deal with the hiring manager's indecision or extra steps. Listen to their request, give them a chance to explain why and be ready to push back if you do not agree or if it is counter to candidate experience best practices.

The best way to push back is to calmly listen, be sure to respond thoughtfully (not react) and use data and prior examples to highlight why their next course of action may not be the right one to take. Recruiters can always ask talent acquisition managers, HR business partners (HRBPs) or other trusted TA members for help when needed.

Interviews

Interview training

Interview training results in better hires overall because well-trained interviewers can promote a consistently better candidate experience and protect against unconscious bias. Interview training must include the basics – what questions are legally acceptable to ask – but that is just the beginning. Here are some considerations for evolving interviewer training:

- **Who in the organization is qualified to be an interviewer?** There are no common standards here, but companies can consider whether a new employee should be with the organization for a period of time before interviewing, whether to make interview training mandatory and what seniority levels can interview for which positions.

- **Go beyond the basics.** Explain their role as an interviewer. Interview training should cover interviewer expectations like their role as company representatives and for candidate experience. Show them how the interview invitation will look and where they can find the résumé and details on the candidate. Sometimes when interviewers are rushing from room to room and using only their mobile devices, the invitations are truncated, and they cannot see the résumé. It could be as simple as making sure they 'show all notes' in the invitation.

- **How and when they are expected to give feedback.** Will the hiring manager collect feedback or will the recruiter host a debrief meeting? Set these expectations in interview training so interviewers know what is expected of them. You can train them on how feedback will be collected.

- Compassion International, another multi-year CandE winner, implemented a training programme called 'Hire Up', a three-and-a-half-hour course, that all of their people managers are required to attend. 'Hire Up walks hiring managers through the entire Compassion hiring process, and explains their roles and responsibilities in recruiting, starting with candidate experience, and how important they are to Compassion's employment brand and our process. As a result, Compassion has received great feedback from the hiring managers who have gone through the program and are now better equipped to extend candidate experience in the interviews.'[4]

PointClickCare, another CandE winner, implemented a training programme called 'Hire to Win'. All employees involved in the interviewing process are required to go through the internal training programme. It cements the vital nature of a good candidate experience and the impact of a positive, authentic employer brand. Since initiating the programme, PointClickCare has seen an increase in support and commitment from each member of the hiring team.[5]

- **How to administer interviews consistently across the organization.** Interviewers should also learn about how to administer certain parts of the interview, especially if you have a case study, code review or other assessment.

- **Unconscious bias training.** This teaches interviewers to understand the important difference between hiring for someone who 'fits' the culture and someone who 'adds' to it. One excellent method is to interview for alignment to company values rather than to company culture.

- **How to pivot from sensitive topics.** One of the most challenging aspects for interviews is how to be personal and build a relationship with candidates while remaining professional without crossing the fine line that exists. It takes experience and practice. Interviewers may have a good understanding of which questions are legally acceptable and which they must avoid in the interview, but it is always good to remind them. Furthermore, sometimes interviewer conversations can begin friendly and innocently but touch on sensitive topics like politics, religion or even college sports that polarize the room. It is important to teach interviewers on how to recognize if a conversation is headed into a sensitive area and how to pivot back to keep it job specific.

- **What to do if an interview goes poorly.** Companies should have a policy on how to manage interviewers that do not perform well. In the best interest of candidate experience and both parties' time, we recommend having a strategy to talk to either a manager or a recruiter before cutting an interview short and walking a candidate out. This is a worst-case scenario, but even when candidates perform poorly, we still want to treat them with compassion and avoid embarrassing them. Remember, they might be a customer or source of future referrals.

Keep a list of employees who have completed interview training, and frequently audit the list for new employees and newly promoted workers who now meet your qualifications, so you have a constant source of interviewers and the regular interviewers do not burn out.

Companies that do not have formal interview training programmes can still practise best practices by partnering with the hiring managers to set expectations with new hires about interviewing.

Structured, semi-structured and unstructured interviews

Structured interviews are when companies use the same, standardized methods to interview candidates for their open positions; semi-structured interviews are when companies assign interviewers a predetermined area or agenda, but the interviewer is free to ask some of their own follow-up questions; and unstructured interviews are when companies do not have any set format for interviewing. Table 6.2 summarizes structured, semi-structured and unstructured interviews, and when they are best used.

We recommend employing some structure into the interviews. At the very least, the recruiter can strategize with the hiring manager on the makeup of the interview team, select participants and assign each interviewer a specific subject area or discipline to cover. In addition to whether an interview is structured or unstructured, one must also decide between a few different interview methods and formats (Table 6.3). Table 6.3 outlines the most common formats and methods and when they may be best used. Usually, in a more structured

TABLE 6.2 Different types of interviews have pros and cons and are best for unique company circumstances

Type of interview	Pros	Cons	Best use
Structured (most formal; predetermined agenda and questions)	• Most repeatable • Best for interviewers to understand expectations of them • Ensures more consistency across anyone who interviews • Ensures more consistency from selection criteria • Good for eliminating bias • Good for new interviewers • Can capture the best feedback	• Takes more time to train interviewers • Questions must be developed, tested and occasionally updated • Questions could be 'leaked' by candidates • Candidates sometimes feel like the company did not get to know them	• Companies that do a lot of volume hiring • Companies that need more reliable interview data • Companies with less-experienced interviewers
Semi-structured (predetermined area/agenda but interviews may ask related follow-up questions)	• Makes interviewing more personal and engaging when a recruiter uses a guideline but has freedom to explore topics • Simpler to implement with some training and planning • Still allows the company to deliver a consistent interview experience to candidates with a small amount of customization	• Can get off track easier/not get all questions asked • Not always an 'apples to apples' comparison between candidates • Could allow for some bias to enter the conversation if an interviewer is looking for 'culture fit' and mistakes 'like us' as synonymous with culture fit	• Companies with more seasoned interviewers • Companies where workers have more training and an understanding of unconscious biases and how they may arise • Companies with many different types of positions where one process does not suit all roles
Unstructured (least formal; no set format for conducting interviews)	• Easier to adapt to changing times and topics • Can get very in-depth with both answers and questions • The best chance to personally get to know a candidate and build a relationship	• Very challenging to capture consistent feedback on each candidate as it relates to the job • Opens the door for interviewers to compare candidates to each other rather than to the job specs • Less opportunity to evaluate candidates on an equal platform • Important questions may get entirely forgotten • It may give the candidate the impression that the	• There is a better chance of a successful interview if it is a seasoned interview team • Perhaps when used for a hiring manager interview, or final interview with an executive, when the interview loop/panel has structure

TABLE 6.3 There are multiple ways to construct a candidate interview

Format/ method of interview	Description	Best use
Loop (format)	A series of consecutive interviews, usually 1:1, but there may be more than one interviewer present.	Works well across all interviews, when length and complexity of the loop is commensurate to the responsibilities of the job.
Panel (format)	Multiple interviewers at the same time.	Best for structured or semi-structured interviews, where there is some preparation in advance.
Group (format)	Multiple candidates meeting hiring managers and/or interviewers at the same time.	Helpful when companies must hire more than one person for the same role within a short period of time. This format is best for structured interviews, when multiple candidates answer the same question; or semi-structured when the interviewers have been able to prepare in advance.
Behavioural (method)	Designed to evaluate how candidates react to certain situations, or how they reacted to past situations.	Works well across all interviews, structured and unstructured, when the questions are relevant to the responsibilities and requirements for the job.
Case study (method)	Designed to evaluate how candidates solve a problem by presenting a hypothetical business situation, usually true to life.	Work best in a semi-structured format with well-trained interviewers.
Fit (method)	Designed to evaluate how the candidate fits into the organization and team culture. (Be aware of employees thinking that 'culture fit' is the same as 'like us', which can create bias. Encourage them to interview based on fit to company values.)	Best in a semi-structured interview with well-trained interviewers, with company-related questions such as teamwork, innovation, competition, social responsibility; and not personal, unrelated questions like, 'What do you do for fun?'

(continued)

TABLE 6.3 (continued)

Format/method of interview	Description	Best use
Homework/assignments (method)	Sometimes used in conjunction with another interview format, such as a technical interview (with a take home code review) or a case study or presentation.	Best when given before an interview, not after; and the interviewer has time to review it. For example, a coding exam may be given before the technical interview so the interviewer can ask follow-up questions.
Presentation (method)	Designed to evaluate presentation skills, a candidate may be asked to prepare a slide deck and speak to a group.	Best for roles in which public or group speaking is required, such as executive and sales roles. Semi-structure works well, when candidates are given a presentation topic but may field follow up questions from the interviewers.
Technical (method)	Designed to evaluate hands-on technical skills and grasp of concepts, could include a conversation, 'homework', or a whiteboarding activity.	Best in a job-related semi-structured format where candidates are given the same problem or set of questions, but the interview can ask follow-up questions.

interview environment, HR decides on the best formats. In companies that have semi-structured or unstructured interviews, it may be the hiring managers' and/or recruiters' preference.

Selection of interviewers

The recruiter and hiring manager will strategize on the interview participants after deciding which interview methods will be used to evaluate the candidates. Interview panels vary considerably in length, and our best recommendation is to proportion the number of interviewers to the complexity of the job. The more senior a position, the more stakeholders and key relationships they'll have, so it makes sense if a senior director needs to meet with 7 to 10 people. On the other hand, a customer service representative may only need to meet with two or three people.

As we stated above, it is a good practice to introduce at least some structure into interviews. At the very least, the recruiter and hiring manager can assign a type of interview, if there are multiple assessments, or even simply a topic to each interviewer. For example, it makes sense for the most technical interviewers to administer a technical interview and/or code review. Using this approach will reduce the chance that every interviewer asks the same questions. Worst-case scenario, you have six interviewers in a loop that all end up asking the same question, and when you're trying to determine if the candidate is a fit you realize that the team has missed a couple of the most pertinent questions.

A great strategy to avoid that worst-case scenario is for recruiters to compose an e-mail summary for the hiring manager to personally mail to the interviewers, indicating a summary of the candidates, the résumés, why we are interviewing, assigning each interviewer an area to cover and setting expectations for delivering feedback afterwards. Figure 6.1 is a template.

Occasionally, an interviewer will reach out to the recruiter and ask if they have questions they can use for their interview. If so, this might be an invitation to introduce some structure into the interview process if none exists yet.

FIGURE 6.1   This is an e-mail template that a recruiter can use to help prepare and align every interviewer prior to meeting with candidates. The intended use is for the recruiter to give a draft to the hiring manager. The hiring manager can then customize that draft before sending to the interview team

Dear [Hiring Manager],

Following our interview strategy conversation, here is a draft e-mail you may edit. Please send this to our interview team so we are all aligned with our interview plan:

[Interviewers],

Thank you for taking time out of your day to be part of our interview loop for the [open job] position. We are beginning in-person interviews next week and here is a short summary of what we need.

You'll each meet with three final candidates [list names] and their résumés are attached. We selected these finalists after a three-month search in which [Recruiter] reviewed over 80 résumés. I am assigning each of you a specific area to cover.

[Interviewer 1]: [Assigned area, such as behavioural questions]

[Interviewer 2]: [Assigned area]...

The candidate market is very competitive, so we ask you to prioritize this meeting, and allow the candidates to interview you as well. We will debrief as a group after the interviews. If you cannot make the debrief meeting, send your feedback to [Recruiter] and me within 48 hours of your interviews.

Thank you,

[Hiring Manager]

Interview scheduling considerations

- During the recruiter phone screen, the recruiter should always verbally outline the steps to the best of their ability to set expectations with the candidates around the length of time.

- After a candidate passes the hiring manager interview, those steps can be reiterated.

- What are the next steps, and when and where are they expected to take place?

  - Ask the candidate for as much availability as possible upfront to eliminate back-and-forth e-mails. If they hear from a scheduler or admin next, the recruiter can let the candidate know that they will still be there every step of the way, but the scheduler will help ensure a great experience. It's a nice touch to send the candidate the proposed schedule while waiting for confirmation from the interview team so they can 'pencil it in' and start to research the interviewers.

- ○ Will it be in-person or virtual? If the interview is in-person, try to limit it to one day (unless it's better for the candidate to break it up).

- ○ Give directions to office, where to park, how to access the building, who to ask for.

- ○ Special considerations: Do they need ID, will they get their temperature taken, is a mask required, etc.

- ○ What to expect during interview, detailed itinerary, names and titles of interview team.

- ○ Fully coordinated travel.

- ○ Tips for tricky parking garages and difficult-to-navigate buildings.

- ○ What types of interviews will occur.

- ○ Tips to prepare for interview, including research and dress code.

- ○ Clear next steps and consistent follow-up.

- • On the day of the interview, the recruiter should be available, or have appointed another colleague (recruiting assistant or admin, perhaps), to manage the interview, make sure interviewers are on time and who can make last-minute adjustments if needed.

- ○ If the interview is taking place in an office, do you have the interview room booked, and is it clean and presentable for the candidate? Do you have a way to prevent employees from taking your reserved interview rooms?

- ○ Do you have water ready for the candidate?

Interview best practices

- Send the admin, receptionist or front desk a list of the day's interviews so they can expect the candidates when they arrive.
- Foster a company culture that interviews for values alignment and work ethic in addition to skills and experience.
- Understand where unconscious biases may arise in the organization, and take active steps to mitigate them.
- Build in a bio- or snack break.
- Arrange a tour, if possible (even a virtual one).

After the interview, make sure you have a debrief meeting on your calendar with the team or that you can collect feedback electronically within 48 hours of the interview. At the same time, check in with the candidate to ask how it went and say some encouraging words. This is a great time to portray to candidates that you are in their corner.

Walgreens, another CandE winner, has a policy of constant feedback, requiring hiring managers to provide feedback within 48 hours of interviews. Recruiters in turn must give feedback to candidates within 48 hours of receiving hiring manager feedback.[6]

Decision

When the decision is made to hire a candidate, the offer and onboard process begins (see Chapter 9). Since this can take some time to prepare and to gather approvals, let the candidate know that good news is coming and give an expectation of when you will have information for them.

When a candidate is not hired, call them to let them know they are not progressing (see Chapter 7) and disposition them right away. Providing definitive closure when no longer pursuing candidates gives them closure and is the right thing to do. Providing feedback to candidates, especially final-stage candidates, is a candidate experience differentiator.

Delivering a rejection over the phone – as opposed to mass e-mail or text message – can leave the candidate with a positive impression – 29% higher than e-mail messages. Coupling that with feedback on why the organization made that decision could increase the likelihood of reapplication. … Year after year, Talent Board CandE research shows that communication and feedback loops are ongoing differentiators of a more positive candidate experience.[7]

In conclusion, it is important to remember that the screening and interviewing stages are key steps in the candidate journey. This is when companies spend the most time with candidates and the two parties learn the most about each other. Recruiters, interviewers and candidates form, and leave, impressions about each other that lead to impactful decisions about the open position. Companies that practise good candidate experience tactics use the screening and interviews to build relationships with candidates in addition to assessing them for qualifications. As competition increases for qualified workers, it becomes more imperative for recruiters to take a lead role in managing the entire interview process to ensure a good candidate experience. While interviewers take their responsibility seriously to hire the most qualified candidates, they are often not aware of how the market continues to shift and talent acquisition continues to evolve. Sometimes interviewers conduct the meetings the way they always have – for years – and it can lead to a negative candidate experience because the expectations of candidates continue to shift and evolve.

Notes

1 Talent Board. 2017 North American candidate experience research report, February 2018, thetalentboard.org/benchmark-research/cande-research-reports/ (archived at https://perma.cc/KAX2-8L6B)

2 Talent Board. 2021 Global candidate experience research reports, December 2021, thetalentboard.org/benchmark-research/cande-research-reports/ (archived at https://perma.cc/KAX2-8L6B)

3 Talent Board (2018, February) 2017 North American candidate experience research report, thetalentboard.org/benchmark-research/cande-research-reports/ (archived at https://perma.cc/KAX2-8L6B)

4 Talent Board (2018, February) 2017 North American candidate experience research report, thetalentboard.org/benchmark-research/cande-research-reports/ (archived at https://perma.cc/KAX2-8L6B)

5 Talent Board (2019, December) 2019 North American candidate experience research report, thetalentboard.org/benchmark-research/cande-research-reports/ (archived at https://perma.cc/KAX2-8L6B)

6 Talent Board (2019, December) 2019 North American candidate experience research report, thetalentboard.org/benchmark-research/cande-research-reports/ (archived at https://perma.cc/KAX2-8L6B)

7 Talent Board (2019, December) 2019 North American candidate experience research report, thetalentboard.org/benchmark-research/cande-research-reports/ (archived at https://perma.cc/KAX2-8L6B)

07

How to reject candidates with empathy

In previous chapters, we talked about rejecting candidates at different stages in the candidate journey, but now it is time to discuss non-selection in depth. By the end of this segment, you will be ready to communicate status and rejection with all applicants, giving timely and appropriate messages that brings them closure, but also in a way that leaves the door open for the candidates that you would like to re-recruit and keep warm for future roles.

We will discuss the following:

- How to ensure that all candidates receive an appropriate disposition message.
- What candidates want and expect to hear when they are not selected.
- Ways to respond when candidates request feedback from a recruiter.

CandE Benchmark Research shows that when talent acquisition teams focus on the best practices we are going to lay out, negative candidate experience ratings start to improve. Companies build talent pools with greater ease because candidates who might be a good fit in the future stay engaged and apply again. Additionally, non-selected candidates with a good impression of their experience will increase their brand alliance with the organization, continue to refer others and share their positive experience with others.

Why does it matter how we reject candidates?

It matters how we reject candidates because it is a costly mistake not to care. Three main reasons that companies' rejection messages matter include to preserve the employment brand, make it easier to hire in the future and to retain customers.

When someone has fruit trees in their garden, and it comes time to harvest the fruit in the autumn, they find ways to preserve whatever fruit they cannot eat while it is fresh by canning it or making pies, ciders and jams. This way, the extra fruit does not go to waste. This is the same mentality that high-performing, CandE-winning talent acquisition teams have when it comes to candidate rejection: when a company invests time and budget into modernizing the attraction and application stages of the candidate journey, for example on initiatives like enhanced technology and new career landing pages, rejection messages that are crafted with empathy can preserve your engaged and qualified talent pool, so your attraction efforts do not go to waste.

Think back to Chapter 3 (the Virgin Media story) and other anecdotes we've shared along the way highlighting how candidate experience impacts the bottom line of your business. Every candidate touchpoint is an opportunity for a company to make a lasting impression – positive or negative – that influences the candidate's behaviour during this recruitment. For example, have you ever extended an offer to a candidate and wondered why they don't seem excited about it? Usually, when this happens, we assume the candidate has received a better offer from another company, but that is not always the case. Sometimes the behaviour goes back to a simple comment that was made by a recruiter or interviewer that deflated the candidate's excitement.

If so, that impression could also influence the candidates' future behaviour with your company. If the candidate is hired, are they feeling more excited after positive interviews, or lukewarm after a strange interaction? As you can imagine, moments like this carry over to employment and how engaged that new employee is with the company. Even if the candidate is not hired, those initial candidate touchpoints still influence if they apply again in the future, refer others, leave positive or negative reviews and continue to be a customer of the organization.

Companies have a limited supply of candidates. It may seem the candidate pool is endless if we have a good flow of inbound applicants for open positions, but according to CandE Benchmark Research, 50 to 60 per cent of candidates are rejected without any screening or an interview beyond the application for any given role. Additionally, recruiters 'say no' a lot: We reject up to 99 per cent more candidates than we say 'yes' to, since usually only one candidate is hired per open requisition.

Increased job seeker traffic does not mean that our candidate supply is endless or that other qualified candidates are applying. Companies might have more applications if they have a recognizable brand or if they post on a popular job board. A certain job title might attract more applicants simply because it is desirable; or more applications are received if it is a skill set that is entry-level or more widely available in the market. A candidate might read the requirements and think, 'I can do that' instead of 'I have experience doing that' or a company might have a poorly written job posting that does not clearly articulate the true requirements. When there is an economic downturn, or even a localized incident like a store closure, we might get more applicants because more people are unemployed. Some applicants unfortunately think that applying to multiple jobs within a company is a sure way to get a conversation with a recruiter, sort of in a shotgun blast style.

None of the scenarios in the previous chapter mean that more applications are going to lead to a quality hire, and the situation can be exacerbated if we are hiring for a specialized skill, a niche industry or a small geographic area and cannot pay for relocation. However, every one of those applicants matter and will have an opinion of how companies treat them when the rejection message is delivered: if they perceived fairness in the process and if they felt their time was respected, even if they did not make it beyond the application stage.

When a company makes a job offer to one candidate after interviewing multiple qualified finalists for a single job opening, the rejection communication is a critical action in keeping those runners up (or silver medalists) engaged and interested in staying in the company's talent pool to be considered again for future positions. If a recruiter does it right, it could drastically shorten the time to fill a future position when that candidate is excited to hear from the company again and jumps at another chance to work there. Conversely, if the finalist receives an e-mail rejection that is a pre-written template, especially after investing hours into their candidacy, they may experience disappointment so strong that they decide they do not want to be considered with the company in the future. They might also stop being a customer and share their negative experience with others.

A candidate may experience varying degrees of disappointment depending on how far they get in a company's evaluations, but it never feels great to be rejected or told 'no'. As recruiters, we must treat our candidate population with care by offering closure, transparency and feedback where we can and by developing a recruiting team that advises candidates through interactions rather than transactions. 'Recruiters can serve as valuable resources to candidates... and should help candidates position themselves better – even if it is at a competitor. Not every candidate will join your organization. But EVERY candidate will have an opinion on whether your organization is worth joining.'[1]

Why is rejecting so hard?

If connecting people with jobs is the best part of a recruiter's job, it's easy to understand how delivering frequent rejections is arguably one of the most difficult parts of what we do in talent acquisition. It is not fun to tell people no. A lot of times we get personally invested, end up really liking and cheering for a particular candidate and get disappointed when they don't get an offer. Sometimes we deliver a rejection that we know is the right answer because a candidate is not a good fit, but it turns into an uncomfortable conversation that is hard to shake off.

Often, it's the sheer number of 'no's' we give. Let's look at some simple maths for a 'moment in time' snapshot of a recruiter's dashboard:

If we have a mid-sized company where one recruiter has 18 requisitions (according to SHRM, the average recruiter req load is somewhere between 15 and 20) and an average of 50 applicants per requisition, that means 882 of their candidates at any given time will be rejected.

Of course, automation handles the bulk of these through auto-rejection templates.

But if the recruiter talks to 15 people for each requisition, that means they will have talked to 252 of those candidates who will not get hired. Adjusting for candidates that withdraw or accept other offers, let's estimate that the recruiter will end up delivering rejections to 200 of the candidates in play.

That is a lot of 'no's'.

On top of the mental weight of delivering rejections, there are additional factors:

- **Other priorities.** Recruiters are prioritizing offers to their top candidates and keeping interviews moving for promising ones, as they should, but it means they sometimes fail to close a loop.

- **Time.** Recruiters' jobs can have very heavy administrative burdens between updating an ATS, gathering required information for compliance, scheduling meetings for themselves and hiring managers, requesting and following up on approvals, rewriting job postings, keeping candidates engaged and more. (This is where investing in technology that alleviates administrative work to free up time for recruiters to give a white-glove service to top candidates is a game changer.)

- **Training.** No one ever trained them on how to say no. (We'll fix that in this chapter.)

- **They don't want to hurt people's feelings.** We have to re-channel that intent in the right direction because candidates' feelings are hurt worse when they feel that they are left without closure. When we can properly deliver a rejection message with compassion, we are doing the right thing by them.

- **Lengthy decisions.** Sometimes the recruitment for certain positions takes a very long time, or hiring managers and/or recruiters cannot decide whether to advance a candidate. Sometimes feedback on a recently interviewed candidate is great but hiring managers are not yet ready to extend an offer – 'There might be a better candidate out there still' and this is where it's important for the recruiter to remind the team that candidates must be measured against the job description rather than compared to each other. Often, if it is a 'maybe', the answer will probably be 'no' in the long run, and we should let them go rather than hold on just to reject them down the line.

- **They're not supposed to.** Sometimes companies choose to take the most conservative path possible when it comes to talent acquisition, and that means keeping communication to generic, pre-approved templated messages. Organizations are not legally required to give feedback, and sometimes companies choose not to. Guidance like this can come from leaders who are advised that they might get sued for discrimination if feedback is given. Our counter-argument is: How often has that actually happened? If a company follows legal guidelines and modern talent acquisition best practices and chooses to hire the most qualified candidate, the chances that a suit would have merit are very slim.

- **Rely on data,** such as from the CandE Benchmark Research, to highlight this important point to leadership.

What candidates want

As a recap, we know that candidates who consider working for us expect the following to feel that they had a positive experience:

- **Respect for their time and clear expectations.** Letting them know when to expect to hear from you goes a long way in creating a good candidate experience. If you do not have an answer within that time period, you can still check in and say, 'We have not had a chance to meet and collect feedback yet, but I will update you as soon as I am able.'

- **Respectful communication and transparency.** We will discuss this later in the chapter, but we recommend a phone call rejection message for every candidate that has been interviewed. If a candidate has invested time in us, it is a small gesture that we can invest in thanking them for their time, especially when we think they have potential to be evaluated for the company in the future.

- **In 2021, we saw some alarming statistics in the CandE Benchmark Research data:** Of candidates who were not selected for a position, 63 per cent reported they received an e-mail from a 'do-not reply' address notifying them that they were no longer considered after the in-person interview stage, up from previous years. Only 19 per cent received a personal e-mail from the recruiter or hiring manager, and only 6 per cent received a phone call.

- **We also saw that when candidates received a phone call rejection,** their positive candidate sentiment increases.

- **Closure through perceived fairness and exchange of feedback.** Many business leaders often quote, 'feedback is a gift', and it also applies to post-interview feedback when a candidate is not selected for a position. Candidates want to know how they did, why they were not selected and what could they have done better? They are looking for tips on how to improve their performance in their job search in the market, not to go head-to-head and challenge the company's decision. Rather, oftentimes, they know it in their gut if the interview did not go well, and they're simply asking for confirmation.

When delivering feedback in a rejection conversation, think of it as leaving them with a gift and phrase it as coaching for their next interview experience. For example, if a candidate asks, 'What could I have done better?' you can respond with: 'We had two strong finalists between you and another candidate, and we had to choose the one who fits our needs closest. We hope to stay in touch with you and that you'll consider us again if we have another role that is a good match for your experience. In the meantime, I do have a couple of suggestions for you, if you're interested.' Pause, let them react. They will probably answer affirmatively. 'I noticed you had some really great answers, but you tended to meander a bit away from the original question. Really listen to what is being asked and focus on being more specific with your examples. They will really appreciate that.'

According to our annual CandE Benchmark Research, when employers give rejected candidates general and specific feedback on qualifications and job fit, the resentment rate decreases and positive sentiment and fairness increases.[2]

If an organization is staunchly opposed to giving post-interview feedback to non-selected candidates, just give more proactive coaching instead, especially when prepping candidates before the interviews, as we discussed in Chapter 6.

Aerohive, a CandE winner, said:

> We are not afraid to provide transparent feedback to job applicants who are not offered a position with Aerohive unlike many other companies who are 'risk averse'. We realize job applicants seek and desire feedback so they can improve the next time they are called for an interview. We feel they deserve to know this information after investing their own personal time and effort in undergoing a series of interviews with us.

According to CandE Benchmark Research, when given feedback, a candidate's willingness to refer and to increase their relationship with the employer can increase 20 per cent or more. Candidates who were invited to provide feedback to the company after the interview, either in person or through a survey, were dramatically more likely to refer and to increase their relationship with that organization. Feedback goes both ways. When feedback was both asked for and offered throughout the attract–recruit–hire process, it overwhelmingly increased the average candidate's positive impression of the given organization. Offering individualized feedback demonstrates a company's ability to treat candidates as people, not simply as an application to discard.

Similarly, asking candidates to rate their experiences shows a commitment to all candidates, whether they make it to the hiring stage or not, and it helps companies to improve. Deluxe, a CandE winner, said:

> We have a survey that goes out to our candidates immediately following their in-person interview. The survey asks candidates to provide feedback about various stages of the hiring process – from how they became aware of our opportunities to the application process and the interview experience. This data, along with the data that's collected from the CandE survey, goes a long way toward identifying our strengths and areas of opportunities in our candidate experience. More specifically, we heard one recurring theme from applicants that had been a pain point for us in the past: frustration over a lack of follow-up for candidates who didn't get the job. As a result, we began tracking follow-up communication rates for our recruiters and holding them accountable. The next year we won our first CandE award since 2014. Not that this was the only reason for winning the award, but it certainly helped.

How do we turn these insights into best practices for our team?

Rejection prioritization

The further a candidate progresses into a company's recruiting process, the more care needs to go into a rejection message if that candidate is not selected. More time and feelings are invested in each step and disappointment will be felt deeper if a candidate is rejected in a final round than if they are rejected just after submitting a job application.

In Figure 7.1, the top of the pyramid are the candidates who have progressed past the recruiter screen and have met with a member of the interview team. The best practice is that we call these candidates to reject them in a live phone call because these are the candidates who have invested the most time in the company and are arguably the most personally invested in, and excited about, the opportunity. These candidates have learned the most about the company through both research and conversations with employees and have built relationships with interviewers.

The middle are the people that we phone screen or have invited to take some assessment beyond the application. It's still best to call them but we can e-mail them as long as it is a personal message.

While we encourage custom rejections as much as possible, these special considerations are a top priority:

- **Internal candidates.** We discussed internal mobility in Chapter 4 because as we know, we have to constantly re-recruit our employees to retain them; but internal candidates are not always the most qualified for our positions. Having a separate rejection process for internal employees helps retain employees even when they are not qualified for a position because they will feel like they do have a path to advancement and are receiving encouragement and direction from the company to get there. When companies have an internal career portal, it can become a tool through which you can develop employees and further groom them for future openings when they are not currently qualified. Internal candidates need to be rejected with special care. Each time an employee applies for an internal position and is rejected, they will become more discouraged, and it could negatively impact their employee engagement. Here are a few guidelines to avoid this:

  o Share each internal applicant with the hiring manager, even if they are not qualified.

  o When they do not get a hiring manager interview, call them to deliver the news. Coach when possible and give encouragement.

  o When you notice an internal candidate has applied to a few jobs and doesn't seem to be getting traction, proactively reach out for a networking/coaching conversation with them. Even when a company promotes an open internal mobility programme, there will always be individuals who are not comfortable starting the conversation. Just because they're not talking about it doesn't mean they are not feeling discouraged.

  o When the hiring manager has talked to the internal employee, involve the hiring manager in delivering specific coaching feedback to the candidate, including what they can do better or work on for next time.

- **Employee referrals.** It is a very nice touch when companies give personalized rejections to employee referrals, especially when the candidate is very underqualified but either the employee or the candidate might think that their company connection gives them a chance. The recruiter can copy the employee referrer on the message and provide some positive coaching and encouragement to the candidate, such as 'Pay attention to our basic requirements and make sure your experience is a good match, and also that your résumé reflects the alignment. We would be happy to stay in touch with you for future roles that are a better match.' By copying the referrer, you are educating both the candidate and the employee on what to keep in mind. You are also helping the candidate get into a potential situation where they are applying to, and getting rejected from, multiple roles.

- **Passively sourced candidates.** Anyone that we have passively sourced should also at least receive a personalized message and not the standard rejection auto-template. If we solicited them, and they took time to consider our offer when they were not initially interested in us or our company, it is the right thing to do and a very nice touch above other competing companies' practices. The message can include language such as, 'I enjoyed meeting and getting to know you, and I hope our paths cross again. In the meantime, I will send you a request to connect with you on LinkedIn. Also, I'd be happy to consider you for future roles here.'

Other special touches that can go a long way:

- **Veterans and transitioning military.** Sometimes those who have served the country have a challenge translating their military experience into civilian terms. Other times, their leadership experience might not be the right fit for an organization. For example, an ex-army battalion officer who commanded 600 has undoubtedly impressive experience, but it might not be the right fit for a 200-person company where managers play a close-knit career development, training and mentoring role with a small team of direct reports. Always thank them for their service and if your organization has services for transitioning military, make sure to connect them. Give them any advice you can share, or explanation of why they are not a fit. There is always the chance they are an excellent fit, but the recruiter is just not seeing it yet because of how the résumé is written.

- **Serial applicants.** When a candidate applies to multiple roles within an organization and that number of requisitions keeps ticking up, it could give a recruiter pause, especially in larger organizations where there are multiple recruiters. There are many reasons why this happens:

    o Candidates really want to work for your company. If a candidate has a great résumé and the right role just has not emerged, reach out and tell them you've noticed and would like to stay in touch. This simple action can go a long way in extending a lifeline to someone who is frustrated that they're not making headway in working for their ideal company.

    o Candidates think they are qualified. Many times, candidates review a job description and think, 'I can do that.' We recommend that recruiters review their job postings to make sure the requirements are clearly written, as we discussed in our job posting section of Chapter 4. You can send a rejection message with a sentence such as, 'with all of our exciting growth, we are targeting candidates who have accomplished these specific tasks in other organizations that hit the ground running here'.

    o Candidates might think that a 'shotgun' approach to job applications is a good thing, that the more eyes on their résumé the better, when the opposite is often truer. Send them a note with a message like, 'When you are applying to companies, focus on finding the roles that are the right match for your skills and interests so you can articulate your career path. It tells companies that you have a clear path forward, and that is a good thing.'

The bottom of the pyramid are candidates who submit an application but do not meet our minimum qualifications and will not be evaluated further. These represent the bulk of the candidates, and we can use auto-rejection templates to message them but still must follow some basic best practices (see Figure 7.1).

FIGURE 7.1 Rejection pyramid

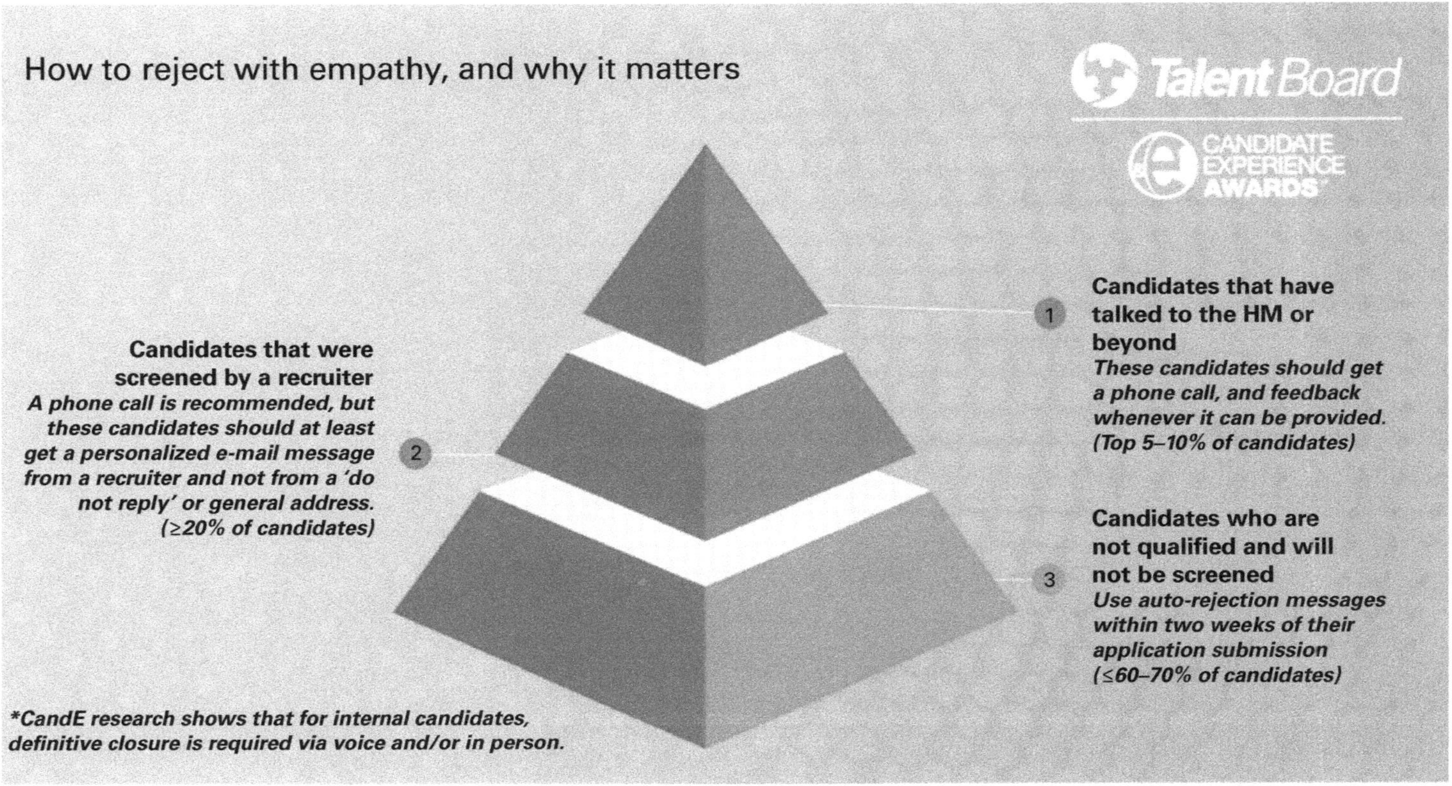

How to reject with empathy, and why it matters

Talent Board

CANDIDATE EXPERIENCE AWARDS

1 **Candidates that have talked to the HM or beyond**
These candidates should get a phone call, and feedback whenever it can be provided. (Top 5–10% of candidates)

2 **Candidates that were screened by a recruiter**
A phone call is recommended, but these candidates should at least get a personalized e-mail message from a recruiter and not from a 'do not reply' or general address. (≥20% of candidates)

3 **Candidates who are not qualified and will not be screened**
Use auto-rejection messages within two weeks of their application submission (≤60–70% of candidates)

CandE research shows that for internal candidates, definitive closure is required via voice and/or in person.

When using auto-rejection templates, make sure that:

- Recruiters are actually sending rejection messages to candidates. Sometimes, after a candidate applies, a company sends a message that says, in summary, 'Thank you for applying. You will be contacted if your resume is a fit.' We do not recommend this approach because it doesn't answer the candidates' needs, including transparent communication and perceived fairness. As we discussed in Chapter 4, candidates are applying to your job posting because they think they are a fit; therefore, they deserve communication, which they usually do not receive after that form of e-mail.

- Your auto-acknowledgement template sent after application, and auto-rejection message sent after résumé review for unqualified candidates, are distinct and clearly written.

- The tone of the rejection message expresses gratitude for their interest and time. Even better is when the template is written in the voice of the company culture.

- It invites candidates to apply again and connect on social media or sign up for job alerts.

- Branding is cohesive with other external communication

Silver medallists

When a company only makes one offer but interviewed multiple finalists, they end up with 'silver medallist' candidates, or runners up. These are candidates who performed well, and we would consider again in the future or hire now if we could open a new role. Strategically it is best when we can get an offer of acceptance from the top finalist before we reject our silver medallists because it makes communication management much easier for the recruiter. However, this turns into a very delicate situation to manage from a timing standpoint because we want to ensure a good candidate experience for all. You can buy time by setting expectations for when you'll have an answer. For example, 'We are meeting this week to make a decision and I should have an update for you by the end of the week.' If they had other pending opportunities, it is good to ask, 'I know you've had some other conversations, too. How are your other opportunities coming along?'

If the first offer is accepted, the best practice is to schedule time to call the silver medallists to deliver the rejection message and be as open as possible about what transpired.

Sometimes the outcome is simple: One candidate in particular was a stronger match because they were more qualified.

> We had strong people apply, but it came down to two, you and another candidate. It was a really hard decision, but our other candidate has deeper experience in _____. There was very complimentary feedback about what you brought to the table. While we needed to make this decision because it is the best for the business, we want to stay in touch with you, too. There will be other roles opening in the near future and we hope you'll consider us again.

When there is constructive feedback to share, remember that feedback is a gift and phrase it as coaching rather than a recount of what went wrong. While we cannot take away their disappointment, we can soften the blow. For example:

> Regrettably, I have to deliver some bad news today. We are not going to move forward with an offer for you. It came down to two candidates, you and one other who had deeper experience in _____.
> You answered many questions very well, but there were a couple of constructive comments that I would be happy to share, if you are open to it.

Pause, wait for a reply.

> Whether it's here or at another organization, we want to see you succeed. One way to improve your interviewing is to focus on articulating exactly what your contributions were in your team roles. Perhaps start with the 'we', what the team did, and then elaborate on the 'I', and what you specifically led.

Notes

1 Mazor, A, Cleary, B and Brender Brandis, N. Your candidate experience: Creating an impact or burning cash? Deloitte, 2017, deloitte.com/us/en/pages/human-capital/articles/candidate-experience-creating-an-impact.html (archived at https://perma.cc/SF2D-5BA6)

2 Talent Board. 2021 North American candidate experience research report, December 2021, thetalentboard.org/benchmark-research/cande-research-reports/ (archived at https://perma.cc/9RAS-KZUW)

08

Get hiring manager support

Building strong relationships from the beginning

One of the Talent Board predictions for over the next decade is that hiring managers and interviewers will need to become more accountable for candidate experience if we are to continue to maintain and raise the bar above other organizations hiring the same talent. It can no longer be the job of the recruiter alone to build relationships with candidates and meet their expectations. Our goal is to evolve our roles from recruiting, which involves filling an open role, to talent acquisition, which involves strategy and input around attracting and acquiring top talent to help our company grow. Often, the first obstacle in this evolution is getting hiring manager buy-in.

One of the most exciting events in recruiting is when a promising candidate makes it to the interview, but it can quickly spiral into one of the most frustrating events. What recruiter hasn't experienced one of the following?

- An interviewer is late.
- An interviewer doesn't show up at all.
- An interviewer cancels the interview at the last minute because they have a conflict or a deadline they must meet.
- The interview starts on time, but afterwards the candidate tells you about an awkward exchange they had with one of the interviewers.
- After the interview, the candidate is even more excited about the role, but afterwards one of the interviewers gives vague, lukewarm

feedback that influences the others who previously had positive feedback, and now the candidate might not be moving forward.

- After the interview, the candidate is excited about the interview, but you do not receive any decision from the interview team.
- After the interview, the hiring manager tells you it went well but they want to review more candidates before making a decision.

It is up to the organization to deliver interview training company-wide that sets expectations around hiring priorities, the importance of timely feedback; and even unconscious bias training so interviewers learn to measure each candidate's experience to the open position rather than comparing candidates to each other.

Interviews are sometimes an unknown variable in our quest to improve candidate experience because they are out of our control. Since we cannot be present to monitor our hiring teams and ensure best candidate experience practices during interviews, sometimes it is only afterwards that we hear about undesirable interview behaviour. In Chapter 6, we learnt about crafting interview loops and panels, and prepping both candidates and interviewers for success in the in-person interviews. For now, let's focus on building stronger relationships with our hiring managers.

As recruiters, we can minimize these occurrences ourselves and influence more productive outcomes. Recruiters who are coached to approach their role as a business partner, in a consultative manner rather than a customer service one, will be able to build stronger relationships with hiring managers. In this chapter, we will help you to discover how.

Why the recruiter–hiring manager relationship is important to the candidate experience

Candidate experience is influenced by the relationship between recruiters and hiring managers in many ways, including:

- You can develop a strong understanding of the job need and create a job posting that is concise and specific. Strong job postings give candidates a clearer understanding of whether they are qualified before they decide to apply (helping prospective candidates self-select out means fewer candidates you have to reject). The job post is also more intriguing to the qualified candidates you want to attract.

- You can prioritize your time more effectively because you know the ideal candidate persona. Your kick-off meeting and subsequent check-in meetings with the hiring manager continue to home in on what is most important in the role.

- You can elicit more participation from hiring managers sharing the opportunities to their networks and directing the team to do the same; and a better platform from which the hiring team can be educated by you and the hiring manager about the ideal candidate persona.

- More participation in proactive outreach and sourcing in their own networks because you have educated them about the demand challenges of the market and urgency around high-demand roles.

- More cooperation from hiring managers in getting candidates screened and interviewed, and hiring managers who are more amiable when you have suggested next steps that might take them out of their comfort zone.

- Faster responses to all your inquiries, for their feedback and also greater assistance in getting the interview team's feedback.

- The candidates get an impression of the spirit of collaboration that exists between recruiters and hiring teams and is more intrigued in a role with your organization.

Why don't hiring managers care about candidate experience?

Hiring managers do care about the experience of the candidates they want to hire. When we build our hiring manager relationship effectively, we can help them understand hiring challenges in today's competitive market so they care about the candidate experience of people they may want to hire in the future as well. The reality is that many hiring managers simply aren't aware of competition in the market, the importance of candidate experience, the effect it can have on the bottom line of the business and the importance of them participating in the process, from the candidate's perspective. Here are some common ways we can improve their understanding:

Pipeline visibility. Often, hiring managers do not have visibility into the total number of candidates that we review and screen, or what is known as the candidate 'funnel', and they simply lack understanding of candidate experience from the full-cycle talent acquisition perspective; just as we may not understand how to build an ER nurse schedule, configure the corporate firewall or suggest the best strategy for retail shelf-stocking procedures. When we present three to five screened and qualified candidates to a hiring manager, they are more likely to think, 'This is it?' than 'You have been really hard at work!' unless you share that you started with screening 120 applicants, out of whom 60 passed the assessment, then you contacted the top 30 to phone screen. Out of those, five have already received other job offers and you ruled out 20 who did not meet the preferred qualifications or who raised some specific red flags.

'Time to fill' is one of the most common metrics for recruiting success, arguably because it is the easiest to measure, but what it fails to measure is how much time is wasted when we have to reschedule interviews (we forgive emergencies that occur and are referring to those who think rescheduling an interview is as simple and innocuous as rescheduling a 1:1 with a colleague). We can lose candidates if too much time is spent on scheduling and they take another offer with a company that interviewed quicker than we did. When a candidate is interviewed, 'time to fill' also fails to capture how much time it took the hiring manager and/or interview team to decide regarding the candidate and communicate that to the recruiter.

Sharing candid snapshots of recruiting activity, both the wins and the detail of problem areas, can help hiring managers understand the total investment of our efforts in hiring their position and give them a greater understanding of the challenges you are facing. They can respond to challenges, correct their team and may even have suggestions that improve your next round of screens.

Market insights. When hiring managers are delaying a decision, they might be stressing because they don't want to make the wrong one. They have a clear picture of their target persona and ideal hire, but they may be out of touch with the availability of that persona in the market, the demand for that skill in the market and current rate, or whether someone actually exists with the combination of skills they are seeking.

Sharing intel and market insights as well as any anecdotal support-ing information, such as the number of candidates who did not respond to your proactive sourcing outreach or declined to interview, why candidates are withdrawing before you get the chance to inter-view them, why candidates are declining offers, other companies hiring for similar roles, and – if you can get it – salary offer amounts, will help hiring managers understand the urgency of interviewing and deciding on candidates quickly.

Candidate empathy. It's always impressive to see tenure in a company's employees. Employees who have been with a company for more than five to seven years are keepers of unwritten company history and 'tribal knowledge', and are great sources of information when we have questions. However, the longer an employee has been with an organization, the more potential there is for them to resist change in any capacity, including in hiring. Have you ever heard someone say, 'Well that's just not [our company's] way'? Now, combine that with the fact that longer-tenured employees have been a candidate fewer times and probably forgot what it's like to be on the candidate side of hiring.

Additionally, it is the responsibility of the recruiters to reject and disposition candidates. It is usually not top of mind for hiring managers, and there is often a bit of fear around candidate retaliation or litigation that can make them hesitant to 'close the loop' with a candidate.

Sharing candidate feedback, especially if your organization surveys rejected candidates, is the best way to evolve this way of thinking; combined with any comments on sites like Glassdoor where candi-dates can rate their interview experience. This is also where Talent Board's Business Impact Calculator that we introduced in Chapter 3 can be valuable. Candidate feedback will highlight where candidate expectations fell short, and it can also illustrate to hiring managers that candidates are only looking for closure. When everyone involved in hiring has done their part to ensure a good experience and that the best candidate was selected, there is little reason to fear retaliation or litigation. Non-selected candidates will indeed be disappointed, but, if the recruiters do their job, candidates can be left knowing that it is not a personal rejection, and they are encouraged to apply again in the future.

Consultative recruiting. Sometimes companies purposely hire less experienced recruiters. In this case, hiring success can be impeded in three ways: 1) By a recruiting team that lacks practice with challenging communication like giving feedback and negotiating. 2) Where the hiring manager is seen as an authority figure rather than as a key stakeholder. If a hiring manager expects to be treated as stakeholder, those expectations may not be met by recruiters who are more task-oriented. 3) When a hiring manager expects to give direct orders to the recruiter, but the cycle of negative candidate experience is perpetuated because neither the hiring manager nor the recruiter knows better.

In this case, it is helpful for the talent acquisition team/leader to develop service level agreements (SLAs) for the business that each recruiter can share with the hiring manager when they first meet.

How can I build a better relationship with my hiring managers?

Getting their buy-in starts with the recruiting kick-off meeting. Many times, our schedules are not our own, and we move from meeting to meeting with barely a breath in between. Some of those meetings we can listen to or participate in on autopilot. Whether you are meeting with a hiring manager for the first time or the 20th time, each new requisition is an opportunity to set new expectations by conducting a dynamic kick-off meeting.

Best practices for conducting a successful kick-off meeting

SCHEDULE YOURSELF 30 MINUTES TO PREP BEFORE EACH KICK-OFF MEETING.

- Job descriptions are an internal document for your organization, and a tool for organizational design that describes the level and responsibilities of a particular role. Usually, they are the basis for a job search.

- The challenges are: 1) Job descriptions usually do not contain key details that you need to know about the current team or project. 2) Job descriptions are not written to attract candidates to a job opening.

- Job postings are the first impression for an organization, and we want to put our best face forward and present a document that is interesting, engaging, informative and free of errors. We're going to start prepping for the kick-off meeting with the job descriptions to bring a clean copy of our future job posting. Sometimes in kick-off meetings, recruiters focus on the job description and review it line by line alongside the hiring manager, which takes up the entire kick-off meeting. That practice is fine but is not optimal in our efforts to appear more strategic and establish our authority as a business partner in the hiring space.

- Start editing the job posting before you meet with the hiring manager. Your goal is twofold: 1) Transform the job description into a job posting – an ad – that catches the eye of candidates you want to attract. After all, it is not fair to get frustrated with candidates for not reading our job description if we do not provide a document that is readable. 2) Use the hiring manager's time during the kick-off meeting to discuss strategy and set expectations, not to go over the job description line by line.

- You'll gather some of the details about the ideal candidate persona in the kick-off meeting, but you can start by adding a catchy sentence that describes the company, and start narrowing down the bulleted lists of responsibilities and requirements by removing unnecessary bullets like, 'Other duties as assigned.'

- Look over the document, fix formatting errors and make note of suggestions you'll want to ask the hiring manager. A good rule is to ask before you make major changes to the content and be ready to explain why you are suggesting it. For example, you may suggest changing the name of the job posting, calling it 'Lead Project Manager' instead of 'PM IV'. Explain that your intent is to make the posting title more universally understood outside of your organization and also to help the wrong people to self-select out (avoid unnecessary future rejections) if they do not have 'Lead' experience.

- Be prepared to present a couple of profiles at the kick-off meeting. Your objective is not to hit it out of the park with the ideal candidate in your first meeting. (If that happens, kudos to you!) The real objective with preparing three profiles ahead of time to share with the hiring manager is: 1) To help calibrate your search and make sure you are on the right track, especially if it is a highly specialized position that you're not familiar with. 2) To show the hiring manager that you took time to research beforehand. They will appreciate it and be impressed you did some homework, even if they don't say it upfront. 3) To highlight anything that may not be in the job description already or may not have come up in conversation (especially if you're able to share résumés of previous candidates and they recall why someone was not a fit). Overall, using profile examples will help guarantee a more successful search and you will save a lot of time going back and forth with meetings.

- You can source résumés from the applicant tracking system, from either current employees recently hired into a similar role or from runner-up candidates (silver medallists) who did not get an offer. You can also search on LinkedIn.

- Sourcing is an important skill for every recruiter to understand, especially if you are not getting the applicant flow you need to fill a particular role, or if qualified applicants are not applying. It's a desirable skill to be able to go find a couple of qualified profiles quickly without asking for extra resources. When you present qualified profiles, it tells the hiring manager that you know what you are looking for. From a candidate experience perspective, it's important to understand that sourced (passive) candidates must be treated differently than active candidates who have applied to our roles. It is okay if you are not a sourcer, we presented some tips on sourcing in Chapter 4.

Conducting the kick-off meeting

So, what do you really need to find out in the kick-off meeting? You have to do a bit of detective work. You want to understand things like, does your hiring manager know what they're hiring? If so, your job is to use them as a source of knowledge to build a strategy based on past successes and failures so that you are not tasked with reinventing the wheel.

Maybe they're new to the organization, but you happen to be a veteran with this search. Or, maybe it's a new position that hasn't existed in the organization before, a 'buzzword' they heard and now they're convinced they need it, and now it's your job to go find it.

Hiring managers have big jobs. They're responsible for important parts of the business, keeping things afloat and building new ones, and the pressure to grow is high. We have to give them a little bit of forgiveness, but we also have to take good notes during the meeting so we can recap them later in an e-mail and remind the hiring manager of what we agreed on because they are people, too.

We must apply a bit of psychology to our jobs. Every meeting is going to be different. Some hiring managers seem really easy going up front but are highly critical of recruiters later. Some hiring managers love to teach and will spend 30 minutes every day with a recruiter until the role is filled. Your managers will come to meetings distracted. They are afraid to take risks and make the wrong decision. They do not know the market like we do.

Sometimes, hiring managers may be good at portraying confidence they do not really feel, when under the surface they're quite stressed and feeling under pressure. It is our job, as partners, to give them trust in our relationship and capability: We can help them to succeed with their hiring needs.

WHAT TO ACCOMPLISH IN THE KICK-OFF MEETING:

In a 30-minute meeting, you will usually have about 20 minutes to gather key information, agree to some basic expectations and deliverables, and demonstrate that we have a plan that is doable and repeatable.

Here is a sample agenda:

- >5 minutes for either of you to run late from a previous meeting (but do try to be on time).

- >5 minutes to exchange greetings.

- >5 minutes to communicate the purpose of the meeting to the hiring manager, which is to collect information about the open role and build a strategy with them for a more successful search. If this is a hiring manager you've worked with in the past, you can call it a new initiative to improve hiring by enhancing the format of the kick-off meeting. Your goal is to get their buy-in so that later in the meeting, you can ask for them to uphold certain responsibilities around the search.

  - Explain how 'hiring' is not just the offer and onboarding. It is the entire candidate journey we need to keep in mind and the experience of our candidates and how it affects the bottom line of the business as well as helps us to hire faster now and in the future. This is a great place to share data you may have, perhaps from the CandE Benchmark Survey or other candidate experience survey. At the very least, you can introduce the Virgin Media and Kimberly-Clark case studies from Chapter 3, which is always impactful because it is a well-known brand. Even if you are not in a business-to-consumer (B2C) organization, explain how more than just purchasing is affected.

  - Request their partnership in the effort to improve candidate experience. You and your team have proven best practices, and partnership from the hiring manager around sharing faster feedback and coaching the interview team will make a difference.

  - Offer specific suggestions that may make a difference. For example: 'One challenge we faced in the past is getting candidates scheduled with you quickly, I know your calendar is very busy.

Would you consider creating a weekly interview block on your calendar for the next few weeks, perhaps on an afternoon that works best for you? That way, I have a weekly deadline to bring you new profiles, and you can devote the time to screening them.' Or: 'During our last search, one of the interviewers on the panel cancelled last-minute three separate times, and we lost a candidate because we weren't able to reschedule fast enough. If that interviewer is key to this panel, it would be helpful if you could talk to them in advance and set the expectation that they need to prioritize these interviews. Thank you.'

Ask questions to learn more about the role and the ideal candidate persona.

- We have a list of sample questions to get you started. They include asking about:
  - Why are we hiring this position? (new/replacement).
  - Persona (is there someone we hired similar).
  - Internal or external hire.
  - Timing.
  - Characteristics the team can/cannot live without.
  - Budget.
  - Where did we find them before?
- Some of your questions need to be designed to get lessons and context from previous searches so that you do not reinvent the wheel every time.
- This is also where you should understand the hiring manager's biggest priority and concern around filling the role. Is it budget-related? Is it filling the role as quickly as possible? Is it finding the candidate who meets a long list of must-have qualifications?
- Share the profiles that you sourced. After hearing the description of the role, they may not be relevant; that's okay, share that information with the hiring manager and say you'll get a couple more based on the new information. If they are a fit, pay attention

to feedback that the hiring manager gives – you may generate some pertinent follow-up details.

Form a strategy and plan, and communicate it to the hiring manager. Do you need to research more data, such as the market rate for a particular role or availability of candidates in your market? Will you post this role via the normal means (i.e. job board and Indeed) or will you post to specialty sites? Do you need to source? Will you use a staffing agency?

- This is a good time to request that the hiring manager post the role via their personal network and encourage their team to do so as well. You can explain that warm referrals are always a trusted source of candidates. When a company has referrals, they usually are hired faster, have longer tenure with the organization and are more productive.[1]

- Identify the steps for candidates. Does the hiring manager want to review all résumés? After you talk to the candidate (or watch their video interview), does the hiring manager screen them next? What will the interview look like, and who will the interviewers be?

  o You may have to advise the hiring manager about having interview loops that are too long or have too many steps. Also, pay attention to the interview team because your organization may have guidelines around who is qualified to interview, and sometimes hiring managers are not aware of them. You can either push back and suggest substitutes, or see if there is a way to get those individuals trained up on interviewing in the next couple weeks so they can participate.

Here is where we need their buy-in: You need to both agree to basic expectations around participation and timing.

- Communicate the service level agreements (SLAs) that you will uphold around follow-up items like additional research, sending new résumés and other requests to get the search started; and agree with the hiring manager on SLAs they will uphold for you, including accepting and keeping meetings, turnaround time for feedback and managing the interview team.

Attempt to find a good time for a recurring check-in meeting.

Send an e-mail to the hiring manager that recaps the plan and SLAs. If you have additional questions or are able to gather any outstanding research, attach them.

The importance of this step should not be underestimated. There is a lot of information in a kick-off meeting, and if this is a new practice for you, it is good to reinforce the message, especially if you have a manager who tends to multitask. It is good to have the conversation documented so you can refer back to it anytime. Stay flexible, but hold everyone accountable.

During subsequent check-in meetings, use the plan to measure your success and whether you need to change your strategy for better results. Strive to deliver what you promised and meet your SLAs. Building trust with your hiring managers will serve you well now and in the future.

Lastly, good candidate experience can positively impact the hiring manager, too. The professional reputation and personal brand of hiring managers is affected by how they treat candidates. Hiring managers are used to being shielded by the recruiting teams from having to deliver negative news to candidates, but it has meant that they can make hiring decisions without having to explain them, or they don't have to respond when they do not want to. Nowadays, information is pervasive, and it's easy for applicants to find out who hiring managers are for specific roles and get a pretty good idea of who the teams are. Think, for instance, about one of the first things most of us do when we are introduced professionally to someone else: We look them up on LinkedIn. The more employer branding a company does, the easier it is to get information about the role and discover who the team is and who their manager might be. When candidates have been interviewed and had an unpleasant experience with a hiring manager or interviewer, they may name them in feedback surveys or, worse, on publicly available review sites like Glassdoor or Indeed when rating their interview experience.

Not only are we extensions of the company brand, but extensions of each other's professional brands. To keep professional bridges and reputations intact, it is imperative we work more in union than ever before.

Note

1 Maurer, R. Employee referrals remain top source for hires, SHRM, 2017, shrm. org/resourcesandtools/hr-topics/talent-acquisition/pages/employee-referrals-remains-top-source-hires.aspx (archived at https://perma.cc/AJZ8-EQCW)

09

Improving the hire phase

Offer and onboarding

Congratulations! We have reached the penultimate hiring stage of the candidate journey: Extending job offers to the most qualified candidates and hiring and onboarding those who accept. By the end of this chapter, you will be more confident in closing candidates and ready to enhance your onboarding process with engaging content designed to keep future employees from the time they are selected to Day 1 and beyond.

In the offer and onboarding stage, there is usually a hand-off of responsibility from recruiters to HR or onboarders at some point after offer acceptance. This stage is important because multiple workers are usually involved and yet candidate experience work does not stop once an offer is made. Rather, it flows into employee experience and every component of offer and onboarding must be performed with care to ensure a great candidate journey. The HR workers or onboarders who process the new hire might be more focused on the administrative and compliance side of onboarding a new employee rather than on delivering a consistent experience to that new hire. Without that natural flow and consistency in experience as the candidate becomes a new hire, the alternative is that the candidate could feel their experience was inauthentic.

It's important to take time to visualize ourselves in the new hire's shoes at this point, especially if recruiters and onboarders have not been a candidate themselves in quite some time. What is the candidate, soon-to-be new hire, feeling and experiencing? Getting a job is very exciting and feels like a self-actualizing accomplishment, but it can be quite stressful.

Regardless of experience level, the new hire is making what could be a monumental life change to join a different organization. Some of the stresses a candidate could experience when switching jobs include:

- Personal accountability or guilt over leaving the previous employer.
- Ending relationships, especially direct reports.
- Possible counteroffer from the current employer.
- Other competitive offers. How will they know they're choosing the right one?
- Someone in charge of a large project may want/need to finish it before they can put in notice.
- Reaction of current employer when news is given/being 'walked out'.
- Walking away from large bonuses.
- Change in routine that disrupts family, like no longer being able to stay home or take children to school.
- Leaving a comfortable job for a 'riskier' one with a bigger impact, like in a small company.
- Longer commute.
- Switch in environment.
- Potential relocation.
- Potential increase in travel.
- Fear of the unknown.
- Nervousness.
- First job ever.
- Gap from last pay cheque at old company to first pay cheque in new company that may leave them hurting for cash.

When a candidate does not have a good experience during the offer stage, it can amplify the stress they are already feeling and either cause them to decline the new role or could affect their employee experience later. Additionally, in competitive talent markets, there are many factors that can jeopardize a successful outcome and cause candidates to change their mind even after they have accepted a job offer. When an excellent candidate experience turns into a clunky onboarding, it opens up the door to doubt. This doubt is the seed that grows into less engaged new hires that are willing to move for better opportunities.

A company can have world-class candidate experience from attraction to offer, but if the onboarding does not meet the candidate's expectations, the candidate might not join, or they might join and be a less engaged employee. The entire candidate journey must be consistent and flow from end to end.

Therefore, a recruiter cannot consider the job to be finished until the candidate is at their new desk or logged into their new work computer. After all the time and effort invested, the last thing anyone wants is to have to start a search all over again.

What candidates want

At a minimum, candidates are looking for everything we discussed in previous chapters: Transparent and responsive communication, information and quick decision-making.

They want to know quickly whether they are selected for the job or not. This could be because waiting for a decision is agonizing; but it also could mean that they're engaged with multiple companies and have competing offers on the way. Perhaps one company's position is the candidate's top choice and they are anxiously awaiting a decision to know whether they are selected and meanwhile they are receiving pressure from another organization, which has given them a good offer along with a looming deadline by which they need an acceptance.

Even if the candidate does not have an offer deadline, it is natural to want to compare offers alongside each other. (It is no different than when we want to interview multiple candidates at the same time to compare and contrast, rather than one at a time.) While timing does not always work out for this to happen, it is a situation that will influence candidate behaviour – particularly in hot talent markets or for in-demand skill sets. It could be why sometimes a candidate will pressure a recruiter for an answer, whether they divulge the other offers to the recruiter or not. Understanding this will help recruiters to manage candidate expectations, understand motivations and be savvier in negotiations.

When a candidate is not selected for a position, they want – and deserve – to know why so they can freely pursue other opportunities and make a decision without jeopardizing those opportunities because of timing. If they are not selected, they want to know why the decision was made, so they can get closure. They also want to understand what the feedback was, so they can improve for next time.

When a candidate is selected, they need a guide in navigating next steps and decision-making. When a recruiter is using candidate experience best practices, they become that guide. The opportunity might not fully become a reality for the candidate at this point even if they are fully engaged in the process. The recruiter does not just deliver the offer to the candidate. They can influence a positive outcome when reminding the candidate about what said they are looking for in a new role, which could include:

- An attractive offer that is competitive with market rates and commensurate with their experience.
- Finding meaningful work and make an impact.
- Adding value for themselves and for an organization.
- Joining an organization that will propel them forward in their career and life.
- Doing meaningful work with a good team.
- An attractive financial future or more money now.
- Finding a workplace culture that they can identify with and fit into.

When a candidate accepts a position, they want and expect to feel welcomed into the organization and feel like they belong. The company must be ready for the new hire on Day 1 with workspace for the employee, equipment and technology, and an onboarding plan. On the first day, a new hire can feel uncomfortable if left alone without an itinerary or someone to reach out to for guidance.

In the following sections we will break down the steps of offers and onboarding and discuss best candidate experience practices.

Salary discussions

It is a best practice to start talking about compensation early, and often, to make sure that the candidate and the company are aligned in their salary expectations. Open conversations around sensitive topics like salary help to establish trusting relationships between a candidate and a recruiter. If a recruiter has built a strong relationship with their candidates based on communication and transparency, they are on track towards getting their candidate to accept a job offer. They understand the candidate's motivators and have a better chance of knowing how they're feeling about the opportunity in general and whether the candidate has other offers. As the evaluations continue, the compensation parts of the conversation can grow more in depth.

By talking about compensation often, both the recruiter and candidate can set expectations with each other without premature negotiation. That way, a candidate is not 'locked into' a rate too early; but potential surprises can be avoided, and they can identify any possible dealbreakers since this much time and effort is put into the selection process.

Offer prep and the pre-close

When a decision is made, the recruiter should reach out to the candidate as soon as possible. There is positive news to deliver at this point, and it is exciting! The recruiter has an opportunity to connect with the candidate as an advocate, show genuine excitement for that individual and congratulate them since their hard work has brought them to this point. At the very least, the recruiter can deliver a short message to tell the candidate that they have been selected and educate that the next step is to put an offer together, how many days they expect it will take and that they will be in touch as soon as possible. A message like this keeps the conversation going along with the momentum of excitement the candidate is feeling about the role. It keeps the company top of mind for the candidate especially when there are other competing opportunities that might be taking longer or not as transparent about the candidate's status.

This is an excellent opportunity to 'pre-close' the candidate and generate excitement about the offer. The recruiter should share some of the positive feedback from the interviews, reiterate how they see the candidate adding value to the team and work, review the career growth opportunities and also how the company's culture and the role fit with what the candidate is looking for. The pre-close is important in revisiting compensation to make sure that there are no surprises: Is the candidate targeting the same offer amount or has their request changed? Are there other opportunities that arose since the last time the recruiter asked? Are there other offers? Does the candidate have any upcoming vacations or are they more nervous about leaving their current company in the lurch, and so they might ask for four or five weeks' notice instead of the typical two weeks?

Throughout the entire journey, the recruiter should also be collecting and sharing as much data as they can with the human resources and compensation teams. Work with HR to ensure that your salary ranges are fair and equitable – and competitive – because candidates expect an attractive offer. If you are part of a large, national company with a centralized recruiting team, make sure you are using salary surveys for each region, rather than basing all salaries off one area's salary data. Companies rely on salary surveys for data on compensation ranges, but there can be big differences in what rates the market is bearing if it is a very in-demand skill set, if there is a particular area that is experiencing a technical boom and the salary data is older, or if the company is hiring a skillset that exists outside the company's industry and therefore not accurately represented in a specific salary survey.

When determining salaries, candidates and companies are usually looking at different data points. Companies use reports based on the cost of labour within geographies, industries and roles; and candidates usually have access to crowd sourced data on salary ranges for the job titles. Also, when relocation is involved, candidates look at the cost-of-living differences in their current city compared to where they would relocate versus the cost of labour.

Offer amounts should also be closely balanced with internal workers in the same job to ensure that equity is retained and that the recruiter is not creating an outlier, with either too high or too low of a salary, in the career band.

When possible, attempt to prepare a document or talking points to share the monetary value of the total rewards so candidates understand the full value of the package and see it as a whole number versus only looking at the base salary. Focus on meaningful and competitive total rewards, especially if you know your salary ranges are slightly under the average. For example, if your organization has an excellent 401(k)[1] match that is higher than most other organizations, a recruiter could do some calculations to show that if an employee invests a certain amount into the 401(k), it means the company would match a certain amount in a full calendar year. (A 401(k) plan is a company-sponsored retirement account that employees can contribute income, while employers may match contributions.) Rather than including just the percentage, sharing that an employee could make 'up to $__' could help illustrate the true value and trigger the employee to consider the total rewards amount and not just the salary.

Even minor, fringe benefits could create real value for some candidates, so it is good to focus on benefits that are unique to your organization and different from others in the industry.

Compensation is also a powerful tool for sending messages that reinforce the desired brand image and for relaying to employees the things the organization deems important... Southwest [Airline]'s pay scale is comparable to that of its competitors. However, Southwest pilots are paid by the flight rather than by the hour. Like other employees, they also have stock options and profit sharing, which serve as incentives and create a sense of ownership in the company.[2]

Extending the offer

In order for the best possible chances that the candidate will accept the offer, recruiters need to do everything possible to reduce the interview to offer time. Usually at this point, recruiters are pursuing approvals from busy executives that do not often check e-mail and offers can get lost in the system.

According to CandE Benchmark Research, if employers make the offer within one week of the final interview, the candidates' willingness to increase their relationship increases exponentially and they are more likely to say yes – and what a retention starter! Any delay means that the candidate could be second-guessing their fit, start to doubt the confidence that they will be selected or interview with other companies that are able to move faster and extend an offer before your company.

The recruiter should call the candidate to give the good news and convey genuine excitement for the candidate. The recruiter can talk through the details of the offer, including offer components and next steps, and also make time to answer any questions the candidate has. This phone call is also a great opportunity to 'pre-close' the candidate and either get a verbal acceptance or at least get a sense of the candidate's excitement or hesitancy. It is okay for a candidate not to accept the offer on the spot, but a recruiter can take note of any hesitation.

There is nothing wrong with it, and hesitation could stem from a number of factors:

- They were taught to 'play the game' and do not believe in saying yes right away.

- Sometimes candidates simply want time to look through everything and run the numbers.
- They want the offer in writing before responding.
- They want to prepare to negotiate a higher amount.
- Sometimes they want to talk it over with a spouse.
- They do not want to make a snap decision (or, at least, seem like they are making a snap decision).
- They are going to try to get another company's offer to compare or they have another company's offer and want to compare it.
- They are expecting a counteroffer.
- They are not excited about the offer.

These factors are normal. A recruiter can influence most of them if they have practised good candidate experience and developed a good rapport with the candidate over the candidate journey. Candidates might respond this way because they think it is the right way to 'play the game' or if they are receiving coaching from a parent, spouse, peer or friend behind the scenes. Sometimes the factors that cause candidate hesitation come from previous experiences when the candidate did not have a good experience or a mistake they think they made in the past when they didn't get a satisfactory offer. Because of this, recruiters need to allow candidates this time without reacting with too much pressure. The hesitancy also might surface if the recruiter was unable to develop a good relationship with the candidate. Sometimes, despite our best efforts, candidates hold their cards close, and we are unable to create that bond.

Regardless of whether the recruiter gets a verbal acceptance, it is important to end the call well (respond, don't react), reiterate excitement and extend congratulations to the candidate, and reaffirm that the candidate is their top priority, and they will make themselves available for future conversations.

Next, the recruiter should send the written offer letter to the candidate soon after talking with them. When picking a date by which the company needs an answer, give at least 48 business hours, and extend that time if they ask.

Competitive and counteroffers

Recruiters cannot expect 100 per cent disclosure from every candidate about other competitive job offers and why certain offers are more attractive than others. The best way we can defend against competitive offers is to build the best relationship possible, give timely information, be transparent and ensure they have a great experience when they are being interviewed. When candidates do share information about competitive offers, it is a gift to a recruiter. The best thing a recruiter can do is listen, thank that candidate for confiding in them and have an informed discussion about options, which often lead to negotiating a higher salary.

A recruiter who has built a good relationship with candidates can ask, 'Please keep me updated on your other offers, and if you are favouring one opportunity over another,' or, 'When you receive the other offer, I'd really appreciate hearing about it, so we have a chance to respond. If it comes down to something negotiable, I hope you'll give us a chance.' Competitive offers are often an unknown variable. When a candidate has a competitive offer, it likely means that their salary request will increase, as well, which means recruiters need to be open to renegotiation.

We will talk about negotiations in the next section below.

Recruiters can take a more proactive stance against counteroffers, which occur when the candidate's current employer increases the candidate's compensation or gives them a bonus to stay. As part of the verbal offer script, the recruiter can advise the candidate that the company might counteroffer. The recruiter can remind the candidate about why they said they wanted to change companies in the first place and help the candidate to determine whether more money would solve those challenges or if it is a temporary fix that is nice but does not take away their dissatisfaction.

At publishing time, we are experiencing an increase in competition within the talent market. There are fewer job seekers actively applying, a higher volume of withdrawals from consideration, more offer declines, higher salary requirements and we are spending more time on complex negotiations with candidates. The following suggestions are ways that recruiters can influence positive outcomes from counteroffer situations throughout the entire candidate journey.

- **During the initial candidate screen.** The best way to manage potential counteroffers is to anticipate them from the beginning – the moment you meet with a candidate. If you're interested in the candidate, expect future competition!Prepare yourself with an understanding of your candidate's motivations. If recruiters are used to 30-minute phone screens, they might consider scheduling 45 minutes so they can take the time to understand candidates' goals, dreams, passions and frustrations. Even if their conversations do not last the whole 45 minutes, they can use the remaining time to record what they heard from the candidate. The extra time conveys honest interest in the candidate's story and shows the recruiter's commitment. It can help set the stage for a positive working relationship.

- **During the screen, a recruiter can ask probing questions, such as:**
  - What's prompting you to look for a new position right now?
  - Besides the role, what are you looking for in your next company?
  - What do you enjoy doing?
  - What job responsibilities are you not excited about?
  - Describe your ideal environment to me.
  - If you could change one thing about your current role, what would it be?

- **Next, the recruiter can share their own personal story.** Why did they choose their company? Why are they passionate about it, and what do they find exciting? The rapport and trust that recruiters build can be the secret weapon later, especially if another offer enters the picture.

- **When making an offer of employment,** before a counteroffer: Coach candidates that they might receive one. Talking points include:

  - 'The job market is very competitive right now. When you put in your notice, there is a chance you might get a counteroffer from [current company]. They may increase your salary with a promotion to retain you. My best advice is to remember why you thought about leaving in the first place and ask if more money or a promotion is going to solve those issues in the long run.'

  - 'Sometimes when people put in their notice, managers even respond by putting some pressure on candidates. They may respond with statements like [list the following] but stay true to what your gut is telling you and make the right decision for yourself and your family.'

    - 'I'm really shocked. I thought you were as happy! Let's discuss this further before you make your final decision.'

    - 'We had you in mind for some exciting and expanding responsibilities. That will have to stay confidential now.'

    - 'You were slated for a raise in the next quarter, but we'll make it effective immediately if you stay.'

    - 'What company is it?'

    - 'We were really counting on you for this major project, that is unfortunate to hear.'

- **After the candidate tells you they received a counteroffer.** The recruiter can ask some initial questions to gently challenge the counteroffer. Talking points include:

  - 'Thinking back on our first conversations, I remember you mentioned the reasons why you were looking for a new opportunity. [Recap reasons from interview notes.] How many of those key reasons have changed?'

  - 'When we first talked, it sounded like you had decided firmly to leave. Why do you want to stay now? Are they just giving more money, or can they actually address the things that caused you to look in the first place?'

- 'Our offer is because [hiring manager] and the interview team see and comprehend your value. You really impressed them with [list some of the most positive feedback]. If your current employer wanted you to stay, they could have taken action to keep you on before you were forced to act yourself to get what you need and are worth.'

- 'Is our offer less attractive now? Please tell me why.'

- 'Your manager wasn't willing to give you what you wanted a few days ago. How has their mentality changed?'

- 'Why do you think they are giving you this counteroffer now? Why do they want you to stay?'

- 'Are you surprised by the counteroffer? Did you ask them for a raise or promotion before you started looking for another opportunity? If so, why did you have to get an outside offer before they gave you a raise/promotion?'

- 'In two or three years when you are due for your next promotion, will you need to get an outside offer again for them to respond? That's exhausting!'

· We will talk about negotiations in the next section. However, **when candidates ask for more money** in a counteroffer situation, recruiters need to understand that this is normal candidate behaviour. It is okay for them to ask for more, even beyond what they put in their application. It is up to the recruiters to choose how and when to respond; and the research and investigation to determine if the offer can be increased should include the attention of the hiring manager and HR. When candidates ask for a higher offer, our immediate response can be:

- '... Again, thank you for sharing this information with me. I must do some research because these decisions are not up to me. I don't know what the outcome will be, but I promise you that I will ask. You are a priority, so I will get back to you as soon as I am able.'

Extra talking points about the opportunity could include:

- 'We are committed to developing employees because people are our biggest resource. As we reach our goals, this is such a great time to get in the door and grow into a leadership position in the future.'

- 'We have a very dynamic career model that evolves as we grow. That means that there isn't just one path for you to follow and you have a chance to shape how your future career looks here.'

- 'We are a small team and so you will get a lot of one-on-one focused attention and career development.'

- 'Our company recognizes employees and rewards progress along the way. Your manager will work alongside you to prepare you for more responsibility and future promotions.'

- 'We have a culture of internal responsibility. We encourage employees to explore different career paths within our company and have open conversations with their managers about what they want to accomplish.'

When candidates are conflicted about their choice, recruiters should show empathy by using phrases such as:

- 'I understand that this is a hard decision. What can I do to help you make it?'

- 'I understand that you have strong relationships there and it is hard to leave people you enjoy working with. But those relationships will still be there even if the role ends.'

- 'Would another conversation with [hiring manager] help? I would like to connect the two of you to discuss this in more detail.'

When a recruiter wants a stronger challenge to the counteroffer, they can use phrases such as:

- 'If you accept the counteroffer, your relationships there might change, especially with management. They might see you as a risk moving forward or question your commitment.'

- 'Where is the money for the raise coming from? The next time you want a raise, they might refuse altogether and say, "Remember we just gave you that huge raise a year ago?"'
- 'Do you think it is going to feel awkward there now? Will it create tension? Are you going to be happy staying, or is the extra money just making it more tolerable in the short term?'
- 'Are you compromising what's best for you if you accept the counteroffer and stay? More money is nice, but will you be happy there? For how long?'

If a recruiter finds out that they've lost the candidate to the counteroffer it is best to wish the candidate well and be gracious using phrases such as:

- 'I am disappointed that I won't get to work with you, but we are genuinely excited for you and wish you well. I will send you a request to connect on LinkedIn and I hope our paths cross again. I wish you continued success.'

Negotiation

Recruiters should be trained on basic negotiation best practices because it should be assumed that a candidate will negotiate their offer amount. The amount of negotiation may vary based on the job type (more likely for salaried workers versus entry-level hourly), the experience level of the candidate, the role itself (a salesperson may negotiate more) and how in-demand the skills are.

A change to a candidate's salary requirements is not ideal, but it should not be unexpected. A recruiter cannot expect to lock a candidate into a salary or a rate early in conversation, especially before a candidate has had a chance to learn about the role, its challenges and its nuances. If an open job ends up being more complex than initially advertised, it is fair for a candidate to ask for a higher rate for a higher effort. Additionally, as candidates learn more about the total compensation structure and benefits of a company, their salary requests might change, especially if the company they are interviewing with has a smaller medical benefit plan or less robust insurance offerings. As we discussed in the previous section, we can also expect counter- and competitive offer situations that will change our offer strategy.

More experienced recruiters may be better at negotiating than junior recruiters. Sometimes junior recruiters do not have the same exposure to negotiations that their candidate does, and sometimes it comes down to a difference in the amount of confidence and life experience. In Chapter 9, we discussed one of the best ways to respond when a candidate asks, 'What's the range?' is by sharing a target figure instead of the entire range. If the recruiter is hiring in a state that requires pay transparency, then the recruiter should disclose the range but give additional detail, such as, 'typically we hire in the 2nd quartile and 85 per cent of people hired into this role are below midpoint', to give context and set expectations with candidates. A larger team could consider having a 'closer', a recruiter who either helps 'close the deal' with the candidate in person or by offering advice to the recruiter behind the scenes.

Of all the touchpoints in the candidate journey, sometimes this is the place where complete transparency may not work out in the recruiter's favour. It is because the candidate is 'playing the game' of negotiating and the recruiter needs to recognize this and play along. A recruiter cannot simply decide not to play the game or change the rules.

For example, sometimes recruiters with the best of intentions want to do the right thing and extend their best offer right away because they know they have an excellent candidate, and they believe in transparency. The recruiter may have also disclosed the pay range for the position. In this example, we will say that the pay range is $80,000 to $100,000 and the company typically hires to the midpoint of a range. With good intentions, the recruiter wants to give the candidate a great offer that gets accepted and so they offer $90,000 immediately. The candidate will be grateful but most likely expect to negotiate off that number rather than recognizing it as the company's best offer. The candidate will thank the recruiter but may ask for $95,000, which instantly means that the recruiter must hold firm and potentially lose the candidate or they will be hiring past midpoint, which could disrupt internal equity in the role.

Offering your 'best and final' offer as your first offer, and refusing to negotiate, is not successful because:

- It's essentially an ultimatum, even if we don't intend for it to be one.
- Candidates have expectations about playing the negotiating game.
- Candidates want more control. It appears as you created the situation, want complete control and they have no involvement even though it affects their future.
- They may have salary data that supports a higher offer, and it is important to hear them out because a company's salary data may be incorrect or outdated.
- It's perceived to be a 'social contract' and a recruiter can't suddenly make up their own rules.

Prepare for a negotiation

When a recruiter has done their due diligence, surprises at this stage will be limited; but there should still be an expectation of an impending offer negotiation. Even if a recruiter does not enjoy or feel comfortable with negotiating, it is part of the game and candidates will want to negotiate so they feel they are getting a good salary/rate. The amount of negotiation a recruiter has with candidates could differ depending on the level of the position and experience of the candidate. Do not be dismayed with their request, rather, admire them for asking and gently correct any wrong assumptions they have through transparency. Thank them for trusting you with this information. Even when a candidate has an unreasonable request, the recruiter can respond, 'At the very least, I can promise that I will research.'

It is key for a recruiter to think and talk about the total compensation package and not just the base salary. Understanding all aspects of the total rewards and benefits plan, beyond the basics, and being able to translate them into tangible value for the candidates, is a strategic skill. Sometimes there are components to an offer, like RSUs[3] or an ESOP[4] that recruiters do not fully understand (especially if they are new or early in their career) and therefore do not fully explain to the candidates. These total rewards components should be sold to the candidate, just like the opportunity itself. Sometimes the candidates do not fully understand an offer component that a recruiter might assume to be common knowledge.

Another common negotiation point for candidates is around their bonuses. Bonus plans can differ greatly from company to company. They are variable compensation but should not be an unknown factor. Most companies have annual bonuses, but sometimes organizations give quarterly bonuses and others give regular spot bonuses. There is usually a target bonus percentage, but some companies cap the bonus and others do not. Usually, bonuses are dependent on both company and individual performance. Some companies have a conservative bonus structure and regularly achieve their goals, while others have a very large target bonus but regularly only achieve 50 per cent of it. Whatever bonus structure a company has, it is helpful when a recruiter can use historical data from the past few years to illustrate what a candidate can expect for a bonus.

The recruiter needs to understand what flexibility they have to raise the offer amount, as well as what their limits are and when they need approvals. Sometimes, limitations exist purely due to budget. Other times, salary limits are in place to ensure that companies are not creating outliers when hiring a new worker into an existing career band at a level that is higher than the current employees. If there is a limit to the salary that a recruiter can offer, there might be flexibility with another offer component. Sometimes, there are creative solutions to offer candidates the amount they are seeking while staying within the targeted salary range for the job. For example:

- Raising the annual bonus target.
- Committing to a quarterly review in the first year with potential to give a step increase if they meet goals and objectives.

- A sign-on bonus.
- An extra week of vacation.
- A flexible work schedule.
- Hybrid on-site/remote model.
- Equity.
- Raising the level of the position (if the candidate qualifies).

By building a relationship with these candidates throughout the journey, you are also now in a good position to ask them about any other offers they have or are expecting. This is more intel for you and your team, as well as leading towards more successful offer negotiations.

When a candidate accepts the offer

When we are able to successfully reach an offer acceptance, it is time to take a moment and celebrate! Getting here is a big feat. However, the recruiter's responsibilities are not done until the new hire is logged into their computer. The time between job offers and onboarding can vary greatly from company to company. It can be as short as two weeks (or less!) or as long as six months, especially when hiring from campus programmes. While we hope for a smooth onboarding, there are variables that can take companies by surprise. A good rule of thumb: No matter what size your organization is, the job is not to be considered 'filled' until the candidate is at their desk on Day 1. That does not mean you are actively interviewing for the role after someone accepts the job offer, but a lot can change in between the time that a candidate accepts an offer and is scheduled to start.

For example, let's say Company A ended a year-long search for a software engineer with very specific experience and extended an offer that was accepted by Sally on 1 May. Before Sally can join Company A, she needs four weeks' notice. Company A's hiring manager has vacation planned, and so the team has settled on a start date of 5 July because the company only has new hire orientation every two weeks. Sally was actively interviewing before Company A extended the offer, and her first choice was Company B's role, but it was placed on hold in April, right about the time she started talking to Company A. However, Company B was able to reopen the position in Q3, and they called Sally and immediately made her an offer, since they had already interviewed her in the spring. If Company A hasn't kept in touch with Sally between 1 May and 5 July to keep her engaged and excited about joining, she might decide to change her mind and go with Company B after all.

Keeping candidates engaged from offer to onboarding is a strategy that involves multiple people in the organization, but the recruiter is an important component since they were likely the first relationship that the candidate had with the company. Recruiters should think of the offer to onboarding period as a transition, rather than a hand-off. When possible, let the candidate know what to expect and who might be contacting them next so that confusion is minimized. In larger organizations, candidates may hear from recruiters, HR Operations, onboarders, immigration, relocation and others; and it can be overwhelming. Sharp Healthcare, a CandE winner, told us:

> One of our largest projects was centralizing our onboarding within recruitment. We have six human resource departments, so a candidate can get lost in the system. Now each new hire is assigned an onboarding specialist, who acts as the point of contact every single step of the way. We keep in touch with candidates through phone calls and in-person meetings from the beginning to the end of the onboarding process. This has resulted in candidates telling us how smooth the process is, and the hiring managers have appreciated that there is only one point of contact. Even though this change of process was painful, we knew that improving the candidate experience was our top priority. And even now, we continue to get better. This has ultimately resulted in a 10 per cent decrease in the time to onboard a new hire.

A good engagement strategy is important. Actions like specialized marketing messages to new hires, congratulations and welcome gifts, inviting new hires to company social events like picnics or happy hours and involving the entire team to give them a personal touch reduces the chance that a new employee changes their mind and decides not to join the organization.

So, candidates are not overwhelmed with administrative onboarding activities on Day 1, companies can send new hire documents to the new hire to complete before their first day. Ensure their equipment is set up and ready for them and be sure to give them a warm welcome into the organization. Structured itineraries over the first days, including at least one or two planned lunches, are an excellent idea to help the new hire learn the company, office building and role. Assigning a mentor/coach/buddy gives them a point of contact when they have questions.

When a candidate does not accept the offer

Unfortunately, there will be times when a recruiter did everything in their power to connect a perfect candidate with a job opening, but the candidate decides to go with another offer. It can be a blow to a recruiter, especially if you have workers who take their job so seriously that they tend to internalize disappointment. It's important to teach recruiters that they are not going to win over every candidate and that, if they've done their job correctly, they can't take the rejection personally. Just like a recruiter is not necessarily rejecting a candidate personally if a particular job is not the right fit, a candidate is not rejecting a recruiter personally when they decline an offer.

When a recruiter receives a reply from a candidate that they are going to decline the offer, they should immediately try to schedule time to talk with the candidate over the phone or via video chat rather than communicating via e-mail. The first item to ascertain is whether the offer is salvageable. Is there a competitive offer, and would the candidate give the company a chance to respond to it? Sometimes, if recruiters act quickly, they can salvage an offer and turn a decline into an acceptance. Sometimes a candidate declines the offer for more personal reasons, such as deciding they can't relocate and pull their children out of school or the other company's mission and culture resonate stronger with the candidate. A candidate may receive a competing offer that is so strong that there is no way the company can compete with it, especially if it is a smaller organization and the competing offer is from a large enterprise.

There will be instances when offers can be salvaged and some where the recruiter will have to know when it's lost. Either way, it is good to understand why the candidate made their decision, record it and give the data to the business to see if any trends are emerging or if insights can be gleaned.

The recruiter should try to leave the candidate just as they would during a rejection; that the door is open for future consideration, they should connect on LinkedIn, congratulate the candidate and be happy for them in their new role.

Best practices during offer and onboarding

Ask for referrals

When a new employee is hired into an organization, part of the conversation should be around employee referrals and whether the new hire has contacts that the company should reach out to. In fact, some organizations give new hires a special bonus, for example a double referral bonus for any hires made from referrals during the new hire's first 90 days of employment. It is a great time to capitalize on the onboarding momentum and also on potentially meeting ex-colleagues that the new hire is remiss to leave behind.

Ask for feedback

Feedback is a constant theme throughout the candidate journey, and we have discussed the importance of giving and receiving feedback in nearly every chapter. At this stage, many companies ask new hires for feedback on the candidate experience, and then do a 90-day check in;

but we can make a bigger impact on new hires by asking key 90-day questions such as:

- Did we deliver what we promised?
- Did anything surprise you?

CandE winning companies hold themselves more accountable for the overall recruiting process and resulting candidate experience while measuring it regularly and consistently. According to AdventHealth, a multi-year CandE winner, this includes continuing to ask for feedback:

> Executives and leaders live by the data, not anecdotal feelings or hunches. Our executives expect metrics of us, and we expect it of them. As a result, we have developed service level agreements for every step of the process, not only for our recruiters but our managers as well. We use the metrics to start with an understanding of why things need to change. Our candidate survey tells us whether individuals were so unhappy with the process that they are not willing to use our services as a healthcare organization. This is impactful to them and this helps drive change management. We also develop committees with different stakeholders to get everyone involved in the solution. If they design it, they will implement it. Then we constantly measure our progress each month to show success.

Notes

1 A 401(k) plan is a company-sponsored retirement account that employees can contribute income, while employers may match contributions.
2 Miles, SJ and Mangold, WG. (2005). Positioning Southwest Airlines through employee branding. *Business Horizons*, 48 (6), 535–45.
3 A restricted stock unit (RSU) is a type of stock-based compensation that employers might offer as a benefit.
4 An employee stock ownership plan (ESOP) is an employee benefit plan that gives workers ownership interest in the company; this interest takes the form of shares of stock.

10

Overcoming resistance to improving candidate experience

When recruiting departments want to implement candidate experience best practices within their organizations, sometimes they are met by resistance from the business leaders who don't fully understand the business impact. We invite you to review Chapter 3. In addition, these are some of the common reasons that businesses resist candidate experience and how talent acquisition can prepare a response.

Resistance to candidate experience No 1: it's too expensive

Today's organizations are transforming to keep up with technology and the demands of modern commerce. HR budgets are stretched thin and usually reserved for items like digitization and AI. In Chapter 3, we mentioned that companies spent $508 billion on *customer experience* (CX) technologies in 2019 globally and that spend was expected to increase to $641 billion in 2022. Only 10 per cent of companies have a dedicated budget for *candidate experience*; yet a company's candidates and customers are often the same individuals.

In hot talent markets, trends turn to making quick hires at the lowest costs possible. Companies churn through transactional encounters with their candidates instead of building long-term relationships with them. The common belief held is that candidate experience seems nice, but it is too expensive to implement and too costly to distract recruiters away from making more hires. The businesses believe that there are other priorities that need to be met. The reality is that quick, low-cost hires sound like the best strategy to employ but the businesses' bottom line will suffer in the long run. These organizations would benefit from building strategies around engaged pools of candidates who are interested in working for an organization and will wait for the right job opportunity.

Candidate experience a fairly standard industry term within talent acquisition and is top of mind for many recruiting professionals. Outside the recruiting role, other workers involved in hiring (hiring managers, interviewers, schedulers) don't often prioritize it. Sometimes in organizations, candidate experience is important but only applies to candidates they intend to hire. In other organizations, candidate experience is synonymous with 'user experience' rather than 'customer experience' and involves their digital interactions – application, social media and onboarding – but does not involve the interpersonal touchpoints like the evaluation, communication and follow-up with candidates. Candidates do not care what it is called; they just want to be treated fairly.

When the conversation turns to resisting candidate experience programmes because of the cost of implementation, we argue that it is more expensive *not to* implement good candidate experience programmes. The focus should not be on how much such a programme would cost, but how much money it will save – or earn – for the company. This certainly applies to candidates who are customers and will increase their relationship with an organization when they've had a good experience; but even B2B companies will benefit:

- Lower turnover rate because employees built strong relationships and are more engaged.
- More referrals because candidates, whether or not they were hired, had a good experience with the organization and will speak highly of it.
- Hire offer acceptance rate from top candidates, including ability to beat out offers for more money when a good candidate experience

is provided. Hiring top workers means companies have a better product or service.

• Faster offer conversions mean lower cost per hire.

Resistance to candidate experience No 2: compliance comes first

There are companies we've heard state that they work in highly regulated industries and cannot focus on improving candidate experience because their legal counsel wants them to limit their candidate communication and feedback.

Being an Office of Federal Contract Compliance Programs[1] (OFCCP) or government contracting company does not mean you cannot focus on candidate experience. In competitive job markets, candidates have the upper hand. As we showed in previous chapters, more candidates are withdrawing during the application step when applications are too complex or lengthy, telling others about their negative experiences and also choosing not to continue their brand alliance to the organization when they have had a negative experience.

The recruiter's job is to make sure that candidates feel good about your company so they remain engaged throughout the candidate journey. In addition, focusing on a good candidate experience can reduce potential bias in the hiring process and therefore aid with diversity recruiting requirements and initiatives.

Here are some tips:

• Application:
    ○ 'Mystery shop' your own job applications, paying attention to the length and complexity. Eliminate questions that are not required to determine whether a candidate is qualified for the position. For example, it is not necessary to collect professional references on every candidate if you only check the finalists' references. Instead of requiring every candidate to unnecessarily gather reference information for your organization, consider removing the question and instead directing recruiters to ask for references after a positive interview.

- Communication about internal mobility. When internal candidates apply to new positions, the recruiting team can have a process by which recruiters are alerted of potential upcoming vacancies so they can manage communications with any silver medallist candidates from similar searches. This way, they can get a head start on backfilling a vacancy and save a candidate who would otherwise get rejected. Since there are often some time-related steps to be compliant, recruiters can verbally set expectations with candidates, so they know what to expect.

- Interview:
  - Hold compliance-focused questions until the very end when you're sure that you want to move forward with that candidate. That way, just like with the application, you're creating a good experience by not asking questions.
  - Get wording right on compliance questions. Having an interview aid for compliance questions is helpful so that recruiters can follow a consistent, approved format when asking questions that can be sensitive, for example with immigration.
  - Sensitive topics. Train interviewers to pivot away from conversations that can lead to bias, like talking about colleges, children or football teams.

- Dispositioning:
  - Ensuring an excellent candidate experience means giving candidates timely feedback.
  - When recruiters and hiring teams can come to decisions faster, it improves the candidates' experience but also helps recruiters to accurately track dispositions and communications, which will reduce flags in case of audits.

Sometimes recruiting departments focus more on the reporting aspects of compliance programmes so their department is covered in case of any regulated audits. The entire purpose of recruiting compliance is to uphold laws that ensure minority groups have a fair chance in a company's recruitment efforts and are not treated unfairly, so that the most qualified candidates may be chosen. The most qualified candidates can be selected when both the interviewers and the candidates themselves are able to determine if the job opportunity and candidates' skills are a good match. This hiring decision is completely reliant on the evaluation process, and companies that are focused on fair treatment, have transparent practices and share feedback with candidates are in a better position to have the best data to make those hiring decisions in the most informed manner possible. Therefore, candidate experience reinforces the intent of compliance programmes.

Resistance to candidate experience No 3: it's one more thing the recruiters must do now

When there is an unfilled position in a company, everyone on the team feels the burden and are at risk of burnout or feeling overwhelmed. Hiring managers need to recruit to fill the open position in addition to their daily responsibilities and productivity suffers more the longer the position is unfilled.

Sometimes, organizations are reluctant to implement candidate experience programmes in the organization because they are resistant to any activity that will distract recruiters from maintaining high productivity levels and contacting more candidates. However, this is a mistaken viewpoint because candidate experience best practices do lead to greater productivity since time to hire is decreased and top candidates are less likely to withdraw from consideration or reject offers.

Implementing candidate experience practices is a good use of everyone's time in the organization because the company is able to keep top candidates engaged and achieve better hire conversion rates as a result.

Resistance to candidate experience No 4: it's too 'fluffy'

Candidates view their experience during interviews as an indicator of how much the company values its workers. Sometimes interviewers mistakenly believe that interviews are one sided, and it is only the candidate who needs to impress the interviewer. However, in our definition of candidate experience, we learned that every interaction and touchpoint matters to our candidates. Sometimes a candidate's decision can come down to one interaction, either positive or negative, that they had with an interviewer.

Candidate experience is a bit 'fluffy', but it is what candidates are asking for after the tumultuousness of the early 2020s. The recruiting and selection process has always been a scary process with unknown variables, but after the social, economic, cultural and health challenges we faced around 2020–2021, candidates were faced with even more uncertainty. They wanted human connection, even during business transactions, with others who shared similar life experiences, challenges and values.

Job seekers are more wary than ever and more likely to withdraw from consideration when a job application or assessment is more difficult or confusing than necessary. Also, in times of greater stress, negative candidate experiences may seem amplified, and a candidate could be more likely to leave a negative company review. A negative interaction between a candidate and an interviewer may be an isolated instance, but it can contribute to a company reputation.

Candidates are looking for deeper meaning in the work they are doing, including DEI, social impact and community involvement. The more a company promotes and educates its audience on the work they are doing, the more likely it is to attract candidates.

Resistance to candidate experience No 5: it's not how we do things

We know that work is changing rapidly due to globalization, technology and health issues like the COVID-19 pandemic. There is simply no way that companies can be competitive in today's candidate market without significantly altering recruiting practices. For the first time in history since the birth of the internet, the 2020s saw recruiting change just as fast – if not faster – than technology. Today's recruiters need to be comfortable stepping into a consultative role where they manage the recruiting process. They must be experts in the talent market and in influencing behaviour of their hiring managers.

There are numerous companies who have enjoyed a top place in their industry for decades and have developed a reputation among their competitors as a top place to work, but they are struggling to build their technology teams. Part of the reason is the great demand for technical talent in relation to the limited supply of qualified workers.

Another reason is because, a few niche roles aside, technical talent is not industry-specific. As companies bring newer technologies into their organization, such as cloud, they are competing with more industries for a subset of workers with key experiences. (The company's own tech workers will also be exposed to more competitive offers. The mid-sized credit union that just implemented a cloud-based CRM system may suddenly find its employees are receiving an escalated number of outreach messages from other organizations looking for that specific experience. Some might come from the CRM company themselves... along with much larger offers than the credit union can compete with.) Suddenly, the company's good reputation and position as an industry leader is less relevant to candidates and company leaders cannot understand why offers are being declined and they're losing employees. But that same company may still not invest in improving candidate experience because its existing recruiting practice is just fine.

Think about it this way: In the IT department of any company that is building and releasing new software or technical features either for internal use or for customers, *business analysts* are hired to document requirements from the business – what they need the software to do – and then translate it into technical specs for the developers to create. The business leader does not tell those workers how to gather requirements from them; they hire BAs with requirement gathering, user story and documentation experience.

Let's say a business is not as familiar with the software development lifecycle (SDLC) but they are in the process of adopting it. Then, *organizational change managers* are hired to analyse, communicate and coach workers through the transformation. Once again, the organization is bringing experts into the organization to analyse, consult and lead a component of key change.

Why do those business leaders still expect to direct the recruiting activity through their recruiting partner and use the same recruiting process they have always used? Why keep this process static when every other technical element is rapidly changing around them?

Today's recruiter needs to feel comfortable analysing the challenge at hand and suggesting changes to alter the way that searches have historically been carried out, using data to emphasize their position:

- If a recruiter is working with a hiring manager who wants to be present for and affirm decisions at every step of the hiring process, the recruiter or talent acquisition leader needs to question why.

- If a director is the default hiring manager for all of their teams' new hires, even though each group has their manager, the recruiter or talent acquisition leader must question why they are not empowering their teams to make decisions or delegate this responsibility.

- Why is that hiring manager taking so long to give feedback regarding candidates?

- Why is that hiring manager who wants to see more and more diverse candidates still upholding practices that allow unconscious bias to seep in?

Note

1 The Office of Federal Contract Compliance Programs is part of the US Department of Labor. OFCCP is responsible for ensuring that employers doing business with the Federal government comply with the laws and regulations requiring nondiscrimination.

11

Getting leadership buy-in to improve candidate experience

The nods have it – or do they?

Some of the most interesting reactions we get every year when sharing our candidate experience benchmark research are the nods in the room and on the Zoom calls. Even when we can't see the people attending our session or event, we get comments in the chat box that say, 'Yes, agreed.'

What are we talking about here?

We're talking about the potential business impact that you've already read about a few times in the first few chapters of this book. The fact that each and every candidate's experience applying for a job at your organization impacts whether they ever apply again for another job, refer others to your organization, remain a fan of your brand and/or make purchases from your company if you're a consumer-based organization.

HR and talent acquisition leaders and their teams usually nod at the above and concur that candidate experience does on some level impact their business and their brand. But it's what happens after that that is disheartening: lack of data supporting the above leads to inaction on the part of the TA team. They feel like there's no business case to make and/or that leadership above them won't listen because of other competing business priorities. The fact is, there are always business impacts affecting organizations big and small across industries:

- leadership changes;
- recruiting team changes;
- mergers and acquisitions;
- new product and service launches;
- changing business priorities;
- economic fluctuations;
- a pandemic.

What's frustrating is the fact that recruiting and hiring (and retention) are some of the most important activities for organizations. Their employees – full-time, part-time, contract – are the people who help to grow and sustain the business. Period. But sometimes there's a disconnect between the very business impacts listed above and the continued investments into hiring and retention strategies. When the market takes a dive, recruiting takes one of the first hits. When frenetic hiring ramps, like what happened in 2021, then recruiters are hired back like crazy, and they end up with way too many job requisitions to fill and not enough time to deliver a quality recruiting experience. Even when the right recruiting technologies are in place to help source, screen, hire and communicate automatically, the human-communication part of the equation suffers – the recruiter and hiring manager experiences can deteriorate and ultimately the candidate experience suffers. It's more about getting people in the seats and forget about the sheer volume of people that will never be hired, yet can leave a lasting impact on the business and the brand.

Why measuring candidate experience is where you start

We work with hundreds of employers, big and small, across industries around the world every year that benchmark their candidate experience. But one of the questions that always comes up for hundreds more is – why? Why should we do this? You may have asked it yourself at your organizations as well, your leadership may be asking that and your talent acquisition team may be asking that. Why? What's the point of doing that?

Well, imagine this. Out of every 100 candidates that research your organization and apply for a job, on average, 99 of them are not going to get hired at the end of the day. Now, start running numbers with that number, and add that up over time. The sheer volume of people who don't get hired, either by outright rejection or they never hear back, could potentially have a much bigger impact on your business and your brand over time. Especially compared to those who actually get hired.

The hires are always very important. That's why you have a recruiting and hiring process, and why you screen candidates to find those that you want to work for your organizations or you're sourcing them directly, however you find them. But there's still going to be this volume of people that have some level of experience with your business and your brand. Out of the sheer volume of those people who research and apply, that's as far as they're going to get at the end of the day. So, while how much experience candidates can have with your organization will vary, it will always impact their perception of fairness about your recruiting and hiring process. And that ultimately impacts whether or not they decide to ever apply again, or whether or not they decide to refer others and, if you're a consumer-based business, whether or not they want to have any brand affinity, as well as making purchasing decisions or influencing purchasing decisions of others.

Even if you're not a consumer-based business at the end of the day, a candidate's brand affinity – how much association with your business and your brand they want to have – will impact how likely they are to refer others who may fit those roles you're hiring for at any given time. So, one of the things that we recommend, initially, is that you need to have some data. You've got to have a baseline, a benchmark, of where you're at – what do your candidates think about your recruiting and hiring process? One place to do that, of course, is Talent Board, where we run the candidate benchmark research programme, but, whatever the case, get some data first – how do the candidates feel about your recruiting process, at the end of the day, is number one.

Then, identify some areas where you can make improvements. Often, you'll find that it doesn't take huge change management initiatives to make improvements in your recruiting and hiring process. Frequently, it comes down to consistent communication, setting better expectations with candidates, asking them for feedback, providing them feedback, especially final-stage candidates, being more transparent and accountable about the entire process and ensuring that it's a positive experience. And that your candidates feel it was a fair experience.

Next we're going to share some case studies excerpts from our research on why measuring candidate experience is so important and how to demonstrate the business impact of candidate experience to make a business case for change. The companies listed below regularly ask their candidates and new hires for experience feedback, giving them a baseline of data to garner leadership support to make improvements. You can also refer again to the Virgin Media and Kimberly-Clark case studies referenced in Chapter 3.

We'll then end this chapter with the steps to build your own business case.

CandE case studies

AdventHealth

The TA leadership team knew that the best element to excel in change management was their metrics. Their leadership team lives by the data, not anecdotal feelings or hunches. As a result, they developed service level agreements for every step of the recruiting process, not only for their recruiters but also for their hiring managers. They use metrics to start with an understanding of why things need to change. Their candidate surveys tell them whether individuals are unhappy with the recruiting process and whether they are willing or not to use their services as a healthcare organization. This is impactful to the business and in turn helps drive their change management. They also develop committees with different stakeholders to get everyone involved in the solution. If they design it, they will implement it. Then they constantly measure their progress each month to show recruiting and hiring success.

Boehringer Ingelheim Pharmaceuticals

In order to ensure that, as a talent acquisition organization, Boehringer were all equally committed to and aligned with the importance of the candidate experience, and it included the whole TA team in its journey-mapping exercise from the beginning stages. In addition, there were open discussions about its candidate experience being a top priority for the organization. The journey map exercises and consistent discussion of its candidate experience helped create a basis for conversations with its hiring managers and business leaders. During these important conversations, the company highlighted the importance of the candidate experience and shifted its hiring managers' perspective to view recruiting through a candidate lens. This was especially relevant in discussing interview teams (especially their size and complexity) with the hiring managers. It also built the candidate experience into its interview training sessions, creating an exercise to help hiring managers and interviewers recognize the gap between focusing only on what was wanted and needed as a company versus what the candidates wanted and needed.

New Balance Athletics

As a global organization, New Balance Athetics has important sales figures to hit each year to remain successful and fuel the growth of its business. When the candidate experience is put into business terms, customers can be either be lost or gained from that very candidate experience. Not only could you lose that potential customer from a bad candidate experience, but they also spread that negative message to their friends and family. So, putting these experiences into business terms allows it to demonstrate to its key business partners how important the candidate experience is.

Reynolds American

Reynolds American engaged an Advisory Team of hiring leaders and HR partners to review, guide and champion processes and expectations to ensure that TA was meeting the business needs during the year. This group was asked to demonstrate support for the change, provide insight as to changed process adoption, satisfaction, challenges, etc. The Advisory Team provided input and supported implementation of the communication, training and resistance management plans. They were key in proactively identifying and managing resistance to change. They conducted voice-of-the-customer focus group sessions drawn from a select group of cross-functional hiring and TA leaders and a separate session for the talent acquisition team to discuss perceptions of their roles, needs and feedback from the business. Hiring manager outreach was important to complete a baseline survey, provide additional insight and information, meet with their recruiters to launch changes meetings and to build relationships with talent acquisition leadership.

CSAA Insurance Group

CSAA Insurance Group built support and commitment within its talent acquisition team and across the enterprise. Candidate experience surveying required vulnerability on the part of the talent acquisition and interviewing teams, and doing it enabled them to look under the hood in real time to see what's working and what can be improved. It established an environment where its team understood that the data were intended for continuous improvement. In addition, the company met with business leaders and interview teams to discuss the connection between customer experience and candidate experience. It shared talent acquisition's priorities and reinforced the simple behaviours and changes leaders could demonstrate to have a positive impact. These included speed, follow-through, adhering to the interview guides and using a conversational interview style to create a comfortable and inviting interview experience. It developed and deployed tools to guide these leaders' thinking and updated working agreements so that everyone knows how their support impacts the recruiting process and candidate experience.

Walgreens

Walgreens knew its candidates were its customers as well, so the importance of a positive candidate experience was critical to its business, and not only when it makes a hire. The company knew its candidates were its customers as well, so the importance of a positive candidate experience was critical to its business, and not only when it made a hire, but also, more importantly, in situations where it did not hire the candidates. It coaches not only its recruitment team but also its hiring managers. Hiring managers are continuously educated to empathize with candidates throughout the hiring process and about the importance timeliness serves in creating a positive candidate experience. It knows that speedy feedback drives positive results, whether it's the candidate joining the company or being allowed to move on to other opportunities.

BASF

Like many other companies, the impact of COVID-19 turned BASF's entire recruiting and hiring upside down. The outpouring of empathy across the world echoed the realization internally that people are what truly matter. The support from its leadership team to personalize its approach and put candidate needs at the forefront of how they operated was widely felt throughout BASF, and the call to action was quickly embraced by its teams. After reviewing the previous year's candidate experience feedback data and comments, areas of improvement were very apparent. It wasn't hitting the mark for a high touch candidate experience. Insights about the lack of diversity on its interview panels were revealed along with a new understanding that its candidates didn't necessarily understand what they were looking for during the interview process. Overall, its numerical data supported the commentary, so it had a true understanding on how to impact their candidate experience quickly.

Southwest Airlines

For the last several years, Southwest Airlines compiled candidate experience data into a presentation that it have been able to share with all its recruiters, senior leadership and other relevant stakeholders throughout the company. It shared its year-over-year scores and pulled out relevant feedback that told the story of what its action items should be for the upcoming year. It also set goals for its recruiting team around its candidate experience score, celebrated the awards they've received and been committed to hiring recruiters who share their Southwest values and prioritize providing incredible hospitality to its candidates. This is because it knows each year, pandemic or not, that candidate experience directly impacts the bottom line.

Build your own business case

Based on input from some of our closest talent acquisition leaders in our CandE community, it's really important to think about the following 11 items as you start to build your business case:

1 **Define the business problem.** Think about what the problem is that you and your team are trying to solve. What recruiting strengths and weaknesses have you identified? Have you prioritized what's causing a negative candidate experience? What metrics have you gathered to validate your project? *Example: Improving candidate experience by increasing the budget available to train the talent acquisition team.*

2 **Define the vision.** Describe the intended benefits of the proposed project and what you want to accomplish. *Examples:*

a) *To better candidate engagement with current applicants and stronger competitive edge against competitors who are hiring.*

b) *Each year the annual CandE Benchmark Research reveals a significant percentage of candidates surveyed had poor candidate experience (i.e. what we call the resentment rate) and were willing to end their relationship with the business and brand they had applied to. That means they would not apply again, refer others and/or make purchases from consumer-based businesses. For B2B companies, this means fewer referrals, an important candidate experience metric, which ultimately can impact the recruiting and hiring bottom line (and should be a primary source of hire). While more difficult to quantify, usually large portions of your recruiting budget are for targeted marketing and advertising (i.e. programmatic advertising for midsize to large companies), and even if you track your source of hire, a poor candidate experience will impact it. Conversely, a great candidate experience can pay dividends to your organization in potential revenue and referrals, which is your ultimate goal.*

3 **Define your strategic objective.** Describe how your project contributes to the strategic plans of the organization? To your hiring plans and objectives? Does it align to the mission, vision, values of the company? *Examples:*

a) *With 25 per cent YoY [year-on-year] growth expected, we plan to add 100 net new positions to the organization.*

b) *One of our values is Welcome Everyone but we rule out many candidates early without giving them much feedback. This training will teach the team how to be more welcoming to candidates.*

4 **Define the sponsors and stakeholders.** Name the individual, department or group sponsoring the business case. *Examples: Chief Operating Officer, Chief Human Resources Officer.*

5 **Outline the economic and business landscape.** Give history. Describe the business landscape and current situation. Call out gaps between the current process and what the new solution could achieve. *Example: The competition for talent continues to be challenging, even during the pandemic and economic downturn. On top of that, 2020 and 2021 have brought increased turnover. There is concern that we will not meet our future goal of 100 new hires without additional training for the recruiting team. We missed our hiring goals by 20 per cent over the past two years, even after engaging search firms. While we made a record number of offers, we had a 75 per cent acceptance rate. Out of the 65 people that we hired in 2019, five took a job at another company before their start dates. We have also started to see an increase in negative reviews about our interviews on Glassdoor and Indeed.*

6 **Determine your expected return on investment.** Year over year, how much money can be saved or earned with this project? Note: See the Business Impact Calculator for the cost of a negative candidate experience. *Example: Currently, our average cost per hire is $2,500 and our time to fill is 65 days. We believe that we could bring both of these numbers down, resulting in a cost savings of at least $30,000 a year.*

7 **Define your project benefits.** Provide evidence of the benefit of your project. Note: Review throughout this book the proven benefits of a good candidate experience based on 10 years of CandE Benchmark Research and insights. *Example: Methods to build relationships that result in pre-warmed candidate pools for future jobs. This will reduce time to fill and the need to rely on third-party search firms and postings. Better reviews on Glassdoor and other sites, which will strengthen our employer brand. Hiring pre-engaged candidates means that onboarding is more meaningful and they have a higher likelihood of staying with the company longer. Increase our offer acceptance rate and learn methods to keep candidates engaged from their offer acceptance through their first day on the job.*

8 **Define your approach and determine your estimated costs and resources needed.** List what is needed to complete the project. List expected funding, need for special resources, team members, etc. *Example: We need to participate in the CandE Benchmark Research to collect candidate experience data. Also, the cost of the candidate experience learning program is $X per employee, for the five members of our recruiting team. These are different ways they can learn what improvements are needed and how to better implement them.*

9 **Determine the estimated timeline.** The time it will take to complete. *Example: It will require xxxx hours of their time for xxxx weeks.*

10 **Determine limitations and constraints.** List what could prevent the success of the project, such as the need for expensive equipment, bad weather, lack of special training, etc.

11 **Anticipate naysayers and pushback.** Based on previous conversations, do you expect any opposition that you can plan to answer now? Prepare your response! *Example: Leadership might come back and say that we have limited resources, so we cannot hire any more recruiters. Also, because we must fill 100 new hires next year, we cannot afford to take so many hours away from their sole function, recruiting, to get trained. They need to make more calls and talk to more candidates. Your response: Based on my analysis of alternative solutions, this is the most cost-effective and rewarding choice, because....*

Gather your metrics

Unfortunately, when it comes to process improvement in recruiting and hiring, too many companies often go with their gut in fixing all their woes by adding team members, downsizing and/or purchasing new technologies, all without doing their due diligence and making a true business case. But how are they going to know it even works after 6 to 12 months? And do they have the data and the metrics to back that up as they build on that non-existent business case? This is why you need to do your research to better define your project, your vision and your strategic objective. You also need to make the time validate where you're going with data and metrics, and to reveal what is actually happening in your recruiting processes before you build a business case to pitch.

So, what kinds of data and metrics are you going to gather to make your business case? There are three different kinds of metric questions that you should really ask yourself about when you build your business case:

1 Does it increase the speed of our processes?

2 Can we shorten that time-to-fill or the time-to-start, or can we shorten the time that the applicant applies for a position or as they move through the process, the assessment, the testing, the interview phase, perhaps the pre-boarding and onboarding phases?

3 How will this new product, service and/or process change we're considering positively impact our current key metrics?

A recommendation would be for you to conduct a time study of how long recruiting interactions are taking at your organization. This can be gruelling for your recruiting team for sure, but the investment can really pay off getting a baseline of recruiting metrics (or updating your probably outdated metrics). For example, plan to take two to four weeks and have your team individually record every single activity that they engage in every single day, aggregate and round to the nearest hour. If possible, you should also encourage your hiring managers to participate in this exercise.

Have them track things like: How long are they on the phone each day? Are they following up with a candidate and how much time are they investing? How long are interviews taking? Are you consulting with candidates? How often are you meeting with hiring managers? How long is the offer to onboarding activity taking? Again, record every interaction and determine how long it's taking with every activity from pre-application to onboarding.

You also want to consider any financial metrics you have in recruiting. What are the recruiting costs for all the time invested in your operations highlighted above? What is your cost per hire? How much does it cost your organization when open jobs go unfilled for any length of time? Also, is there a way for you to decrease the recruiting spend for each hire or in just your TA operations cost of doing business? And, once filled, how much revenue are those new hires generating for your company? How soon do you project recovering the improvement investments made?

Hopefully, you also figured out that you can leverage all the work you did with mapping your candidate journey (see Chapter 5) and roll that into your business case. Remember that too much time in the recruiting process can cause you to lose critical candidates and deteriorate your overall candidate experience. You need to think about how each minute is spent on developing the requisition, launching it, recruiting for it and ultimately making the hire. Understanding how long it's taking to fill each job type is critical to knowing what your strengths and weaknesses are in conjunction with any candidate experience surveying you're hopefully doing.

Gathering direct candidate experience feedback will give you another important set of metrics to use to validate your business care. Whether you participate in the CandE Benchmark Research programme, or collect continuous survey feedback from your new hires and non-selected candidates, this data will help you understand your recruiting and hiring strengths and weaknesses through the eyes of the candidate. Each year we see a hesitancy to ask candidates for feedback, but we highly recommend you do so. There are many different candidate experience survey platforms on the market today, including Survale, Starred and Qualtrics. You might also consider mainstream survey platforms like Momentive (formerly Survey Monkey) and Alchemer (formerly SurveyGizmo).

The questions that always come up when it comes to surveying candidates (and employees) are:

- How many questions do we ask?
- What questions do we ask?

- Who are we asking?
- How often do we ask them (frequency)?

You should be asking a minimum of 5 to 15 questions about their experience at different stages of the recruiting process, whether they were hired or not. Keep it within 1–3 minutes for candidates to complete. No matter what, you want to make sure you're asking sentiment rating questions about their experience, and whether they would apply again in the future or refer others to your company. Each year our programme makes the questions we ask candidates available publicly from our website. Your ratings scales could be 4-point, 5-point or 11-point Net Promoter Score scales.

You also want to ensure that you're only asking candidates for feedback once per month, and don't duplicate the asks if candidates have applied for multiple jobs. Of course, this will all vary based on your hiring volume and job type variance. In the end, this data will give you the positive and negative experiential feedback you need to understand what's working and what's not in your recruiting and hiring process.

Presenting your case

Using the completed business case outlined above, how are you going to present it? In today's virtual world, most people are using slides to highlight what they're pitching, as well as preparing an executive brief to be sent ahead of time. Make sure that you've identified the best way to present your business case, focusing on delivering the key points behind your business problem, how you plan to solve it, your investment needed, your potential return and all the data to back it up. How is solving this problem going to save you time and money, and buy you time and money? What are other success metrics? How will you track over time to ensure the return on your investment is sustained?

Because once you get approval for your project, you're going to have to report to leadership your metrics and outcomes, good and bad and all in between. This is why we also encourage you to do a peer review prior to presenting by contacting TA leaders that you're connected with in other organizations. Walk them through your business case presentation and ask them to provide feedback, what works for them based on their own experiences and what they recommend you do differently based on those very same experiences.

It's best to be able to deliver progress reports each step of the way so that each stakeholder in the approval process understands what that progress will be, so they're informed along the way. Will you give quarterly reports, monthly reports, perhaps daily reports? But you want to let them know in advance that they will be getting a progress report and what will be included, ideally, if you could see the metrics and the data change along the way through the implementation so they could maybe start to see some quick wins with the implementation or just start to see that progress is actually being made.

Remember, running through all the steps above, gathering metrics and asking for peer feedback prior to delivering your business case takes time, but making the time will make a difference in the end and maybe give you the approval edge you'll need. You don't have to wait until it's 100 per cent perfect because that will never happen. Our rule is to get it to 80 per cent solid and then go, go, go! As a talent acquisition professional, it's really important to learn and practice the return-on-investment process and building a strong business case.

Process improvements can ensure a quality candidate experience

Again, we can't emphasize enough that the best business leaders use sound data to make informed decisions about their organization's strengths and weaknesses, where they should invest further to increase growth, what needs to be cut from the bottom line and the people they'll need to hire and retain to grow and sustain their businesses. Getting candid candidate and employee feedback, whether from an annual benchmark programme like the CandEs, or from continuous feedback from all rejected and hired candidates and current employees, can provide you the data you need to make the business case when:

- Making process improvements focused on improving communication, feedback, expectation setting and more.
- Researching new recruiting technologies for the organization to improve recruiting efficiencies and automated communication.
- Identifying other team members and recruiting resources needed to make process improvements from pre-application to onboarding.

As mentioned multiple times already, for consumer-based businesses, where candidates are customers and vice versa, the potential revenue impact looms large. A case study conducted by Virgin Media and Ph.Creative a few years ago showed that Virgin Media was losing more than $6 million annually in sales revenues due to poor candidate experiences – which they were then able to turn into a $7 million revenue stream (see Chapter 3).

Most companies, particularly publicly traded companies, aren't willing to share this kind of quantitative data publicly, and for good reason. But many today are internally quantifying the cost of a poor candidate experience, which can be in the millions of dollars or pounds per year, and incremental improvements to recruiting processes and candidate experience can go a long way to increasing revenue and referral networks. That's why we also created an online candidate resentment calculator for HR and talent acquisition professionals that generates potential lost annual revenue by plugging in average recruiting numbers: how many hires per year, how many applicants per hire and the average annual value of a customer. Companies can use this calculator to help them with their business case and get the internal dialogue moving around the cost of a poor candidate experience.

While the resentment calculator only produces a rough estimate based on the hiring numbers used, it helps to make the business case that improving recruiting processes and the candidate journey will benefit companies' bottom lines. Even B2B companies can use it as a conversation starter because ultimately if they don't have the candidates they need to grow and sustain their businesses, it will potentially impact their revenue.

Even with all the potential business impact highlighted above, whether candidates will apply again and/or refer others based on their overall candidate experience is a vitally important outcome of the candidate experience. While most companies would argue that they don't want all the candidates applying again, they do want those deemed future fit to apply again. They most certainly want their final interview silver medallists to apply again and to refer others who may also be the right candidates for future roles. Ultimately, identifying areas of improvement, building the business case and getting approval to make the investments in recruiting and candidate experience today can ensure a greater return on employment brand and quality of candidate tomorrow.

12

Diversity, equity and inclusion candidate experience considerations

Even though we've been talking about diversity, equity and inclusion in the workplace for decades, the social injustice and inequity reckoning of 2020 highlighted how important it is to candidates and employees. Both candidates and employees called for inclusive transparency and change, and it seemed as though employers were no longer just checking the boxes and drafting a DEI mission statement for their career sites. Many employers committed to change in concrete and measurable ways, and continue to do so. Just a few short years ago, however, things were very different. To put this in context, let's time travel back to 2010.

That was the year University of Connecticut researcher Peter Turchin wrote an article for the London-based journal, *Nature*.[1] In it he warned that political instability and social upheaval were bearing down on the United States. Things would reach a boiling point, he estimated, somewhere around the year 2020. Turchin stirred a bit of debate at the time, but many were doubtful or flat out unconvinced.

Of course, we now know his forecast was uncannily accurate, especially the timing. But he failed to fully capture the harsh reality of 2020. To be fair, there's no way he could have. No one could have foreseen the perfect storm of horrifying events and their repercussions that would unfold.

The COVID-19 pandemic brought fear, death, record unemployment and major shifts to the way Americans lived (obviously we're still living it at the time of this writing and well into 2022). The shocking murder of George Floyd in Minneapolis at the hands of police fuelled national outrage and protests against police brutality, which resulted in a tide of violence, looting and political opportunism. The social and political fallout of the 2020 presidential election further divided Americans more than at any other point in recent history. Add to all of this the ongoing turmoil created by ongoing wealth inequality, the threat of recession, surging national debt and an epidemic of gun violence, and it's easy to understand why 'unprecedented' became the overworked but all-too-accurate adjective of the year.

Obviously, the United States wasn't alone in coping with turmoil throughout 2020. Plenty of other countries and their citizens struggled with the pandemic, political unrest, social upheaval, economic hardship and more.

It's hard to imagine anything good emerging from the chaos of that year, but, as always, there were blessings to be counted. One such blessing has been a renewed and long-overdue focus on racial injustice and inclusive hiring environments for marginalized groups everywhere. Uncomfortable conversations continue to take place. Unpleasant truths continue to be spoken. Systemic bias continues to be pushed into the spotlight in the United States and elsewhere.

Thankfully, these changes weren't just impacting 'society' or our personal lives. They were impacting the workplace as well.

DEI under the microscope

In the wake of all this, a growing number of employers realized their diversity, equity and inclusion (DEI) practices were being scrutinized like never before. Boards of directors, shareholders, customers, employees and job candidates – everyone was taking a hard look at just how committed to DEI companies really were.

Consequently, employers began committing to more aggressive diversity targets, greater inclusiveness in their management ranks and more openness about their hiring practices and company cultures. To be fair, there were more businesses that had been moving in this direction for a while, but 2020 thrust them flailing into accountability. From a talent attraction and acquisition perspective, this is more than wise. It's essential. Most people across the planet now want to work for employers who are openly, demonstrably committed to DEI:

- A 2021 CNBC poll shows that almost 80 per cent of today's job candidates want to work for companies that value DEI.[2]
- A 2021 Gallup report reveals that Gen Z and younger millennials, in particular, want to work in diverse and inclusive workplaces. The report states, 'DEI is not a "nice to have" for this generation; it's an imperative that is core to their personal identities.'[3]
- Recent iCIMS research also reveals that younger generations of workers expect authenticity in employers' diversity efforts.[4]

The era of getting away with only checking boxes on DEI is clearly waning, and employers must either put their money (and their policies) where their mouths are or risk losing the critical, never-ending battle for the very people who help to grow and sustain their businesses.

As a recent SHRM article put it, more and more candidates 'will make job choices based on their assessment of a company's visible DEI commitment'.[5] Recruiters, in turn, must increasingly focus on DEI, diversify the talent in their pipelines, enforce diverse slate policies (policies requiring recruiters and hiring managers to fill positions using a diverse pool of qualified candidates) and work with hiring managers to make teams more inclusive. In fact, Talent Board's latest benchmark research already shows that recruiters are indeed intensifying their focus on DEI: recruiters themselves now rank DEI as their number two recruiting priority, topped only by the candidate experience.

DEI and the candidate experience

Given how important diversity, equity and inclusion are to candidates these days, it's absolutely vital that you integrate them into your company's candidate experience. Here are a few ideas for doing just that.

Implement strategies and tools for reducing bias

In 2021, Talent Board did a joint research survey with iCIMS, a company that provides recruiting software for the entire talent acquisition lifecycle. We surveyed talent acquisition and HR professionals working within organizations of all sizes and across a variety of industries, and more than 350 anonymous survey responses were collected between 3 May and 27 May 2021. What we learned has us feeling everything from surprise and encouragement to disappointment and concern.[6]

For example, roughly half (49 per cent) of the respondents rated their companies' diverse hiring efforts as 'superb' or 'excellent'. However, a significant percentage are missing golden opportunities to track diversity data and utilize metrics and targets to support their diverse hiring efforts. For example, asked which diversity metrics their companies do track, participants' top five responses were: 60 per cent track ethnicity, 58 per cent track race, 50 per cent track disability status, 43 per cent track veteran status and 31 per cent track age. Given how crucial metrics are in tracking and assessing a company's progress on diversity, we hope to see higher figures in the near future.

Here are a few of the other findings that have us on an emotional rollercoaster:

- 52 per cent of participants' companies have not used diversity-related data or analytics beyond what is minimally required for Equal Employment Opportunity Commission (EEOC) compliance.

- 60 per cent of participants' companies have diverse slate policies or diversity-focused recruitment/hiring goals. But only 34 per cent say their companies set diversity-related service level agreements (SLAs) or specific targets for both recruiters and hiring managers. Nearly half (45 per cent) set no SLAs or targets for either group.

- 47 per cent of participants' companies have implemented technology to reduce unconscious bias in their recruiting and hiring. Although 53 per cent have not implemented such technology, one-third of this group plan to do so in the future.

· 62 per cent of participants said their companies have designated an individual to promote DEI in the hiring process.

Here are three key opportunities for improvement based on the joint research we did with iCIMS:

1 **Put DEI data and metrics to greater use, which will increase accountability.** The adage, 'If you don't measure it, you can't manage it,' rings true when reviewing the substantial percentage of our survey participants whose organizations aren't leveraging or tracking specific diversity metrics, SLAs, targets and diverse candidate slate goals. In line with our own findings, Josh Bersin's report, Elevating equity and diversity: The challenge of the decade,[7] says that 76 per cent of the organizations it surveyed have no diversity or inclusion goals. It states that roughly 80 per cent of organizations are 'just going through the motions' of DEI and 'not holding themselves accountable'. Employers who want to increase accountability would be wise to gather clear, reliable data about their DEI-related hiring, and then set realistic, attainable goals for the future, along with a clear timeframe for getting there.

2 **Implement more strategies and tools for reducing bias.** This research found that less than half of participants' organizations have implemented technology to reduce bias in their recruiting, interviewing, screening and hiring; and only 21 per cent of recruiters and 26 per cent of hiring managers are trained in conducting structured interviews to help reduce bias. Another Talent Board article[8] offered several additional insights on simple ways to reduce bias in recruiting such as weeding out microaggressions in interactions with candidates, rewriting job ads and descriptions to eliminate gender- or culture-specific words and phrases, and scrubbing rejection letters and e-mails, which can easily stray into biased language. Of course, this is just the tip of the iceberg. Employers might also consider using a variety of talent sources to ensure inclusion, utilizing a collaborative or group interviewing process to reduce bias on the part of one or two individuals and switching to validated assessments that have been pre-screened to remove bias.

3 **Showcase DEI more prominently on careers sites.** This research also revealed that many employers are not using their careers sites to full advantage when it comes to highlighting their commitment to DEI. Frankly, it's more important than ever that they do so. As iCIMS' Class of 2021 report and many other sources have noted, today's workers expect authenticity in employers' diversity efforts and they're choosing to work for organizations where inclusion is embedded in the fabric of the culture. Astute organizations can showcase their commitment to DEI early in the talent attraction process by ensuring their careers site features assets such as photos and videos of employees, testimonials about DEI at the organization, diversity-related hiring statistics, personal messages of DEI support from senior managers, information about employee resource groups (ERGs) and a strong, well-defined DEI mission statement.

We've also written several additional insights on simple ways to reduce bias in recruiting such as weeding out microaggressions in interactions with candidates, rewriting job ads and descriptions to eliminate gender- or culture-specific words and phrases, and scrubbing rejection letters and e-mails, which can easily stray into biased language. There's more on this below. Of course, this is just the tip of the iceberg. Employers might also consider using a variety of talent sources to ensure inclusion, utilizing a collaborative or group interviewing process to reduce bias on the part of one or two individuals and switching to validated assessments that have been pre-screened to remove bias.

Here are more examples of what you can do today:

1 **Eliminate microaggressions.** Microaggressions are ways of acting and communicating (both consciously and unconsciously) that signal a person's or group's dominance over others. A recent *Forbes* article[9] highlighted three types of microaggressions that should be rooted out in the workplace – and these definitely all apply to the candidate experience:

a) **Microassaults** include purposefully behaving or speaking in a racist way (e.g. making a racist joke, knowing the joke is racist, yet claiming the joke is harmless), never acknowledging a Black employee during a meeting and ignoring a minority coworker's attempts to share ideas.

b) **Microinsults** are verbal and nonverbal behaviours that are rude and insensitive and that demean a person's race or gender (e.g. a White male asking Black or female coworkers how they were able to get their job, implying they didn't win the role on merit).

c) **Microinvalidations** are ways of communicating that negate, exclude, or ignore a person because of race or gender (e.g. a White employee asking minority coworkers where they're from – a question they don't ask White coworkers and one that implies they don't belong).

2 **Improve your job descriptions.** When crafting job descriptions, recruiters and hiring managers may use gender-specific words that affect who applies to these jobs. Words such as 'salesman' and 'foreman' are obvious examples, but as a SHRM article[10] points out, even subtle word choices can have an impact on your applicant pool. 'Research shows that masculine language, including adjectives like "competitive" and "determined", results in women perceiving that they would not belong in the work environment,' the article notes. Racial and cultural microaggressions may be conveyed when a career site and job postings refer to specific holidays, ethnic events or characters, references to 'native speakers' of a language as opposed to 'fluent speakers', etc. There are software tools and organizations that can help you review and revise your company's career site and job postings to remove bias and microaggressions, which will help to open up your candidate pool.

3 **Interviews.** Clearly, interviews are a major touchpoint where microassaults, microinsults and microinvalidations can occur, as they're the most unscripted and immediate forms of communication between candidates and your recruiters and hiring managers. There's simply no denying that even today interviewers sometimes make racist jokes, use insensitive phrases and language, and make misogynistic and ageist comments. Sometimes these transgressions are intentional, but often they're not. This is one reason I've been a long-time champion of structured interviews (asking every candidate for a job the same set of pre-defined questions).

- By structuring interviews, you help to reduce the chances that interviewers will veer off-road into microaggressions, at least in their questions. As the SHRM article above states, structured interviews also 'minimize bias by allowing employers to focus on the factors that have a direct impact on performance'. I'm also a big believer in diversity and sensitivity training for your entire TA staff, but especially recruiters and hiring managers who are on the front lines of representing your company and its culture to potential employees. Interviews also offer your team an opportunity to implement *microaffirmations* – small, simple acts that affirm others' competence and value (e.g. giving candidates their undivided attention, not interrupting but nodding in response instead, backing up what a candidate says with something from their own experiences, etc.).

- There's no way to entirely eliminate the risk of microaggressions in candidate interviews. After all, we're talking about human interactions here. But training and structured interviews can go a long way toward creating a fairer and more inclusive candidate journey.

4 **Rejection communications.** One of the hardest things TA professionals must do is to reject candidates, especially those who make it into the later and final stages of the recruiting process. We need to be honest, and it helps candidates when we give them specific reasons they didn't make the final cut. But we need to make certain that our recruiters and hiring managers don't venture into those three areas of microaggressions in their explanations. Again, training can help ensure that their rejection communications stick to the issues of job fit (education, skills, background, years of experience, etc.). Rejecting candidates with empathy is critical and we discussed that in detail in Chapter 7.

The business case for DEI

While it's important to have diverse slate policies and diversity-focused recruitment/hiring goals, inclusive hiring is just good for business. We cringe when we hear business leaders state that they just can't find the talent they need because we know that's not true.

They're just not looking hard enough, and they aren't empowering their recruiting and hiring teams to find them.

That's not to say that we've gone from constricted hiring in 2020 to frenetic hiring in 2021, with more candidates looking for the work they want on their terms, quitting their jobs by the thousands because they're unhappy with their status quo. At the time of this writing, the volume of people applying for jobs has also decreased upwards of 30 per cent according to many companies in our CandE community.

But there's more to sourcing candidates than simply using LinkedIn, and most of you reading this book know that. There are more underrepresented groups out there to source from including race and ethnicity, age, gender, veteran status, people with disabilities and more. The talent pool is so much bigger than what our biases are willing to acknowledge. There are thousands of organizations and associations representing groups of all kinds – employers need to empower their recruiting and hiring teams and give them the time, budget and tools to invest in finding people who may want to work for them, no matter what the world looks like. Recruiters carrying 80, 90 or even 100 open job requisitions do not give them the breathing room to invest the time needed to source diverse candidates. That's just the 'get the butts in the seats' mentality that can most definitely accelerate biased recruiting.

Just like we outlined in Chapter 3, when you improve the experience for all types of candidates, their perception of fairness is higher, and the sentiment ratings are higher. These ratings have powerful, direct impacts to your bottom line because candidates who increase their relationship with your company are more willing to buy your products and services, recommend your company to other buyers and job seekers, and spread positive reviews about you on social media and across their personal and professional networks.

Morally, it's impossible to argue against greater diversity, equity and inclusion in the business world. However, moral imperatives that aren't tied to the bottom line often fail to take root in business. Take what you've learned from this book so far on improving candidate experience across the recruiting cycle, combine it with Chapter 10 on making the business case and make the business case for DEI.

Fortunately, there's a growing body of evidence (from McKinsey,[11] Gallup[12] and The World Economic Forum,[13] for instance) showing that DEI strengthens a company's innovation, decision-making and overall performance that will help with your business case. Investing in DEI also lifts employee engagement levels and commitment to the organization. And, as several previous data points made clear, DEI is more crucial than ever for employers that want to hire and retain new talent, especially younger generations of workers.

It's safe to say that companies – whether motivated by morals or the bottom line – are now well aware of the benefits of committing to DEI, as 96 to 98 per cent of organizations with 1,000+ employees have invested in DEI programmes, according to Boston Consulting Group's research[14] in 14 countries.

Despite these investments, a large number of TA and HR professionals believe there's still plenty of progress to be made on DEI in the workplace, particularly in medium and small organizations. iCIMS's 'Class of 2021' report reveals that 65 per cent of HR professionals are 'somewhat concerned' their organizations aren't doing enough to promote DEI; nearly half of this group are 'extremely concerned'.

The latest CandE Benchmark Research underscores it all

Clearly, DEI are good for business, and companies need to work harder to become more diverse and inclusive. (I've written about this recently here and there.) Happily, there's a ray of hope showing some progress in at least one area – the candidate experience. And this isn't about compromising the candidate experience for the sake of one group over others – it's about improving inclusivity for all groups that historically haven't had the same equality.

Talent Board's 2021 CandE Benchmark Research revealed that women and people of colour rated their 2021 candidate experiences more positively than older candidates, male candidates or White/Caucasian candidates did. This may be due, in part, to the more inclusive language and examples of diversity that employers are bringing to their career sites, candidate communications, job ads and other marketing collateral for their employment brands.

In fact, the top recruitment marketing content for women and people of colour in our benchmark research this year included:

- diversity and inclusion;
- company culture;
- why people want to work there.

This aligns with the recruitment marketing content employers told us this year they made available before candidates applied:

- company values (99 per cent);
- diversity and inclusion (83 per cent);
- why people want to work there (80 per cent).

This is the first year that Talent Board asked candidates who participated in our benchmark research to identity their race and ethnicity. Here are a few other DEI-related points of interest from our 2021 data:

- **Willingness to refer others**. Black male candidates have the highest positive ratings when it comes to willingness to refer others, based on their candidate experiences – 72 per cent higher than White males, in fact. They're followed by Hispanic females, Asian females and Black females.

- **Perception of fairness in assessments**. Candidates who identified as Black, Hispanic, Asian and Native Hawaiian/Other Pacific Islander rated the fairness of their behavioural/personality assessment process up to 12 per cent higher than Native American/Alaska

Native and Multiracial/Biracial candidates. There was little to no difference between women, men and non-binary individuals.

- **Perception of fairness in interviews**. Candidates who identified as Hispanic, Native American/Alaska Native and Native Hawaiian/ Other Pacific Islander rated the fairness of their video interview process up to 8 per cent higher than White and Black candidates. There was little to no difference between the rating of women and men.

- **Ageism**. This continues to be a minor but consistent theme in the candidates' comments from our research, so it's no surprise that younger individuals rated their candidate experiences higher than older individuals did.

The importance of perceived fairness

Notice that the previous three bullets above are all related to the perceived fairness of the candidate experience. This is a major factor in an employment brand's reputation and the ratings it receives from candidates.

When candidates feel like their overall experience is a fair one (i.e. they're truly 'in the running' for jobs they're qualified for), they tend to rate their experiences more positively regardless of their gender, ethnicity, race and age. Their perception tells them their experience is fairer and more positive whether that's objectively true or not! And their perception and ratings go even higher when they receive steady communication and engagement activities from an employer at appropriate times during their experience.

It almost goes without saying that candidates who actually get the jobs they apply for rate their experiences higher than those who don't. So, looking closely at ratings from candidates who didn't get hired can tell you a lot about the perceived fairness of an employment brand. For example, when we look at only the candidates who didn't get hired in our benchmark research (which accounts for 87 per cent of the candidates and more than 127,000 individuals in North America alone), Black males who were more likely to refer others had a 120 per cent higher NPS rating than White males. Black females who were more likely to refer others had a 54 per cent higher NPS rating than White females. The results are similar for Hispanic and Asian females and males. Remember, these are all individuals who didn't get the jobs they applied to and yet were likely to refer others based on their positive experience.

It's a similar story when we look at gender and generation. Female Gen Z candidates who were more likely to refer others had a 51 per cent higher NPS rating than female Millennials and a 77 per cent higher NPS rating than female Gen Xers. Male Gen Z candidates who were more likely to refer others had a 60 per cent higher NPS rating than male Millennials and a 106 per cent higher NPS rating than male Gen Xers.

Other rays of hope and areas of opportunity

Outside of the candidate experience there are other small signs of encouragement regarding DEI in the business world, but there are several critical opportunities to support greater DEI that employers are still not leveraging adequately. And this isn't about compromising the candidate experience for the sake of one group over others – it's about improving inclusivity for all groups that historically haven't had the same equality.

For example, the Talent Board/iCIMS research referenced earlier of TA and HR professionals revealed that a mere 34 per cent say their companies set diversity-related service level agreements or specific targets for both recruiters and hiring managers. Nearly half (45 per cent) set absolutely no SLAs or targets for either group. Also, more than half of their companies have not used diversity-related data or analytics beyond the minimum required for EEOC compliance.

Again, these are just a few of the opportunities employers are still missing out on to nurture DEI in their workplaces, and that have a major impact on their recruiting brand and their ability to attract and hire diverse talent.

The COVID-19 pandemic has altered our lives dramatically and forever. We're all coping with greater uncertainty, the feeling that we lack control and the spread of misinformation. The potential impact of all of this on our workplaces – in the forms of bias, racism and xenophobia – is equally dramatic. That's exactly why our companies must re-commit to DEI… and then follow through with concrete and measurable results. Will the improved candidate experience for women and people of colour be sustained in 2022 and beyond? What about for any and all groups? We'll have to wait and see.

Notes

1 Turchin, P. Political instability may be a contributor in the coming decade, *Nature*, February 2010, nature.com/articles/463608a (archived at https://perma.cc/H29U-TGGN)

2 Caminiti, S. Majority of employees want to work for a company that values diversity, equity and inclusion, survey shows. CNBC, April 2021, cnbc.com/2021/04/30/diversity-equity-and-inclusion-are-important-to-workers-survey-shows.html (archived at https://perma.cc/EGB2-KYXD)

3 O'Boyle, E. 4 things Gen Z and Millennials expect from their workplace, Gallup, March 2021, gallup.com/workplace/336275/things-gen-millennials-expect-workplace.aspx (archived at https://perma.cc/C7UW-MJCW)

4 iCIMS. Class of 2021 report, 2021, icims.com/class-of-2021/ (archived at https://perma.cc/55EM-Z7R2)

5 Maurer, R. 2021 recruiting trends shaped by the pandemic, SHRM, February 2021, shrm.org/resourcesandtools/hr-topics/talent-acquisition/pages/2021-recruiting-trends-shaped-by-covid-19.aspx (archived at https://perma.cc/XD4W-W9GZ)

6 iCIMS and Talent Board. (2021, June). DEI research report: The state of diversity, equity, and inclusion in the workplace, Talent Board, thetalentboard.org/benchmark-research/special-research-projects-dei/ (archived at https://perma.cc/DY3R-UBVD)

7 Bersin, J. Elevating equity and diversity: The challenge of the decade, February 2021, joshbersin.com/2021/02/elevating-equity-and-diversity-the-challenge-of-the-decade/ (archived at https://perma.cc/7THB-7VMK)

8 Talent Board. (2021, June). DE&I: It's not just about how we treat employees, Talent Board, June 2021, thetalentboard.org/article/dei-its-not-just-about-how-we-treat-employees/ (archived at https://perma.cc/Y89F-QB6L)

9 Sarkis, S. Let's talk about racial microaggressions in the workplace, Forbes, June 2020, https://www.forbes.com/sites/stephaniesarkis/2020/06/15/lets-talk-about-racial-microaggressions-in-the-workplace/?sh=11fa6a875d28 (archived at https://perma.cc/T5SL-6E3C)

10 Knight, R. 7 practical ways to reduce bias in your hiring process, SHRM, April 2021, hbr.org/2017/06/7-practical-ways-to-reduce-bias-in-your-hiring-process (archived at https://perma.cc/S558-WDA5)

11 McKinsey & Company. (2020, May). Diversity wins: How inclusion matters, McKinsey, May 2020, mckinsey.com/featured-insights/diversity-and-inclusion/diversity-wins-how-inclusion-matters (archived at https://perma.cc/YSH9-29XM)

12 Gallup. (2022, January). Include All Voices in Your Workplace Culture, Gallup, January 2022, gallup.com/workplace/242108/diversity-inclusion-perspective-paper.aspx (archived at https://perma.cc/2K7N-WGBK)

13 World Economic Culture. (2019, April). The business case for diversity in the workplace is now overwhelming, April 2019, hbr.org/2020/11/getting-serious-about-diversity-enough-already-with-the-business-case (archived at https://perma.cc/V8Z4-TN3M)

14 Krentz, M. Survey: What diversity and inclusion policies do employees actually want? *Harvard Business Review*, February 2019, hbr.org/2019/02/survey-what-diversity-and-inclusion-policies-do-employees-actually-want (archived at https://perma.cc/PA95-ATHC)

13

Recruiting technology candidate experience considerations

The first 'recruiting technologies' – job boards, applicant tracking systems and candidate databases – hit the market around the mid-1990s, on the heels of the early internet. They were built to solve two very basic problems: to help employers disseminate their open jobs, and to capture and store accurate information about candidates in their pipelines.

We've come a long way since then. There are now literally hundreds of recruiting tech companies building solutions to automate, streamline, strengthen and simplify every aspect of the recruiting and hiring process. These recruiting technologies span applicant tracking systems (ATSs), candidate relationship management (CRM) software, candidate sourcing platforms, conversational AI technologies (chatbots), video interviewing platforms, background screening platforms, testing and assessment tools and onboarding systems, to name just a few. Talent Board works with a great group of these companies that sponsor our mission of improving recruiting, hiring and the candidate experience.

These technologies are available as standalone point solutions or integrated end-to-end solutions and as on-premise or cloud-based solutions. And many of them are undergoing a major evolution thanks to AI and machine learning.

The point is, these are boom times for recruiting technology – and that's a good thing. At the time of writing, the HR and recruiting technology market will have had $6 billion in investment in 2021, according to WorkTech founder and industry analyst, George LaRocque.[1]

Frankly, companies of any hiring volume and scale across the globe need these technologies more than ever to keep up with the demands they're facing:

- With talent acquisition now a top priority of CEOs and, TA teams are being charged with finding qualified talent better, faster and at a lower cost than ever.[2]
- The COVID-19 pandemic created a dramatic rise in the need to conduct virtual recruiting and onboarding.
- The number of job requisitions is skyrocketing, as businesses worldwide recover from the pandemic.
- Employers now need to replace record numbers of employees who are jumping ship or looking to do so.[3]

According to founder and industry analyst Madeline Laurano at Aptitude Research:

> Recruiters need solutions to help them improve efficiency, create experiences and attract quality hires. Many companies today are using antiquated recruitment technology or investing in too many disparate solutions to see the value of their technology investments. Currently, companies are using 10 or more recruitment solutions and 50 per cent of companies are not measuring the ROI of that investment. Companies must consider the role of technology in automating talent acquisition processes and empowering recruiters to be more successful in their roles, while dignifying the experience for candidates.

The ongoing workforce impacts of the pandemic have been particularly challenging to TA teams and an unfortunate boon to recruiting technology, as an article in Recruiting News Network observed:[4]

> The worldwide coronavirus pandemic that began in early 2020 upended talent acquisition, sending employers scrambling to hire and recruit

remotely and looking for the best talent acquisition (TA) technology... The pandemic has presented employers with unusual and urgent needs that aren't going away any time soon and have changed the playing field permanently. With the average time to fill a position at 45 days, recruiters and hiring teams need help to reduce that timeline and improve hiring results.

Technologies across the candidate journey

Of course, recruiting technology doesn't just benefit employers and TA teams. It also helps to create a better experience for candidates at each stage of their journey. Many technologies also extend across the candidate journey (see Figure 13.1).

For example:

- **At the talent attraction stage** – There are several technology solutions that help employers attract the right candidates and that help candidates research employers that might be of interest. These solutions include:
  - candidate relationship management systems (CRMs);
  - candidate survey systems;
  - job distribution tools and platforms;
  - virtual sourcing solutions;
  - programmatic job advertising;
  - video-based job descriptions;
  - chatbots.
- **At the application stage** – A difficult, disjointed, lengthy or repetitive application process is one of the main reasons good candidates bail out of the recruiting process. This is important to note since over 60 per cent of the candidates in our benchmark research only make it to the application stage. Fortunately, some

FIGURE 13.1 Candidate Experience Journey technology considerations

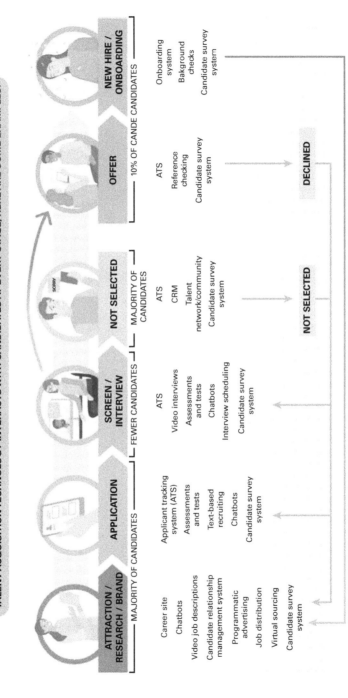

CANDIDATE EXPERIENCE JOURNEY
TECHNOLOGY CONSIDERATIONS

🦋 Talent Board
CANDIDATE EXPERIENCE AWARDS

TALENT ACQUISITION TECHNOLOGY INTERACTS WITH CANDIDATES AT EVERY STAGE, HERE ARE SOME EXAMPLES:

ATTRACTION / RESEARCH / BRAND
— MAJORITY OF CANDIDATES —

Career site

Chatbots

Video job descriptions

Candidate relationship management system

Programmatic advertising

Job distribution

Virtual sourcing

Candidate survey system

APPLICATION

Applicant tracking system (ATS)

Assessments and tests

Text-based recruiting

Chatbots

Candidate survey system

SCREEN / INTERVIEW
— FEWER CANDIDATES —

ATS

Video interviews

Assessments and tests

Chatbots

Interview scheduling

Candidate survey system

NOT SELECTED
MAJORITY OF CANDIDATES

ATS

CRM

Talent network/community

Candidate survey system

OFFER
10% OF CANDE CANDIDATES

ATS

Reference checking

Candidate survey system

NEW HIRE / ONBOARDING

Onboarding system

Bakground checks

Candidate survey system

NOT SELECTED

DECLINED

very good technologies are helping employers to make the application process faster and more pleasant for candidates. These technologies include:

- applicant tracking systems (ATSs);
- assessments and tests;
- text-based recruiting solutions;
- mobile application solutions;
- chatbots;
- candidate survey systems.

- **At the screen/interview stage** – When candidates make it to this stage of the recruiting process, it's crucial that their experience remain positive. These are likely the candidates employers want to retain in their pipelines and encourage to apply to other jobs in the future. Technologies that are useful at this stage include:

  - applicant tracking systems (ATSs);
  - video interviewing solutions;
  - interview scheduling solutions;
  - assessments and tests;
  - chatbots;
  - candidate survey systems.

- **At the offer/onboarding stage** – This final step in the recruiting process can be a touchy and emotionally charged one. Employers need to move quickly but strategically at this point to close the deal and make the potential new hire feel motivated and ready to start their new role. Technologies worth considering for this stage include:

  - applicant tracking systems (ATSs);
  - onboarding systems;
  - background and reference checking solutions;
  - candidate survey systems.

Recruiting automation

One of the key benefits of recruiting technology is that employers of any hiring volume can use it to automate labour-intensive and repetitive processes. This is a huge draw for most recruiting teams, which generally got leaner during the pandemic and therefore needed to rely more heavily on automation technologies. The good news for their candidate experiences is that candidates *expect* employers to use these technologies; they're fine with automation as long as it helps to make the recruiting process smoother, faster and more effective.

Keep in mind, candidates don't care about your company's tech stack. They really only care about getting a job, and yet, the recruiting technologies you implement definitely impact their experience at nearly every stage of the recruiting and hiring process. As mentioned above, most candidates who are interested in any job at any company will conduct a bit of research and apply, and that will be the end of the road for them. They'll have little to no human interaction and will be dispositioned automatically because they don't fit the role. Or worse, they just never hear back from the company after they apply.

This vast majority of candidates understand this is the reality, and they only want a few things from employers during their brief candidate journey: 1) clear acknowledgment that their application has been submitted successfully; 2) consistent communication throughout their experience (no matter how brief); and 3) definitive closure when they aren't going to be pursued any further. Recruiting technologies not only help to provide all of this but they also make these actions easier and far more efficient for employers.

Interestingly, Deloitte's 2020 Global Human Capital Trends Report found that employers aren't adopting automation and machine-learning tools to replace human recruiters: they see automation as a means to augment and optimize the performance of their TA team.[5] One important way that automation technologies support a better candidate experience is by increasing communication. Chatbots and mobile text campaigns are perfect examples.

Technologies on the rise

Here are a few other technologies that aid better candidate communication and a positive candidate experience:

Video interviews

Video interviewing technology is another critical part of the modern candidate experience, especially in the post-pandemic era. Video interviewing not only offers greater personal safety, but it also speeds up recruitment, reduces the costs associated with travel and frees up time for the recruiting team and candidates alike. Not surprisingly, the use of video interviews soared in 2020 and beyond.

Remember, candidates want to know what to expect from the video interviewing process, so the more preparation you offer, the more likely candidates are to have a favourable impression. The number of candidates reporting a positive experience increased by 51 per cent when they were provided with a video preparing them for the digital interview process.

Mobile text campaigns

Enabling candidates to research and apply for jobs via mobile devices has become an imperative for today's employment brands. Our research shows the use of mobile text campaigns jumped dramatically since 2019. The number of candidates reporting a positive experience increases significantly as well when candidates can launch a job application directly from a text message alert, and it rose 35 per cent when candidates receive text message reminders about their next steps.

Job simulation assessments

Job simulation assessments are basically tests that help employers evaluate candidates' ability to perform the jobs they're applying to.

There are a variety of job simulation types, and they're available to embed at various stages of your recruiting process. According to Talent Board's benchmark research, the use of job simulation assessments has increased steadily over the years.

Candidate survey systems

Candidates want feedback and they want to give it as well. Talent Board research has shown again and again that candidates who are asked for their feedback or are given helpful feedback at every stage of the recruiting process are more likely to increase their relationship with an employer (apply to future jobs, purchase their products and services, recommend the company to others, etc.).

Candidate survey systems are an ideal way to build feedback loops into the candidate experience. When employers ask candidates for their honest opinions about their experiences, it's a powerful sign of respect, and it shows that these employers very likely have a work culture that's built on respect as well. As Survale (a trusted provider of candidate surveys) notes, getting feedback from candidates helps employers in several ways including:

- Discovering what' working and what isn't during interviews and other phases of the candidate experience.
- Eliminating recruiting choke points.
- Uncovering job seekers' motivators and desires.
- Aligning recruiters and hiring managers around specific findings and metrics.
- Addressing negative candidate experiences before they impact your employment brand on social media and employer review sites.

Chatbots, AI and machine learning

Recruitment chatbots were once only popular in consumer marketing, helping potential buyers get questions answered. That's no longer the case. Talent Board research shows the use of chatbots in recruiting and hiring has risen significantly over the past few years. In fact, they're now being used by all types and sizes of companies to assist with a variety of communications tasks including initial candidate sourcing, answering basic questions on a company's careers page, updating candidates on their application status, scheduling interviews and much more. Chatbots help to keep the candidate experience engaging and informative, and they make applicants feel as though employers are respectful of their needs and their time.

Talent Board benchmark research shows just how effective chatbots are at creating a positive candidate experience: the number of candidates who are 'extremely likely to refer others' to an employer increased by 25 per cent when a chatbot answered questions on a careers site, and it rose 29 per cent when a chatbot answered questions during the application process.

According to a 2021 article in Recruiting News Network:

> Artificial intelligence (AI) technologies have become an essential component of the recruitment process, particularly at the early stages when grabbing candidates' attention, targeting the best prospects, and making a good impression are extremely important.[6]

However, as the article points out, Phenom's 2021 State of Candidate Experience benchmark research found that most Fortune 500 companies are not taking advantage of AI to streamline the hiring process and personalize the candidate-recruiter interaction.[7] More than 90 per cent of Phenom's respondents didn't even have a recruiting chatbot. These are large companies with deep pockets, which makes these findings somewhat troubling. But in a very real sense, these are still the early days of AI and machine learning, and many organizations are still trying to learn about and understand these technologies.

The Recruiting News Network article highlights several of AI's most potent contributions to recruiting, including more effective decision-making through predictive analysis (e.g. 'AI will crawl the web to find profiles of candidates who may seem like a good fit for the organization... based on millions of data points') and software that automates the resume screening process ('the software analyses candidate profiles to determine how fit they are for the job opening').

Vetting recruiting technologies today

According to WorkTech founder, George LaRocque, there was a lot of due diligence done in the late 1990s around the financial viability of the early internet platform vendors on the market. A buyer's appetite for risk as an employer varies whether choosing a point solution or targeted app versus an end-to-end solution that will run all recruiting and hiring. That's just as important today as it was then, but a large valuation doesn't mean it's the smartest money.

A big valuation is validating, yes, and some of the tech companies on the market today deserve it. And then there are those companies that have never done anything with any real momentum except raise money, which is why it's important to review their current customers and their revenue run rate, a method of projecting upcoming revenue over a longer time period (usually one year) based on previously earned revenue. Buyers should ask their CFOs or accounting team to help evaluate the stability of the companies they're vetting.

In our experience working with recruiting technology companies, there are two factors that drive how organizations buy technology: size and industry. These factors have the biggest impact on what recruiting buyers buy, when they buy it, how they buy it, how often they replace it and everything that goes into these decisions.

In fact, you can have a company that consists of 50 employees, whether it's been around for two years or 100 years, and its technology considerations are going to be quite similar. The difference is the complexity of the workforce that you're working with and industry layers on the other side of that. So, 50 hourly workers are very different to 50 contingent workers, versus 50 product managers. These are the things that have the greatest impact on what type and number of technologies you have and/or need to buy for your organization. It's the same scenario as you grow to hundreds and thousands of employees.

Here are some additional technology considerations and recommendations to keep in mind as you explore your options:

Don't get caught up in what's 'hot'. Many companies tend to get enamoured of what's hot now, like today's artificial intelligence technologies in recruiting and hiring. That's why it's highly recommended that prior to making any decisions you understand:

- what your business needs are;
- what problems you're trying to solve for;
- and who should be involved in the process of evaluating and purchasing the technology.

There's a lot more to consider these days with regards to user interface (UI) and user experience (UX). This is because technology in the last decade has driven an expectation that any device we use is powered by software built specifically to do stuff quickly and efficiently – like our smartphones. Many industry experts have called this the consumerization of software, and basically that's what it is. We want what we want when we want it and no questions please. This impacts how we do our jobs in HR and recruiting and we must look beyond just the lens of HR into how we interact with technology in our day-to-day life. If we don't mimic that in our particular industry, we will lose our people because we are just driven by on-demand technology with greater user experience today.

When you're in the early phase of identifying what your problem to solve is and what your needs are, you should always have an executive sponsor. That could be your CEO or president if you're a small company, or it could be your CFO, COO, CHRO, etc. – someone who's a leader in the organization and who can get things done. But it can't be an arbitrary or ambiguous business need the executive is a champion of – they must understand why they want it and what metrics will change the organization for the better in the next 6, 12, 18 months and beyond.

Also, be sure someone owns the 'problem' and potential solution (i.e. the technology in question) and is responsible for the metrics that

will change the organization for the better. They're not just the implementer either; they're the person who is also responsible for the change management and the adoption, and the maintenance going forward. No easy task even for a larger organization. It must be someone who is more systems oriented and it's not necessarily your CIO or the IT administration for the entire company. It could be, or it could be a recruiting technologist, if you have one on staff.

Consider your organization's growth plan, especially when you're thinking about the type of technology provider you're going to select. The processes and the recruiting technology that enabled may have worked well 12 months ago, but, if growth wasn't accounted for, it may no longer scale at the right pace.

Your implementation process must include HR and recruiting functional people as well as your IT people, especially when you're dealing with data privacy and data security considerations. So, certainly, they'd be involved. Most HR and recruiting tech analyst research firms concur. If you just have functional people to implement, they won't have enough time to do the job, much less their day job. If you only have IT people implementing your technology, they most likely won't understand the HR and recruiting functional side. So, you definitely need both parties on board to implement the technology.

You may want marketing involved, to make sure that whatever you're doing from an employment branding standpoint is aligned with your corporate marketing standards. Plus, marketing can be a tremendous asset when it comes to purchasing and deploying recruitment marketing solutions today.

You've got to have finance involved from the budgetary perspective. They're the ones who eventually must sign the technology contract and the payments, no matter who the executive champion is.

Get everybody on the same page. Regardless of who's involved, it's critical to get agreement and buy-in from everybody. Part of the problem with HR and recruiting tech buyers is that there are a lot of solutions out there with amazing capabilities, features and functionality, but they've been stitching together too many systems for too long and it's not giving them a ubiquitous view of their data. This makes it very difficult to know if they're making the right recruiting decisions. That's exacerbated by teams not talking or working together, so make sure you work together.

When reviewing and vetting HR and recruiting technologies, the free software demo account or sandbox environment isn't always the best for decision-making. The reason being, you and/or your team may not have the time to play in the software, much less understand the use cases and ultimate value for your talent acquisition efforts. In fact, you probably won't have time to play in it. Instead, once you've decided on your short list of solution providers, you'll want to ask for multiple software demonstrations, first starting at a fairly high level and then drilling down to the detail based on what metrics you want to change in your business for the better.

Sandbox environments may work sometimes for smaller companies, but, if you have the time to evaluate, always ask for guided demonstrations where you can still get your hands on the product. Give the vendor a set of examples of what you're trying to solve with the technology and have them prepare an instance where they can guide you through the process of how their tech will enable your team. Have them configure the platform based on workflow you aspire to, what you want your recruiters doing daily, etc. They may even create a workshop setting for the hands-on demonstrations with your entire team, where they walk you through several different use cases, to show what your ecosystem of people can do with the application.

Before you even get to the demonstrations, you'll most likely have had the technology vendors complete a request for information (RFI) or request for proposal (RFP). These are quite valuable for getting to the nuts and bolts and data and security questions you need answered in a document, which you aren't going to get in a demo or even a series of demos if you've invested that time. Within the RFI or RFP, you should:

· **Ask the right questions about data integrity and system security,** and if you have IT representation, they will most certainly cover all this. But there are things you should know as well. For example, where will your data be stored and retained? Do you have to be GDPR[8] compliant (which is being adopted by more countries globally than just the European Union where the law originated)? These days for cloud-based software, your data is most likely stored these days via Amazon Web Services or some similar data-centre service. Plus, most of your recruiting solutions today are going to have some level of data integrations to and from other recruiting and HR systems, so you'll want to know the strategies and tactics for moving data between systems.

- **Ask about your system 'up-time' and when it will be down for software upgrades,** etc., so you can limit user disruption. Also, what redundant systems are backing up your data in case of some disaster of who knows what. How secure is the system and how does the vendor deal with potential hacking of sensitive candidate and employee data? How are login permissions set up and who gets access to what, so that ultimately it's easy to turn off a recruiter's account when they leave your organization.

- **Ask about security.** We see more coordinated attacks on business software today, especially those cloud-based Software as a Service (SaaS) platforms. Corporate cybersecurity efforts to date focus on stopping hackers wanting to access proprietary information and/ or customer data. While this is important for companies to protect against, foreign intelligence services and other related coordinated attacks will need much more in the way of upgraded cybersecurity. Another reason is that you need to have an intimate relationship with IT.

- **Ask whether the technology platform supports enterprise single sign-on and if you have enterprise single sign-on.** Small companies may not have that capability, in which case this vulnerability probably exists at a deeper level. Meaning, there are people who will get terminated but they will still have domain accounts access still. And, in larger companies, you're going to find very good processes in place to make sure that their access is turned off, probably before they leave the building on that very last day of employment. If you're one of those organizations, you would benefit from using HR and recruiting technology that has single sign-on simply because you can turn a person off in one place and that's it, they're shut down everywhere. Again, something your IT team can and should be able to help with.

When it comes to maintenance, you also really need to have a recruiting technology administrator who is strategic and not just administrative. These roles will play a growing role in the future. For smaller companies, this role doesn't have to be a full-time job, and it could be an HR generalist, recruiting generalist or admin in the case of recruiting technologies to help with the ongoing maintenance.

However, this person can't really be a compensation analyst who's just good at technology, for example. It must be someone who has a responsibility and key performance indicators and hiring goals for HR and recruiting; including that it's part of their job description and their role is to make sure that the system is being used, is being maintained, is being updated and that you're getting the most out of it.

The human touch still matters

Technology is very clearly going to become a bigger and bigger component of the recruiting and hiring process. It creates time and cost savings, reduces the daily workload on TA teams, helps recruiters and hiring managers make better hiring decisions and improves the candidate experience – all of which have significant positive impacts on the employment brand and the bottom line.

As mentioned many times throughout this book, consistent communication and feedback loops are critical to candidate experience. We would argue for recruiter and hiring manager experiences as well. Technology helps TA teams manage and scale communications from recruitment marketing to onboarding.

However, human interaction is still essential to candidate experience, even if that's only happening for less than 40 per cent of candidates for any given job according to our research (i.e. those who are screened, assessed, interviewed, made offers and hired). These are also the candidates who have the most interaction with potential employers, tech and human, and are among the ones who truly decide on whether they remain brand champions and apply again, refer others and make purchases (at consumer-based companies). This is why the companies with the highest candidate experience ratings every year in our benchmark research consistently invest in consistent communication and not only ask candidates for feedback on their experiences, they provide feedback to finalists as well. That's good for business no matter what the world looks like.

Notes

1 WorkTech. Exclusive report: $6 billion and nine new unicorns: Global WorkTech soars to record-setting VC investment levels, WorkTech, October 2021, larocqueinc.com/6-billion-and-nine-new-unicorns-global-worktech-soars-to-record-setting-vc-investment-levels (archived at https://perma.cc/KR2B-E5QQ)

2 The Conference Board. C-suite Challenge™ 2021: Leading in a post-COVID-19 recovery, Conference Board, 2021, conference-board.org/topics/c-suite-outlook/c-suite-challenge-leading-post-covid-recovery (archived at https://perma.cc/XFZ7-AJB3)

3 Gandhi, V and Robison, J. The 'great resignation' is really the 'great discontent', Gallup, July 2021, gallup.com/workplace/351545/great-resignation-really-great-discontent.aspx (archived at https://perma.cc/8VBM-QRVK)

4 Cardenas, H. New research on talent acquisition tech trends and solutions, Recruiting News Network, June 2021, recruitingnewsnetwork.com/posts/new-research-on-talent-acquisition-tech-trends-and-solutions (archived at https://perma.cc/H22V-THMF)

5 Deloitte. 2020 global human capital trends report, Deloitte, 2020, deloitte.com/cn/en/pages/human-capital/articles/global-human-capital-trends-2020.html (archived at https://perma.cc/V8Y7-5VT2)

6 Gregorio, J. Lack of AI tech use still holding back large employers, Recruiting News Network, June 2021, recruitingnewsnetwork.com/posts/lack-of-ai-tech-use-still-holding-back-large-employers (archived at https://perma.cc/S84P-AM4K)

7 Phenom. State of candidate experience: 2021 benchmarks, Phenom, 2021, phenom.com/state-of-candidate-experience-benchmark-report

8 The General Data Protection Regulation (GDPR) 2016/679 is a regulation in EU law on data protection and privacy in the European Union and the European Economic Area.

14

Working with recruiting agencies and improving candidate experience

This chapter is not intended as a general how-to guide for working with agencies; rather it is to help recruiting leaders decide how to manage third-party recruiting agency relationships.

The first thing to understand is how ubiquitous the title 'recruiter' actually is. Someone can say, 'I am a recruiter', and without any other context, the person with whom they are speaking could assume they recruit anything from actors or models to athletes to military personnel to contract workers to employees. Some might then respond with, 'Ah, so you are a headhunter', without realizing how different the role of a corporate recruiter is from a third-party agency recruiter.

Agencies have an important role in the quest to find and hire talent. Working with the right staffing partner can save your organization time, money and employee bandwidth, and give you access to a potentially wider network of candidates as well as insider knowledge of an industry or skillset. The challenge is to find the agency that you can trust to be an extension of your professional brand and your company's employer brand. When a company has taken great strides to improve candidate experience, working with the right vendor will amplify that and working with the wrong vendor will diminish those efforts.

Considerations

Structure. Not all agencies are designed the same and you can find companies that do direct hire placement, contract to hire and solely contract placements. There are firms that specialize in certain industry markets, like finance and accounting or utilities. There are agencies that work off commission, retained search only or hourly. Agencies are contracted to fill a particular position and some RPO (recruiting process outsourcing) companies will function as an extension of your internal team, whether you need them for 10 hours per week or 40. Some will even place themselves as an internal recruiter within your organization for the duration of the project so the experience for the candidate and all communication appears to come from the company. Some do only sourcing, and some do full-cycle recruiting. It's important to understand the options and to have an idea of what type of structure will work best with your business.

The type of agency you work with should depend in part on how your company's recruiting team is structured. If you have a single corporate recruiter and a hundred customer service job openings, your needs will be different than a company who is building a large recruiting and sourcing team but is challenged in one particular type of hire.

Prioritization. How did you engage with the agency? When considering using a third party, start within your own professional network. Who do you know currently working in a staffing firm? From there, reach out to your trusted network for referrals to agencies. With the internet and online networks like LinkedIn at our fingertips, we can be less reliant on agencies with whom we have no connections. One potential exception is when we want to engage an agency that focuses in a specialized area where we need help. Even then, we recommend asking for references.

Sometimes, agencies go directly to a company's hiring managers to solicit their services and obtain work and they can find success in companies where talent acquisition professionals and hiring managers don't have strong relationships.

Larger companies have procurement departments who are managing MSAs with vendors and preferred vendor lists. Within smaller organizations, talent acquisition leaders and recruiters should assert themselves as the primary decision makers about which agencies their organization will partner with.

Challenges with working with agencies

Staffing agencies are historically used because they have deeper pools of candidates. Some agencies in fact have very strong relationships with excellent candidates. Others, however, are posting openings on sites such as DICE.com to attract candidates. With modern sourcing tools and platforms at a recruiter's fingertips, we must ask ourselves if this is really the type of help that we need. When you are searching in a smaller geograp ,po0hical market or a specialized skill set, prospective candidates might get double contacted if both you and the agency are reaching out to them for the same role. From a candidate experience perspective, this might not give a positive impression to a candidate.

More résumés do not always equal faster placements. There is a lot to understand about an organization before you can identify the ideal candidate profiles, and this is where internal recruiters have an edge. They understand the culture, pace and personality of an organization.

Working with an agency creates an additional variable that is out of your control when it comes to candidate experience so it is important to thoroughly evaluate the company and their recruiters to make sure you can trust the partnership as an extension of your own brand and extend the same level of candidate experience.

Sometimes, staffing organizations may focus on KPIs around quantity instead of quality. For example, Talent Board worked with one organization who engaged a staffing firm to help with hourly roles in a particular market. While these were front-line roles, there were a few key requirements. In our deep dive to discover why candidate experience scores were low among these positions, we found that the agency partners were reaching out to candidates who weren't necessarily qualified for the positions to show more activity in their recruiting funnel report. This instance was unfortunate in two ways: 1) It set false expectations with the hiring team who were wondering why there was so little to show for a big effort on behalf of their staffing agency partners. 2) Because the agency contacted people who were not necessarily a fit, more candidates had to be rejected. That of course led to more people than necessary experiencing disappointment over not being chosen, which lowered the company's candidate experience score in that year's benchmark research survey. Even worse, this particular agency e-mailed the candidate with a standard rejection template instead of calling the candidates to deliver the message or at least sending a personalized e-mail.

We want to stress that this is one unfortunate example that should not set an example for most agencies out there, but the message is an important one to keep in mind.

TA leaders should enable their recruiters to manage their own searches whenever possible if the recruiters have the skills and aptitude to do so. What motivates a recruiter? Usually, it is the connection they have with candidates, making an impact in candidates' lives by connecting them with opportunity and helping to build organizations. When recruiters are spending a large part of their time managing agency relationships instead of connecting with candidates, their own personal engagement may diminish.

Questions to ask staffing agencies before engaging:

- Where do you find your candidates?
- What do you look for in a candidate beyond what is in the job description?
- How often do you touch base with your prospective candidate pool?
- Can you share a sample outreach message?
- When a candidate is not a fit, what happens?
- May I have a company reference and a candidate reference that I can contact?

Before agencies are engaged, it's a good idea to understand the problem. When a company's recruiting department is understaffed and they need extra bandwidth, agencies make perfect sense. When the problem is that a position has been open for over six months, we must first understand the possible reasons before seeking outside help. Some possible reasons could be: 1) The recruiter is overloaded and the requisition could be assigned to another recruiter. 2) The recruiter may be mismanaging time and need additional training. 3) The qualifications are highly unique and the talent is not currently available in the market at the experience level sought by the company. Perhaps adjusting the required expertise or salary range will bring success. 4) The recruiter may be sending qualified candidates to the hiring manager who may not be adept at making hiring decisions in a timely manner and may need nudging or intervention. 5) Someone on the interview team is not aligned with the hiring strategy or possesses some unconscious bias. If an internal problem is found and resolved, the company may be able to proceed with hiring without outside help. If the internal problem is not resolved, hiring an agency may perpetuate the issue. Even if the firm can find, attract and submit candidates, it's possible that the company will not be able to provide optimal candidate experience unless resolution is found.

When initiating a staffing agency, or agencies, formulate a strategy from the beginning to ensure a seamless process. One of the first things to determine is, will the agency take over the searching, sourcing and candidate outreach, or will it be done in conjunction with a recruiter? Sometimes companies think the more resources searching for a role, the better the results can be. That's possible. However, if the role is for a hard-to-fill skill set and the talent pool is small, companies who use this approach run the risk of candidates being contacted by multiple recruiters for the same position. This is not optimal from a candidate experience perspective. It can be confusing or even give the candidate the impression that the company is disorganized.

During the evaluation, it's important to understand how hands-on the agency will be with a candidate. This is another step with great variation from external recruiters who are extremely hands-on and might even meet a candidate at the company's building before the interview to those who don't engage much after the submission. How much prep will the candidates get from the agency? Will the recruiter be able to step in and prep the candidate?

The most important overlooked step, without surprise, is the candidate rejection. Will the firm that your organization is engaging vow to deliver a rejection message that you approve, at any stage within the candidate journey? Many staffing firms will take great care to reject candidates with empathy because their recruiters are invested in developing strong relationships with people they want to work with over and over again. However, there are staffing firms that are more driven by the commission sales aspect of their business and will move to the next prospect without appropriately closing the door on unqualified candidates. When this happens, the negative candidate experience reflects poorly on the organization as much as the third-party recruiter. As always, candidate experience matters to all candidates, particularly those who are rejected.

15

The future of the candidate experience

Where do we go from here?

After we've built a great candidate experience, what should we focus on next? Where do we go from here?

These questions inevitably come up during our work with Talent Board participating companies and CandE winners. You may be asking them too now that you're nearing the end of this book. After revamping or fine-tuning your candidate experience with the strategies we've recommended, what then? What *should* your top priority be going forward?

Should you invest in new recruiting technologies, especially as AI and machine learning grow more practical and affordable and help free up recruiters' administrative time to focus on relationship building? Should you improve and expand your candidate communications and feedback loops, knowing just how critical they are to winning the right talent? Should you look for ways to broaden the diversity of your candidates and create a truly inclusive experience for them? Or are there other action items worth considering? Should you hire someone whose responsibility is solely the candidate experience?

Our answer is: yes. To all the above.

These are all valid questions and you'd be wise to consider them carefully. But there's a higher guiding principle that encompasses all these issues, and it's really where you should put your focus:

Your number one job after building a high-quality candidate experience is to sustain it over time.

This is what every world-class employer does, big or small in any industry, and it's the secret to maximizing your brand's long-term success in attracting, onboarding and retaining the best people. Sustaining a great candidate experience is also what has enabled a unique handful of companies to win multiple and successive CandE Awards over the past 10+ years. In fact, there have been more than 1,200 companies that have participated in Talent Board's Candidate Experience Benchmark Research Program since it was founded, and only five companies have won annual CandE Awards eight or more times – Intel (in North America, EMEA, APAC and Latin America) and BASF, Colorado Springs Utilities, AT&T, Deluxe and Lockheed Martin in North America.

For example:

For AT&T to get the talent attraction process right they really needed to put the candidate first. So, that's exactly what they did. They mapped the candidate journey to the employee experience. Candidates aren't just candidates when they're first coming through the door. They remain 'candidates' as they move throughout the business; it's one continuous journey for them. They've worked hard to provide a seamless, effortless experience at each transition point of this journey. They've also got better at making sure incoming candidates really understand AT&T's values, culture and what it's like to work there. They created job preview videos that they constantly refresh so candidates get a truly accurate, comprehensive view of what it's like to be in a specific role and a specific environment at AT&T.

The overriding philosophy at Colorado Springs Utilities is to make sure every candidate is treated with the same high level of dignity and respect, and to make sure their applications get the diligent review they deserve. One thing they did long ago was to solicit feedback from applicants about their application form to make sure it's short, easy to complete and gives them only the information they really need. They also looked at every part of their continuous feedback loop – application, phone screen, assessment, every stage of the process – to identify what they could do better. This led them to automate certain things and adopt technology that adds value for the candidate while giving them the specific information they need to make the best decisions.

For Deluxe, they are most proud of the fact that for over 10 years they've been calling their candidates 'customers' and treating them accordingly. They want every candidate walking away from their experience feeling like they matter, whether they get the job or not. Their recruiters and hiring managers spend time with candidates making sure every one of them feels like they matter, even when the person isn't right for the job. They also give candidates feedback and insights into how they can do better in future interviews.

Notice a theme? Communication and feedback loops, every single time.

Sustaining means more than maintaining

It isn't easy to do, this sustaining, because of all the business impacts we talked about earlier in the book that in turn impact recruiting and hiring – a pandemic, social unrest, leadership changes, merger and/or acquisition activity, new products and/or services, and employee attrition, and the list goes on. When we experience an economic downturn, recruiting is the first to go. When there's an upturn, it's one of the first to come back and, as we saw in 2021, with a vengeance, with employees quitting in record numbers and demanding work (and pay) on their terms.

The fact is, sustaining a great candidate experience over time is even harder than building one. You not only have to maintain the higher standards you've achieved, but you also must implement new tactics that keep your experience fresh while navigating all the usual (and unusual) challenges that will impact your business and employment brand in any given year.

However, when companies can sustain a consistent and positive candidate (and employee) experience, they can and do create a competitive people advantage. That's why we recommend making small, continual improvements to your candidate experience even as you work to sustain its overall quality. If you're not constantly distinguishing yourself in today's crowded talent marketplace, you're giving away some of that precious competitive people advantage. Sustaining a great candidate experience takes never-ending commitment and effort. And it's what separates great employment brands from all the rest.

How to get the CandE-winning competitive edge

We've already shared many case study excerpts of how companies are improving and sustaining a quality candidate experience, and we wanted to review some of the more critical highlights one more time. Below are some of the tactics multi-year CandE Award winners have used (and continue to use) to sustain the superior quality of their candidate experiences. Once you've built an experience you're proud of, put these evergreen tactics to work at your own organization.

Communicate at every phase of the candidate experience, from pre-application to onboarding. Timely and consistent communication is, unfortunately, often one of the first things to slide in maintaining a great candidate experience, especially when recruiters and hiring managers get busy or are dealing with competing priorities. In fact, so many companies do such a poor to mediocre job of communicating consistently with candidates that you can dramatically differentiate your employment brand by maintaining steady, timely candidate communications.

Remember, poor communication is one of the main reasons candidates abandon a company's recruiting process. Talent Board's research has found that candidate dropout due to poor communication is 11 per cent in North America and EMEA, 5 per cent in Latin America and 3 per cent in APAC. These percentages may seem small, but they account for thousands upon thousands of candidates year after year.

There are chatbots, texting and IM solutions, and other technologies that help TA teams respond to application submissions, answer questions that job seekers have when browsing a careers site and give applicants critical information when preparing for interviews, etc. These technologies enable both outreach and responses at various communication touchpoints and phases of the candidate journey, and they can be a godsend to busy TA teams.

Get disciplined about the diversity and inclusiveness of your candidate experience. According to a Talent Board/iCIMS 2021 survey of recruiters, a shocking number of companies use little to no diversity-related data or metrics to support their diverse recruiting/hiring efforts.[1] Asked which diversity metrics their companies do track, participants' top five responses were: Ethnicity – 17 per cent; Race – 17 per cent; Disability status – 12 per cent; Veteran status – 12 per cent; and Age – 9 per cent. In addition, more than half of participants' companies haven't used diversity-related data beyond the minimum required for EEOC compliance; 40 per cent have no diverse slate policies or diversity-focused recruitment/hiring goals; and roughly half set no diversity-related service level agreements or specific targets for their recruiters or hiring managers.

These are all lost opportunities for organizations to make real, measurable progress toward diverse recruitment and hiring. In other words, *your company* can distinguish itself and your candidate experience by putting diversity-related data and metrics to use.

Our research also shows that candidates who perceive a high level of fairness in their journey with you (even if they never make it past the application phase) are going to be far more willing to apply to future jobs, recommend your company to their colleagues and friends, spread positive reviews about your company on social media and across their networks, and purchase your company's products and services.

Also, look for and eliminate any signs of bias across your entire candidate experience – on your career site, in job descriptions and ads, on your application forms, in rejection letters and especially in your interviews.

If you aren't already conducting structured interviews, start. Speaking of fairness, CandE Award-winning companies conduct structured interviews 23 per cent more often than other companies. This is no coincidence. Structured interviews add consistency and some level of objectivity to the questions being asked of all candidates. They also connote fairness and help hiring managers more accurately assess candidates' personal qualities and their potential value to the organization.

Keep in mind that candidates mainly judge the fairness of your interviewing process by how well they're able to present their skills, knowledge and experience during their interviews. It's also a huge factor in how they rate the overall fairness of the candidate experience you provide. If your company isn't using structured interviews, make the switch for your own benefit as well as the benefit of your candidates.

Set clear expectations with candidates and always following up when promised. There's no better way to make candidates feel disrespected and even angry as failing to set clear expectations on how your recruiting, interviewing, assessment and hiring processes will unfold. Well, maybe there's one way: set expectations, then fail to live up to them and never bother to explain why. This is a death blow not only to the quality of your candidate experience but to any chance that these candidates will apply to future jobs you post, review your company kindly or buy your products and services. When recruiters and HR professionals do inform candidates of post-interview steps and then follow up within the promised timeframe, Talent Board research shows the number of candidates reporting a positive experience increases by 52 per cent in North America.

Ask for and provide candidate feedback. Getting and giving feedback should be a cornerstone of your candidate experience – and not just at the end of it. You should be soliciting and providing feedback at *every* stage of your candidate journey. The fact that you ask candidates for their honest impressions increases their positive impression of you; and, just as we mentioned above, that means they're going to be far more willing to apply to your future jobs, recommend your company to their colleagues and friends, spread positive reviews about your company and buy your products and services.

As for giving feedback to candidates, they truly want to know how they did in your process. Even when your feedback is negative, if it's actionable and you deliver it respectfully, they appreciate it because it will help them do better on the next job search. (The best feedback you can give rejected candidates is recommendations on what they should do next – e.g. which skills they should sharpen, additional training they might pursue, other jobs to investigate or even other employers they might consider.)

Providing feedback to *finalist* candidates should be non-negotiable for your recruiting team and your hiring managers. Do it. It's a clear point of differentiation for every one of the Top 10 CandE Award-winning companies.

The future of candidate experience is now

A few years ago, we were reviewing a company's candidate experience feedback data from our benchmark research programme, and we were floored by what we heard.

'That's not our data,' the talent acquisition leader replied.

I took a breath and said, 'Yes, it is. These are your candidates' responses.'

'But these ratings are horrible,' the leader said.

I took another breath and said, 'They're extremely negative, yes.'

'But our own ratings are much better than this.'

'Are you surveying rejected candidates?'

The leader paused, then said, 'Well no, but our ratings are much higher than these. We only survey new hires.'

I went on to remind the leader that in our CandE Benchmark Research Program, we survey mostly rejected candidates with only a smaller percentage of new hires in the mix. The conversation only got more uncomfortable after we dissected the data further, with the leader still arguing this couldn't be their data.

The above is a rare occurrence – year after year we run our CandE Benchmark Research – but it does happen. Choosing to survey rejected candidates isn't easy, especially if you've never done it before; you don't want to know what you don't know. Even if there's a general sense of alignment awareness of how a company perceives they're delivering recruiting and how they think their candidates perceive their experiences, there's always some need for realignment when reviewing candidate feedback data for the first time.

Take the number one ranked CandE winner in North America in 2021: Hoag Memorial Hospital Presbyterian. When the Director of Talent Acquisition & Physician Recruitment, Michael Krug, looked at his candidate experience ratings the first time they participated in our benchmark research, he felt like someone had called his baby ugly. They were that bad.

But then he and his team reviewed what their strengths and weaknesses were, made incremental recruiting process improvements over time, sustained those improvements over time and what followed were three consecutive CandE Awards. They shifted their approach to recruiting and hiring from a transactional one to a more relationship-centric approach. The initial components where they made changes were to their candidate communications, process transparency and improving timeliness. They have continued to dedicate their focus to these areas year after year.

And year after year, we hear from companies that just aren't ready to ask their candidates for feedback. To put data behind what they usually already know what they need to improve upon in their recruiting and hiring processes.

Maybe it's their fear of reprisal from business leadership, especially with how competitive and difficult hiring has been the past few years. Maybe it's the hubris of believing they do almost everything right, which is sometimes where we see disconnects between HR and recruiting leadership and their teams.

Whatever it is, we recommend a timely reset. Survey your rejected candidates, external and internal. Survey your recruiting team and your hiring managers. Survey your business leadership. Get a comprehensive understanding of your recruiting strengths and weaknesses. Prioritize your immediate improvements. Implement those improvements. Measure whether the improvements are paying off. Then repeat all the above. Again. And again. And again. That's the key to sustaining a quality candidate experience and ultimately a positive impact on your business.

Recruiting and hiring around the world is only going to get more complex, competitive and costly (for those who don't invest in improving not only the candidate experience but also their employee experience, their recruiter experience and their hiring manager experience). This book is your guide to getting there.

Each year we're asked, 'What's new in candidate experience, Talent Board?'

And each year we answer, 'Absolutely nothing.'

Because, while the world around us changes daily – elevating, promoting and sustaining a quality candidate experience is a constant of consistent communication and feedback loops. This in turn improves the likelihood of quality candidates to apply again, to refer others, to have brand affinity and for consumer-based business to make and/or influence purchases.

This is the business impact of a positive and fair candidate experience, and the future of this candidate experience is now.

Note

1 iCIMS and Talent Board. DEI research report: The state of diversity, equity and inclusion in the workplace, Talent Board, June 2021, thetalentboard.org/benchmark-research/special-research-projects-dei/ (archived at https://perma.cc/48S5-5LCT)

INDEX

Note: Page numbers followed by "*n*" refer to notes and in *italics* refer to figures or tables

abandonment rates 82, 84
AdventHealth 167, 179–80
advertising 68, 69, 74, 79
Aerohive 99, 122
ageism 204
AI 215–17
Alchemer 188
Amazon Web Services 221
annual bonuses 162
APAC 6, 7, 98, 232, 234
    candidate resentment rate 38, 40, *41*, *42*
applicant tracking systems (ATSs) 4, 23, 43,
    45, 46, 64, 72, 79–80, 82–83, 85, 94,
    208, 212
application 82, 83–85, 86, 90
application phase 4, 23–24, 78–90
    candidates needs 80–81
    improving application, practices
      for 81–85
    internal mobility 85–87
    rejecting candidates 88–90
    video interviews and assessments 87–88
Aptitude Research and Talent Board 38
Asian candidates 203, 205
AT&T 232
ATSs. *See* applicant tracking systems (ATSs)
attraction phase 21–23, *32*, 55–76, 122,
    232–33
    CandE global research *59*–60
    candidate profiles, targeting ideal 62
    candidates seeking 56–58
    defined 55–56
    employee ambassador programmes 65
    employee role 60–61
    employer brand, developing 62
    internal candidates, separate processes
      for 67–68
    internal mobility, encouraging 66–67
    job postings 68–71
    live virtual events, creating 66
    organization activities 59–60
    organization information, sharing of 64
    passive sourcing 71–73

    pay range 74
    recruitment marketing, utilizing 62–63
    referral programmes and
      incentives 64–65
    rejecting candidates 74–75
    sharing sourced candidate profiles 75–76
    sourced candidate, contacting 73–74
    using video 45, 66
Auburn–Washburn USD 437 45
automated messaging 16–17, 30–31, 40, 88
auto-rejection templates 119, 126, 128

'banned for life' codes 24
BASF 45, 182–83, 232
Bersin 47, 72, 86
Bersin, Josh 47–48, 197
Black and Indigenous people of color
    (BIPOC) 58
Black employee/Black candidates 198, 199
    fairness of 203–05
Boehringer Ingelheim Pharmaceuticals 180
bonus structure 162
Boston Consulting Group 202
brand affinity 38, 178, 239
business analysts 174–75, 190–92
business cards 65
business case 176, 179
    business case building 35–36, 183–86
    DEI business case 201–02
    presenting 189–90
business impact of, candidate
      experience 37–54, 176–77
    business analysts and business
      leaders 174–75, 190–92
    business case building 183–86
    business impacts that impact recruiting
      and hiring 5–7, *6*, 14, 15–16,
      37–39, 47–51
    candidate experience strategy 169
    communication and feedback loops,
      criticality of 27, 39–43, *41*, *42*
    examples (from past CandE
      winners) 43–46

impact as real 52–54
rejection of candidates impact on
    business 47
business leaders 34, 48, 121, 168, 180,
    174–75, 190–92
ensuring quality candidate experience, by
    process improvements 190–92
in IT department 174–75
Business System Analyst (BSA) 69
business-to-business (B2B) companies 50,
    51, 169–70, 192
business-to-consumer (B2C) 140

campus programmes 163
CandE Awards 81 , 232, 238
CandE Benchmark Research 6, 7, 15, 35,
    38, 45, 46, 57, 59–60, 59–60, 64,
    65, 71, 97, 98, 115, 117, 122, 152,
    176–79, 188, 191, 202–04, 215, 216
CandE Benchmark Research Program 237
CandE Benchmark Survey 45, 46, 84, 140
CandE winner 28, 43, 84–85, 87, 95, 99,
    103–04, 112
CandE Winner Best Practices guide 8, 20,
    21, 29
candid candidate 191
candidate 'funnel' 134
candidate communication templates 45
Candidate Experience Journey 7, 8, 20, 188
areas for improvement 34–35, 35
best practices 8, 20, 21
business case, making the 35–36
candidate personas, defining 29–30,
    30, 62
defined 19–21, 20
example journey chart 32
mapping 29–35, 30, 32, 33
as non-linear fashion 19–21
offer and onboarding 27–29, 145–47,
    163–64, 166–67, 212, 232, 234
see also application phase; attraction
    phase; interviewing and screening;
    non-selected candidates (rejected
    candidates)/candidates rejection
candidate experience measurement
case studies related to 179–83
importance of 177–79
survey platforms for 188–89
see also iCIMS; Talent Board
candidate experience, future of 231–33
CandE-winning 234–37
surveying 237–39
sustaining 233–34
talent attraction 232–33

candidate experience: resistance to
candidate experience practices
    timing 172
compliance programmes 170–72
expensive cost 168–70
from interviewing process 172–73
candidate experience
defined 1–2, 16
scenarios 2–5
sharing positive and negative 5–7, 6
candidate feedback. See feedback
candidate perception gaps. See
    perception gaps
candidate personas, defining 29–30, 30, 62
candidate referrals 50, 51–52
candidate relationship management systems
    (CRMs) 174, 208, 210
candidate resentment 38, 39–40, 41, 42,
    50, 53–54
candidate resentment calculator 49–51
candidate sourcing 55, 59, 62, 71–72,
    208, 216
CareerBuilder report (2016) 79
Centers for Disease Control and
    Prevention 15
chatbots 64, 79, 85, 97, 215–17
check-in meetings 133
CNBC poll (2021) 195
coaching feedback 124
Colorado 71
Colorado Springs Utilities 45–46, 232–33
communication, consistent 16–17, 30–31
communication, criticality of 27, 39–43, 41, 42
examples (from past CandE winners) 43–46
company culture 57, 62, 64, 66, 112
company insight 56–57
company/brand reputation 174
negative candidate experiences impacts 173
perceived fairness importance 204
compensation package 161
competitive differentiators 16–18, 30–32, 34
competitive job markets 170
consumer marketing 215
consumer-based businesses 47, 48, 178, 191
consumers, switching brand 50
COVID-19 e-mail templates 46
COVID-19 pandemic 4, 10, 22, 38–39, 57,
    209, 213, 233
candidate market in pre COVID-19 37–38
impacts of 193–94, 206
perception gaps in Pre COVID-19 7–14,
    8, 11, 12, 13
recruiting practices changing during 46,
    173–75, 182, 206

CSAA Insurance Group 181–82
'Culture Committees' 65
current employees 5,10, 57, 66, 138, 191
customer data 221
customer experience (CX)
    vs. candidate experience 168–69
    CX technologies spending 38
customer service 50

data privacy 219
data security 219
decision-making 147, 148
Deloitte 213
Deluxe 123, 232–33
dispositioning 171
diversity, equity and inclusion (DEI) 21–22,
    58, 97
    business case for 201–02
    creating impacts on employers 194–95
    DEI business case 201–02
    DEI mission statement 193
    historical measurement of 193–94
    implement strategies and tools for
        reducing bias 196–200
    other metics related to 205–06
    race and ethnicity results 202–03
    related to perception of fairness
        203–05
Dr Reddy's Laboratories 43
dropout rate 79

Edwards Lifesciences 69
EEOC. See Equal Employment Opportunity
    Commission (EEOC)
e-mail templates 75, 82
e-mails 64, 74–75, 81, 90, 95, 124, 128,
    139, 143, 165, 228
employee ambassador programmes 65
employee bandwidth 225
employee engagement 66, 68, 87
employee referrals 52, 125
employee stock ownership plan (ESOP) 162,
    167n4
employee value proposition (EVP) 22,
    62, 92
employer brand 21–23, 32, 55, 61, 62, 66,
    76, 89, 92
employers
    on DEI practise 193, 194–95
    empathetic communication with
        candidates and employees 40
    'ghosted' by candidates 37
employment brand 54, 104, 116, 192, 203,
    204, 214, 219, 222, 233, 234

engagement strategy 164–65
engagement/click-through rate (CTR) 44
Equal Employment Opportunity
    Commission (EEOC) 196, 205, 235
Equal Pay Transparency (EPT) Act 71
Erickson and Moulton 86
ESOP. See employee stock ownership plan
    (ESOP)
Eurostar 29
expectation setting 17, 31, 71, 97–98, 100,
    102, 105, 109, 227, 236
external candidates 57, 67

fairness, perception of 17–18, 31–32, 71, 88,
    98–99, 117, 201, 235, 236
    candidates expectation for 80
    impacts form hiring process 178
    perceived fairness 204–05
    results from CandE benchmark research
        (2021) 203–04
Fairygodboss 6, 22
feedback 27, 43, 87, 89, 99, 112, 132,
    135–36, 215, 222–23, 232–33,
    236–37
feedback loops, criticality of 17, 31, 27,
    39–43, 41, 42
    examples (from past CandE
        winners) 43–46
first impression 60, 61, 68
Floyd, George 194
Forbes (newspaper) 198
401(k) plan 151, 167n1
frequently asked questions (FAQs) 64, 97
fringe benefits 151
fun explanatory videos 45

Gallup report (2021) 195
GDPR (General Data Protection
    Regulation) 221
Gen Z candidates 195, 205
ghosting 37
Glassdoor 6, 22, 58, 61, 135, 144
Global Human Capital Trends Report
    (2020) 213
globalization 173
Google Analytics 85
Great Recession (2007/2008) 37

'hard' skills 87
Harvard Business Review 51
high-demand roles 133
hire phase 103, 112–13, 145–67
    accountable and transparency 17, 31, 43,
        45, 46, 160, 161

candidate experience measurement
    importance to 177–79
competitive and counteroffers 154–59
extending the offer 152–54
hiring priorities 132
metrics and date, related to recruiting
    progress 186–89
negotiation 159–61
offer acceptance 163–65
offer and onboarding 27–29, 145–47,
    166–67
offer prep and the pre-close 149–52
offer rejected by candidate 165–66
preparation for negotiation 161–63
requirements for getting good candidate
    experience 170–72
salary discussions 149
salary surveys 150–51
see also candidate experience
    measurement
'Hire to Win' (training programme) 104
'Hire Up' (training programme) 103
hiring managers 25, 28, 46, 92, 98, 99, 102,
    109, 169, 172, 197, 229
AdventHealth of 179
candidate profiles, sharing with 75–76
see also hiring managers support, getting
hiring managers support, getting 131–44
building better relationship with 136–44
candidate empathy 135–36
candidate experience, lack of care
    about 133–36
consultative recruiting 136
kick-off meetings, conducting 139
kick-off meetings, things to accomplish
    in 140–44
market insights 135
pipeline visibility 134
recruiter–hiring manager
    relationship 132–33
see also kick-off meeting
Hispanic candidates 203, 204, 205
Hoag Memorial Hospital
    Presbyterian 44, 238
'Talent Huddle' biweekly
    newsletter 44
HR (human resources) 28, 145, 157, 218,
    219–20, 222, 236
budgets of 168
and talent acquisition leaders 176, 191,
    196, 202, 205
HR business partners (HRBPs) 102
HR Operations 164
Humana 95

iCIMS 195, 235
joint research on DEI practise 197–200
and Talent Board research on
    DEI 196–97, 205
immigration 164
impressions 76, 113, 115
Indeed 6, 22, 37, 61, 144
in-demand skill set 148, 151
insights 57
internal candidates 124
internal candidates 67–68, 89, 124
internal mobility 5, 56–57, 66–68,
    85–87, 124
encouraging 66–67
internal mobility portal 67–68
internal mobility programme 124
internal mobility specialist 68
internal service level agreements (SLA) 94
International Data Corporation (IDC) 38
interviewers
    and candidates 172–73
interviewing and screening 25–26, 92–113
    application screen 94–95
    best practices 112
    candidate experience from 172–73
    candidates want 97–99
    decision 112–13
    hiring manager interviews 102
    interview scheduling
        considerations 110–11
    interview team 92, 93, 97–98
    interview training 103–05
    interview types 105–09, 106
    interviewers, selection of 109–10, 110
    methods 107–08
    prescreening tools 95–97
    recruiter screen 99–102, 99
    screening 94–102
    video interviews 25, 87–88
    virtual environments, transition to 25–26
IT department 174–75

Jacobs 84–85
job descriptions 69, 137
    improving 199
job postings 68–71, 132–33, 137
Josh Bersin Academy 47

kick-off meeting 133, 136
    scheduling before 137–39
    things to accomplish in 140–44
    things to look out after 143–44
Kimberly-Clark 48–49, 50, 179
'knockout' question 100

Krug, Michael 238
Kununu 6

LaRocque, George 209, 217
Latin America 6, 7, 98, 232, 234
    candidate resentment rate 38, 40, *41*, *42*
Laurano, Madeline 209
lifetime value 49
LinkedIn 59, 72, 74, 138, 143, 166
    became sourcing candidates 201
    candidate profiles sharing 75–76
live virtual events, creating 66
Lockheed Martin 232–33

marketing automation tool 63
matrixed organizational structure 85–86
McCamey, Randy 1, 60
McKinsey and Company 57, 83, 202
metrics 179, 183
    candidate experience feedback
        datas 188–89, 191
    and data related to, recruiting
        interactions time 186–88
    diversity metrics 196–97
    metrics questions 187
microaggressions 197–99
microassaults 199
microinsults 199
microinvalidations 199
microsites 44
Microsoft 50, 101
Microsoft Teams 46
Middle East and Africa (EMEA) 6, 7, 98,
        232, 234
    candidate resentment rate 38, 40, *41*, *42*
Miles and McCamey 60–61
Miles, Sandra 1, 60
millennials candidates 195, 205
Minneapolis 194
Momentive 188

'national committee' 65
Native American/Alaska candidates 204–04
Native Hawaiian/Other Pacific Islander
        candidates 203–04
Nature (journal) 193
negotiation 159–61
net promoter scores (NPSs) 204–05
New Balance Athletics 180–83
non-selected candidates (rejected candidates)/
        candidates rejection 26–27, 47, 50,
        74–75, 88–90, 115–30
    candidate rejection, importance
        of 116–18

difficulties in candidate rejection 118–20
employee referrals 125
internal candidates 124
rejection prioritization 123–28
serial applicants 126–27, *127*
veterans and transitioning
    military 125–26
North America 5, 98, 232, 234, 236
    candidate resentment rate 38, 40, *41*, *42*
    candidate perception gaps *11*, *12*, 13
    candidate experience, sharing 5, 6
North American employers 71, 100

offers. *See* onboarding and offers
Office of Federal Contract Compliance
        Programs (OFCCP) 170
onboarders 145, 164
onboarding and offers 27–29, 145–47,
        163–64, 166–67, 212, 232, 234
organizations
    hiring and retention strategies, business
        impacts on 176–77
    CandE benchmark research importance
        to 177–79
    time consideration relating to candidate
        experience 172
    diversity metrics 196–97
    implemented technology, for removing
        bias 197
    organizational change managers 174–75
    positive candidate experience
        impacts 178, 201
    technical talent demands 174
    typical form of candidate experience 169
    weeding out microaggressions
        effects 197–99
Oxford Corporate Consultants 29

pandemic. *See* COVID-19 pandemic
passive candidate sourcing 55, 59, 62
passive sourcing 71–73
pay range 74, 86, 160
perception gaps 7–14, *8*, *11*, *12*, 34
    in Pre COVID-19 7–14, *8*, *11*, *12*, 13
perpetual candidates 27
Ph.Creative 48
Phenom: State of Candidate Experience
        benchmark (2021) 216
phone screenings 25
PointClickCare 104
post-interview feedback 121, 122
'pre-close' 150, 152
pre-employment assessment and selection
        tests 25

print advertising 79
publicly traded companies 191

QR code 65
qualifications 70, 92, 99, 105, 229
qualified profiles 138
Qualtrics 188
quarterly bonuses 162
question and answer (Q&A) 66

recruiter–hiring manager
      relationship 132–33
   candidate experience, lack of care
      about 133–36
   when switching jobs 146
   see also non-selected candidates (rejected
      candidates)/candidates rejection
recruiters/talent acquisition leaders
   consultative role 174–75
   increasingly focus on DEI practise 195
   as nod for candidate experience 176
   see also business case; diversity, equity
      and inclusion (DEI)
recruiting agencies
   challenges 227–30
   considerations 225–26
Recruiting News Network 209–10, 216
recruiting process
   candidates expectations from
      recruiter 120–23
   candidates withdrawal, from recruiting
      process 51–52
   passively sourced candidates 125
   see also hire phase
recruiting technologies: rise of 214–22
   candidate survey systems 215
   chatbots and AI 215–17
   job simulation assessments 214–15
   mobile text campaigns 214
   recruiting technologies vetting 217–22
   video interviews 214
recruiting technology 208–23
   human interaction 222–23
   recruiting automation 213
   technologies across candidate
      journey 210–12, 211
   see also recruiting technologies: rise of
recruitment marketers 63
recruitment marketing 23, 55, 203, 219, 222
   utilizing 62–63
   see also attraction phase
recruitment marketing calendar 63
recruitment marketing teams 60

referrals 50, 51–52, 64–65
rejected candidates. See non-selected
      candidates (rejected candidates)/
      candidates rejection
rejection conversation 121–22
rejection template 228
'the relationship question' 40
relocation 151, 164
renegotiation 154
request for information (RFI) 220–21
request for proposal (RFP) 220–21
researching, the jobs. See attraction phase
restricted stock unit (RSUs) 162, 167n3
résumés 75–76, 78
   and ATS 80
retention, incentives for 53–54
Reynolds American 181
RPO (recruiting process outsourcing) 226
RSUs. See restricted stock unit (RSUs)

salary 71, 97, 100–01, 229
salary surveys 150–51
sandbox environments 220
screening. See interviewing and screening
Seek 6
SEM/SEO 59
semi-structured interviews 105–09
Sharp Healthcare 164
shelf-stocking procedures 134
'shotgun' approach 126
SHRM (Society for Human Resources
      Management) 84
silver medallists candidates 26, 27, 47, 53,
      128–29, 138, 171, 192
'6 Simple Steps to Revitalizing Your
      Candidate Experience' (Adams) 62
SLAs (service level agreements) 136,
      142–43, 196, 197, 205
'social contract' 161
Society for Human Resource Management
      (SHRM) 48, 199
   on recruiters, focus on DEI 195
'soft' skills 87
sourcing 72, 73, 76, 226
Southwest Airlines 46, 65, 183
spot bonuses 162
staffing agencies 72, 228
stakeholders 46, 109, 167, 180, 184
Stantec 46
Starred 188
structured interviews 105–09, 197, 199–200
Survale 188, 215
Syneos Health 44

TA team. *See* talent acquisition team/TA
     team
Talent Acquisition & Physician
     Recruitment 238
talent acquisition (TA) 21–22, 55, 62–63,
     81, 82, 209
talent acquisition managers 102
talent acquisition professionals 73, 83
talent acquisition team/TA team 64, 72, 176,
     209, 222, 235
   consultative role 174–75
   requirements to effective candidate
        experience 170–72
   see also candidate experience
        measurement; recruiters/talent
        acquisition leaders
talent attraction. *See* attraction phase
Talent Board 5, 21, 47, 48, 88, 178–79, 208,
     215, 216, 227
   CandE Benchmark Research 6, 7, 15,
        35, 38, 45, 46, 57, 59–60, 59–60, 64,
        65, 71, 97, 98, 115, 117, 122, 152,
        176–79, 188, 191, 202–04, 215, 216
   CandE benchmark research
        (2021) 202–04
   candidate experience, definition of 2
   candidate resentment calculator 49–51
   on candidates withdrawal, from
        recruiting process 51–52
   on DEI recruiters 195
   founding of 15
   and iCIMS research 196–97, 205
talent inclusion specialists 60
talent market 56, 59, 102
talent pool 72, 86, 229

target audience 62
technical interview 109
'time to fill' metrics 134
transparency 17, 31, 43, 45, 46,
     160, 161
Turchin, Peter 193

unemployment rate 15, 37
United States (US) 70–71
     inequity reckoning of 193–94
unqualified candidates 24, 68, 230
unstructured interviews 105–09
US National Institute of Allergy and
        Infectious Diseases 15
user experience (UX) 169–70, 218
user interface (UI) 218

video interviews 25, 87–88
video using, to attracting candidates
     45, 66
Virgin Media 48, 50, 140, 179, 191
virtual hiring tools 46
virtual recruitment 25–26, 45

Walgreens 44–45, 112, 182
White male(s) 199, 203, 205
workers 169
     authenticity, expecting 195, 198
     with key experiences demand 174
WorkTech 209, 217, 223n1
World Economic Forum, The 202
World Health Organization 15

Zielinski, Dave 84
Zoom 176